THE SPIRAL TO NOW

For my friend Eliah Sentah
May our paths meet again
in this world or the next.
Blessings,
So La Meé
Dec 2020

THE SPIRAL TO NOW

IT'S A JOURNEY OF AWAKENING

Expanded Fourth Edition

SoLaMeé

Author/Publisher contact information
SoLaMeé - (Patricia Heneage)
PO Box 573
Driggs, ID 83422

DBA: Energy Heals.net
PO Box 607
Driggs, ID 83422
www.energyheals.net
www.thespiraltonow.com

CONTENTS

REVIEWS

"SoLaMee', One thing I can say about your book The Spiral To Now is that it is multi-layered...it has lots of material to think about and ponder, a lot of new resources, and it amazes me what you have been through, I can't believe you did some of the things you did! It is so heart filling to see how you have been taken care of by the Universe through it all. You have made it through a lot and you have told your story, that's already HUGE! I am now getting towards the end of your book and I don't want it to end! I have enjoyed so much the chapters with the communion with angels, so beautiful, it struck deep resonance within me." Noreen

"Dear SoLaMee', wow! I found your book The Spiral to Now moving and inspiring. What a wonderful story. It really made me want to get out of my whiney funk and start living again. So many resonances! I want to make another appointment at your earliest convenience. I want you to help me heal as you obviously did my friend. She's going great guns!" Lynn

"If anyone has ever stepped solidly onto the spiritual path, this is one woman's journey of awakening that can offer insights and inspiration to others no matter where in the unfolding development a person is. Ms. Heneage writes with impeccable honesty and right from her heart. I thoroughly enjoyed reading the account of her amazing journey of awakening. The story built and built on one experience to the next until the final chapter. I highly recommend this book to others. Well done, Ms. Heneage!"

"It has been nearly a month since my first session with SoLaMeé. I rarely find it difficult to come up with the words to adequately reflect the impact of a relatively short encounter – but that's the situation I find myself in. Amazingly, my take away was so strong that not a day passes without me considering the lessons I learned and the whole experience. I will be doing it again!" Jeanne

"SoLaMeé, I'm so glad I met you and you worked with me at the Matrix Energetics seminar. It was the highlight for me. I don't know if you installed those wings on me or just allowed them to unfold, but because of that, I am still alive. I know that sounds dramatic, but something happened to me as we were getting home yesterday. I started up the stairs with three things in my hands and I completely lost my balance and started to fall backwards. At that moment something pushed me in the back, so that I started to fall forward instead and then I caught myself on the front storm door. This was miraculous to me. Had I fallen backward from where I was on the steps, I would have broken my neck, my back or even cracked my skull. I am amazed at how the angels are watching over me. And I believe that your working with me helped to open me up to more possibilities and the providence of angels. Thank you!" Pauline

"I just want to thank you, SoLaMeé, for a remarkable session yesterday. I feel like a different person. It's like there's just me. I'm back to wholeness without all the wear and tear of the last several years. I can't thank you enough. I wanted you to know I haven't felt this good in a long time! All of the sudden I have this lightness of being. I can look at everything, nothing changed but everything has changed and I can just be in my heart. You are truly gifted. I am so grateful you're a part of my life SoLaMeé." Maggie

"I've enjoyed a number of sessions with SoLaMeé and although they're all different, I have totally enjoyed each one. As she works I try to sense whether she's using ME or IET – it's impossible to know. The sensation is so soothing that I become lost in waves of total relaxation. Even my busy mind settles down to join the soothing ride. Often our discussion after the session reveals that my sensations jive with what she was noticing and together we draw conclusions that are extremely helpful in the long run. I look forward to enjoying future sessions and greatly value our friendship as well as her talent and knowledge in these healing modalities." Carrie

"Each session with SoLaMeé brings a deep sense of being grounded and connected with my Self. My mind is more than quiet, my body is relaxed/but alert and there is a deep experiencing of just being present. A heightened sense of awareness is evident as I see my surroundings in a way I hadn't "noticed" before. Colors are more vibrant, and details appear that I am amazed I have missed previously. Solameé creates a safe, nurturing environment that allows for my complete release into the restful state that happens as she is working. The long-standing effects of a healing session with her are intrinsically linked to her ability to love and accept each person, as they are, with no judgment." Lorrie

"SoLaMeé is truly in tune with the mind, body and spirit. She also is a very wonderful caring person on this earth. I didn't fully understand Matrix Energetics, but I completely trust Solameé and decided to give this a try. I'm sure glad I did! Not only did my back pain completely go away for weeks, but it was one of the most incredible relaxing sessions I've ever had. I actually felt the pain move from my back and gather in my hand before leaving my body, while beautiful colors of aqua and lime green swirled around me. My back does feel tired from time to time, but has not hurt like it use to!" Liz

ACKNOWLEDGEMENTS

I thank God and the wondrous angels for what has been given and received throughout this journey. Words cannot convey the depths of my gratitude. I want to thank my husband and our beautiful daughter for their love and support during this project despite the scope and intensity that came with it. Their willingness to provide feedback on the timelines in the book early on helped solidify our collective memories of difficult events.

Writing about my life's most sacred experiences has been a journey in its own right. The first two editions in 2015 were pulled together within six months. The process felt rushed and there was little proofing assistance available even through the self publishing system, leaving the book with some errors. I want to thank my husband for his approval of the book in general and his helpful proof reading when able and suggestions for the Third Edition. I also want to thank so many dear friends and clients for their enthusiastic support on Facebook, as the project unfolded over the months in 2015 and over the years as it slowly came to completion.

My mother was always an amazing role model for me as a young woman. She died in 2003. I would have liked her help, wisdom and support for this enormous project, but that was not possible with her early passing. I want to thank my close family for their support at each stage of publication. I am very grateful to my father for his big heart and understanding of my spiritual path. His enthusiastic reading of my book as the later editions came together meant the world to me.

I completed the Third Edition in 2016. The 2017 expanded Special Edition provided updates with many corrections and additions. I added real life photos to enhance important life events. The expanded Fourth Edition included better proofing throughout. I had new challenges with the need for an updated front and back cover that was thoughtfully done by my husband H. Robert (Bob) Heneage. The books graphic layout was done by me with the help of a book template and hours of experimental attempts.

This expanded Fourth Edition outlines important energy dynamics and mystical adventures since 2015 and on up to the end of 2019. My sense is that this final Edition will bring this project to a meaningful conclusion for new readers as well as all who have enjoyed its message throughout the writing and publishing process.

1

GRAND ORCHESTRATION

We are at a time in history when more people than ever feel our world is undergoing great change and upheaval. Do you feel an urge to be set free? We may be like a tiny seed buried in the earth. It comes to life at some point. It will strive with every ounce of its energy to reach the surface sunlight and come into full expression. Many feel inner stirrings that compel us to seek the sunlight of our source and emerge from our cocoons. It is time to awaken, transform and in essence take flight. We are all part of a grand orchestration.

I believe we are the generation of human beings that seek to actualize our full potential. Many of us are even coming around to discovering our inherent capacity for miracles. We are in the age of enlightenment and no one is being left out of this one. It's a journey of awakening for everything and everyone on earth. Our true source or God is infinitely intelligent. It knows our heart's longing for what is more real, universal and even ultimately timeless. Our source has a plan for each one of us to come toward this doorway of discovery. There are many ingredients to a healthy spiritual awakening and restoring our internal communication with our source is just the beginning.

A lot of people have noticed odd sensations in their bodies and discovered that they have new insights into what is possible in the new reality we are all experiencing. The expression "feel that energy" has become main stream and is well understood as the vernacular of this age. Some people have been experiencing a strange sensation in part of their body and believed something was wrong. They thought they had a new illness or some strange malady. Before they could get to a doctor or specialist it disappeared.

We called it a funny energy showing up and then moving on. Many of us are getting a deeper insight into what the body is really all about. Patterns and energies pass through our awareness all the time and the body makes a temporary note of it. I learned long ago that the body is really a communication device, and I am not referring to our mouths verbal capacity. The body reflects the patterns of our mind and wants us to hear it better. It manifests a sign in our cells to get our attention. The condition will clear up, if we get the memo correctly. You may still need a doctor to help out perhaps as you personally focus on decoding the internal signal.

Every step you take toward looking into the energy of the body's sensations will bring you closer to unveiling the patterns that have led to ill health. Once unlocked, these patterns happily bounce back into a groove of vitality and restored health. The heart knows you just want to be whole again. This is why many people are getting the wake-up call from a serious illness. I believe it can help us sort out what life is really all about. We may even realize we need to look at our priorities. Sometimes a person decides to change their lives overnight and it brings about a paradigm shift in their mind, body and spiritual health.

For some people it may also seem like loved ones are passing away too quickly. Exiting this world can be hard on those still here. It has made us appreciate all that *is* here today while we notice all the changes right before our eyes. The ground beneath our feet may be shifting. All in all sometimes we need to make new choices to fully access our true potential.

What if we are called to migrate to new lands or to meet new people? Have you ever felt you were being drawn to visit different parts of the planet or to experience different spiritual groups? We don't always need to relocate, but sometimes we heed the call and it happens almost without our doing. When we do travel, the human body responds at a cellular level to different environments geographically and to different energetic influences or people. We do not always know why we are called to be in a place that feels foreign, but if the heart insists on it, you will do well to let things play out. You may be an essential ingredient to other people lives as well. It may take courage to be the change we want to see in the world. In many ways you could say our collective cultural perceptions and values are changing. We are moving away from a disconnected worldview.

We hear on the news about interesting celestial events taking place every year. Solar flare activity can affect many things in our body and in our world, according to recent studies. On another day, we may be told electrical instruments are doing odd things. We all remember worrying about a change in the Earth's magnetic poles or about other concerns that flood the news.

I believe a cellular activation is under way that is bigger than any solar flare out there. Maybe the solar flares are helping out with the biosphere's upgrades. Either way, what if we all have an inner homing device in our DNA that is waiting for us to say "yes" to this new energy flooding the earth? I believe that there is a powerful spinning field of light calling each one of us up and in energetically.

The next question for some people might be, "How can we assist in this cellular activation?" First, I recommend that you remain calm. I believe that this is a natural process. If you can picture the image of an important metamorphosis, some environments or conditions are better suited to it than others. A change in diet can also really help physical upgrades. We are for the most part, migrating away from chemicals and additives in our food. Many are choosing fresh fruits and vegetables, preferably organic over starchy items and factory farmed animals. Traditional health care isn't the first choice anymore. Many people are looking for options that are natural and holistic.

There are also many useful healing practices and methods popping up all over the planet. I will outline many that I have chosen to study. This is one reason I was led to train in the more advanced healing methods and become more visible. I am like many devoted souls at the ready; available to help others get things back on course in a session or two. Most holistic health practitioners understand that people's bodies are changing and they can assist with diet, supplements, and other recommendations to guide you through your internal changes.

More people than ever are feeling a sense of urgency to wake up to so many things. There is a full scale awakening taking place across the planet. Whether this is all new to you or it's your passion, it is an open invitation to join in. For many of us, it has become what makes life an exciting journey again, and we are ready with bells on! No one can do it for you and you will also need help at some point. My story of awakening may be an eye opening read for some. For those who are beginning to learn and understand what I am presenting here, there could be a literal rising of energy internally as the words convey their vibration or code.

I will be sharing my experiences and insights from many years on this path. I believe it is a journey that each soul must ultimately take in one form or another. This journey has been a surprisingly revealing series of events, not the least of which was a powerful cellular spiritual awakening. I was also shown a path toward a brighter experience of life and all its potential for wonder and awe. It started with a beautiful and potent angelic unveiling of celestial origins. Within a few years it looked more like a full scale rocket launch that propelled me through a powerful doorway in consciousness and beyond to a Greater Reality.

After a significant awakening spiritually, you may feel a certain need to return to the big map on awakening to find helpful hints to stabilize yourself. Ways to integrate all the very human layers was something I instinctively knew was essential for my wellbeing. I found few maps out there that matched my experiences at the time, so I kept notes. I came to know that the source of all light is not of this world, universe, or any other.

Ultimately all light comes in from beyond the veil, not unlike the sunlight as it filters down through the waters of the ocean, refracting as it goes. There is also a light within each of us and its source is not of this world. It emanates as *love* and can be found in every living thing on Earth and then some. Love is who we really are. It is our inner beacon. It was designed to show us the way home to our true self.

Looking back over the years, I can honestly say that my life has been a wild ride. I will begin with my youngest memories and bring the reader along up to the present day adventures in consciousness, healing work and multidimensional awareness. I will also outline the many teachings that played a role in assisting my journey of awakening. They included books on new quantum physics, eastern mystical traditions, ancient Christianity and much more.

Over time, I began to sense that I was making a real map in consciousness for myself. It felt like an energetic trail of crumbs that left a path to use later when necessary. I learned that within the mystical aspects of powerful awakenings, it is useful to discover the important signs of energetic change and find ways to track the unfolding patterns in consciousness. You may need to re engage with some of them at a later time.

I have noticed for years how communication is the cutting edge state-of-things. We are exploring this new frontier every day. We can communicate from nearly anywhere on earth with hand-held phones and, in the course of minutes, send digital images in real time that inspire or horrify millions of people across the globe. The newsfeed of daily existence is so enormous we sometimes need to find silence again just to remember what it feels like to not be electronically connected.

Indigenous cultures for thousands of years communicated across distances without any external devices. For some people all over the globe, this is no longer a lost art. Human consciousness is catching up with the technological advancements, becoming both a compelling and challenging phenomenon. It is not a new scene for some, but it is still an interesting dynamic that we, as human beings, are literally becoming a cell phone capable of making calls from anywhere.

Our inner antenna is coming on line, so to speak. Some people wonder if it is okay to admit they are receiving many signals and tracking calls on many levels; our actual phones feel cumbersome. However, cell phones still are a necessary aspect of life. We need to confirm the energetic insights flooding our consciousness at times and learn to assess the value of other intuitive messages.

A call on my cell phone from someone I sensed intuitively can help me clarify several moments of downloaded sensory awareness the previous day for instance. Information might come from social media newsfeeds, the national or local news on television flipped on for only a minute or two. The signal I have received is confirmed and the intuitive information finds relevance. Another way to look at the new state of affairs is that many souls are learning to surf the inner and outer web of life and all it is messaging.

There is a profound need for a greater awakening for mankind, beyond just advanced awareness and enhanced psychic abilities. With true awakening comes responsibility and opportunity. Over time I learned to embrace so many things. As you move down a spiritual path, perceptions about what is spiritual and what is not fade away as everything takes on an important hue of purpose and thoughtfulness.

For those who aspire to awaken, it will become clear that everything in life matters in some way. Our families and friends matter, even if they do not understand or are interested in awakening. Every encounter with another human being eventually is seen as a mirror for your soul to contemplate. It becomes important to be attentive to the subtle energetic nuances in order to deepen one's experience of the intelligence of all life.

There is also an opportunity to take part in cleaning up the environment and supporting the Earth's need for assistance in energy upgrades. I believe we need all hands on deck for this one. Many are aware of the need to build a sustainable future with natural resources and reassess the dependence on fuel sources that are unclean and even toxic. Ancient civilizations often knew how to live in harmony with the environment and each other. I will offer teachings from ancient indigenous ways that assisted me throughout my journey and are rich in wisdom.

As I wrote this book I noticed that the personal patterning within myself as a young person held keys of wisdom for me. I have also accessed past life traumas and deeply etched memories. They did not surface until the right flow of events came together. We are here after all to heal all that has ever wounded us and continue on where we left off with our spiritual potential.

I encourage everyone to decide to head into the wind towards those difficult patterns and know that all of heaven and Earth bows to your willingness to grow and learn. When we make better choices, push past fears, take the leap of faith and befriend the former enemy, we begin to return to the harmony or true music of life. Even when we are feeling powerless, remember that the sunlight shines across every life on earth, equally; no person is insignificant.

2

BLENDING IN

It all began for me many years ago, with a lot of help from the unseen guides and *fields* of universal possibility. As a young girl, I walked to school every day a few miles down a dirt path that wound along the edge of lush properties. When looking back on my young mind, I remember that I did not like to walk on sidewalks unless it was the safest way. I would take short cuts across lawns to my mother's disapproval. It seemed natural to find a more direct way, as long as it did not disturb something important. I learned over the years that many people insist on staying with the path most traveled, whether as a means of getting around town or following a path with traditional religion. I was not afraid to try a different route to my destination or desired outcome.

It is strange to think that as a young person I really gave some thought to those who might come behind me, down a particular path. I might notice items like broken glass that someone is about to step on. Helping others see it and avoid injury always gave me a nice feeling. I did not need to get credit for doing these things. It was just the right thing to do. I also believed some paths I walked along needed signs saying "Do not proceed further. Find an alternative route!" I was watchful of the things that bring a person to an important path or road in life and will produce a successful conclusion of the process.

My journey began many years ago in a small town in southern California. I was one of five children, all born within six years. My early years included the usual tension and high energy of a large family. Anger bounced around my childhood home from loud sibling conflict. My oldest brother, David, was not happy with his twin brothers being born two years after him. According to my mother, her first born was so easy and enjoyable at first. That is, until the twins came home from the hospital. From then on, all eyes were on them. David became a terrible two-year-old and an even worse older brother brooding often. He was known to creep in, when the babies were finally asleep, and yank hard on their cribs, waking them up, to my mother's heavy dismay. One time she discovered David showering the new baby twins with my dad's shaving cream.

I came a year after the twins and my sister followed two years later. My mom had been an only child and thought lots of children would be great. She assumed we would all love each other! How innocent she was. She knew nothing of sibling conflict and competition for attention. We did all learn to love and appreciate each other, but that would take a few years. In the mean time she had her hands full.

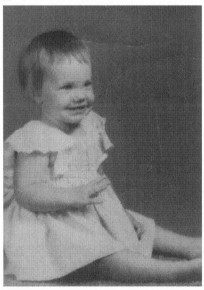

My father was an MD psychiatrist and often came home too tired to sort out the emotional issues we kids had with each other. He had worked hard all day, so his solution was to send whoever was upset or yelling, to his or her room. My mom was left for the most part to develop her own methods. She was initially the stay at home mom, active community club leader and an avid reader. She found ideas from self-help books on parenting and skills like "active listening." She modeled for me the skills of how to listen and be a supportive individual in times of crisis. I would apply these skills throughout my life.

Sound and music were a deeply important part of my personal environment. I loved to sing and tried to do so out of earshot of my brothers whenever possible. If even a hum was overheard the harsh comments would start. Despite this, singing a cappella gave me such a peaceful happiness that I found a way to express myself with my voice whenever possible. I often didn't even know I was humming to the radio, but it felt good.

Years later I would notice that music and specific songs played in my head. They were never random and often were a means for receiving guidance. My mom was a trained opera singer and eventually a professional voice teacher. She performed in many local musical theater productions, as well. My father was also a trained opera singer, so there was a lot of music in our home. The best place for me to sing was alone on our property or in my room when no one was near.

My brothers bullied me any way they could. They would taunt my efforts at singing as well. Perhaps they just enjoyed mocking people and perhaps I was entertaining to taunt. As a child, I never understood why they had such a need to rob me of my joy. It hurt me but mostly confused my nature. Despite this I had a way of being easily distracted by almost anything, if it cheered me up. I could pull myself out of deep wells of confusion and self doubt.

Later I would learn that what annoyed my brothers, for the most part, was my ability to be happy. They wanted to feel better, but did not know how and I reminded them of that. The fighting between my brothers was daily and may have been typical in a family of our size. Often my sister and I would stand at the window and watch with a sense of unease as my mom drove away to do errands. Once again we were left behind and our older brothers were in charge of things. I was able to see the potential for danger before others, but often my concerns went unheard. I cried with great gusto and passion when I was the target. They would sometimes grab and pin me down, bruising me. I would go off with loud screams.

Sometimes they loved to taunt me with a Halloween recording of stories by Edgar Allan Poe and "Tales from the Crypt."These were audio radio plays of murder and horror. My brothers would put the volume on full blast and pin me near the speakers, while my mom was out. She finally put the record out in the trash in a great show of fury. She could not fathom why her sons would do something so awful to their sister! Scary movies on TV were difficult for me as well. Images would encode easily in my mind's eye and I could access real life potential for the dramas that then gave me nightmares.

I noticed at a young age that my brothers had a reduced sense of loyalty or any need what-so-ever to protect me back then. Luckily most of the time I had a way of bouncing back from my brothers cruel jokes or slights. My mother used to say it amazed her how, after deep sobbing tears, I could redirect myself, with my toys or an activity, till I was humming happily again. I tried not to dwell on unpleasant things and found I had a will to live in peace despite the contrary state of affairs. Despite my brothers' cruel ways, I also wanted to be part of the gang, so I tried desperately to not cry and to hold the pet snake, even though it made my skin crawl to touch it.

Because of many things, I thought of myself as average in intelligence. Other kids seemed to receive more encouragement and attention. The first time I was identified as talented at something was when, as a young Girl Scout, our troop went on a horseback ride together. The stable owner and riding instructor pulled my mother, our troop leader, aside to point out how well I sat on my horse. The woman encouraged me to attend her weekly riding class.

I immediately signed up and learned to ride on the trail as well as in the arena doing all sorts of fun things like barrel racing, the game of Polo and performing a few horse show standard skills. I quickly was moved up to her advanced class and even assisted the teacher with her beginner's class by age eleven. It was the first time I felt respected and treated as an equal. In school I noticed how my grades were average, my popularity was average and my attention from teachers was just good. I was not a difficult student, nor was I the one raising my hand often with the answers. I blended in. I made friends but not a lot of them.

When it came to learning to play a musical instrument, I never liked to practice. It began with studying the piano. My teacher would begin each lesson by asking if I had practiced my scales etc. She fired me as a student when after three months, for the third time, I did not practice the lessons. I thought to myself, well at least I was honest about it! I took cello for about five months, but it did not hold my interest. I took guitar and that stuck for three years but again, I did not practice much even then. Repetition of any kind was hard for me. I wanted to move past that awkward stage and learn something quickly.

When we kids were very young, we moved into a comfortably sized home located in the hills of a small town in Southern California. It was an old house built at the turn of the century. With some remodeling over time, it grew in size to include a family room, an expanded kitchen, and even a large pool. I shared a room with my younger sister.

Our property had very tall evergreen and eucalyptus trees, thick shrubs, and natural paths winding down the hillside. Some trees were over eighty feet tall. The lush landscape allowed us kids to play on the property for hours without boredom. My oldest brother busied himself building tree houses in some of the trees, when he wasn't taking out his frustrations on his younger siblings.

At times we played summer games like flashlight tag at night with all the neighbor kids. Whoever was "It" carried around a flashlight and aimed it at the rest of us. You were out of the game if the light beam hit any part of your body. One time our game ended with me getting a minor injury. I had tried to climb over the cedar fence surrounding the pool area, and my foot got caught between the fence boards. I ended up hanging upside down by my pinned ankle. I screamed like I was dying until everyone came running. I felt an uncanny sense of being trapped like an animal. It was a dramatic end to the evening.

I now know that when children appear to over-react in fear to certain situations or conditions, often they have previously endured a far worse, but similar injury or death in a past life. Compassion and sensitivity are the best response. I believe I had been through several dramatic deaths in past lives and some of my childhood traumas were reenactments of the former experiences. My patterns needed to shift into a new phase for overall health and well being to come in.

We lived near the fire station. I liked visiting there sometimes with my sister and saying hello to the firemen. I somehow knew they were the kind of people that care and know how to help people when they get in a jam. I wished my brothers were more like them. Often the sirens would sound off and my brothers and I would attempt to ride our bikes after the fire trucks in the excitement of it all. I would jump on my bike and pedal behind my three brothers down the hill toward the quickly disappearing fire trucks.

One time however, my foot slipped off one pedal, hitting the asphalt. This threw my body over the top of the bike while my handle bars dug into my ribs. I tumbled to a stop. I was bleeding badly on one hand and my knee. My head hurt. I cried and whimpered as I pulled myself out of the road to the dirt shoulder. Soon after this, my brothers headed toward me. They had done what we always did. We would turn around to head home once we knew we could not catch up with the trucks. Without even stopping they passed me by while I lay there. With the comment "Oh she fell... she's fine." They pedaled by without another look. Then I passed out.

When I awoke, a car was slowing down near me and a man was asking if I was all right. This frightened me, because I had been taught that little girls and boys should not talk to strangers. With immense determination I pulled myself up to a standing position and limped with my bike toward home. I had gone only ten feet when I felt myself getting tired so I laid the bike down before passing out again.

This time when I became conscious, a different younger man was walking towards me from his parked van. He asked where I lived and if I needed a ride home. Adrenaline surged through me as I pulled my bike up and began walking again; assuring him I lived very nearby. Nervously, I thought, "No way am I getting into a strangers car, especially a van!" I think I passed out briefly again as I climbed the hill. The van followed behind me slowly.

After I was home, my mom glanced at me with interest. She had not heard about my bike crash from my brothers when they came in the door ahead of me. I felt amazed I had made it home! My mom had seen many scraped knees in our busy house of active children. She decided almost as an afterthought to take me to the emergency room at the nearby hospital, in order to be checked out. The nurse at the ER was all business and zero comfort. She was only interested in my knee and other abrasions. My knee hurt like hell when she scrubbed the area down and bandaged me up. I probably also had a concussion.

I later wondered why my brothers never told my mom that I had fallen and needed her help. At that time in my life it was hard to realize that I had brothers who would not come through for me when I needed them. They all seemed very preoccupied with themselves and each other. I learned the next day from my mom that the young man in the van was the son of one of her friends. Mom smiled curiously at me as she explained how surprised she was to hear more about my bike accident from her friend. That event stayed with me for a long time. Looking back on it, I believe it connected to a broader memory from another life of being left to die. This time I discovered my tremendous will to live and make it all the way home.

I have some hesitance writing about my personal life, but something keeps pushing me to just get it down on paper and it will all start to make sense. Maybe there is a need to give the events of my life a witness, beyond my own memory and the memory of those who may have crossed my path. Several more times, especially in my adult years, I had the experience of being left in a vulnerable state and having to do whatever it took to get to safety.

In several incidents in my adult life I had the privilege of witnessing my hidden teacher suddenly appear out of nowhere. He provided life saving assistance to me. One way or another I was being invisibly watched over and provided with what I needed, even when I did not believe I was.

In other situations I would discover resources within me that pulled me through it all. For example when I was in college one winter and walking back to my dorm room, I was jumped from behind by a young man probably intending to rape me. He said in my ear "I want to "f--- you", as he lifted me off the ground. Before I could even think it through, I had squirmed around to face him. I backhanded him hard enough to knock him off his feet. Granted he was drunk, staggering even. I then ran through the deep snow toward the girl's dorm, making it to safety. I remember catching my breath once inside and wondering where all that strength came from? I had never been taught self defense.

So how does awakening spiritually connect to any of my personal trials as a young woman? I think I needed to establish a clear sense of independence and self preservation beyond all other things. I also did not temp fate, but used common sense for the most part. God had plans for me that would require me to hang in there and trust that events would work out no matter what!

During a full scale awakening, the spontaneous high energy episodes can take tremendous self confidence to navigate through. I would not be where I am today if I did not hang in there and trust that it was all going to come together. If you follow the stories of some far eastern sages, you will learn they often had very difficult phases in their spiritual development, especially in childhood. Very few people understand what they are going through energetically, as powerful forces work to unseat them and or make them feel unworthy. Eventually it all works out and they become beacons of light in our world.

In the 1990's I became familiar with a woman called "Mother Mira" and known by many people as an awakened one. She is considered one of the significant divine mothers currently on our planet. She is about my age and is from India but established herself in Germany many years ago. She reportedly had a very intense spiritual awakening during childhood. As fate would have it, a wise older man understood her spiritual plight when he came upon her. She was about twelve years old at the time. He took her under his wing and became her guardian, allowing her to sort through her trials and complete her process of awakening safely.

I became acquainted with Mother Mira through a friend who traveled several times to Germany to sit with many others and experience Mira's presence. I felt her energy and warmth pass over me while hearing about her story through this friend who knew her. I asked for a picture of Mira and I have it still today. I honor her attainment and activity as a divine mother embodiment on earth. She teaches that there are a number of *mothers* on earth right now to assist humanity through this juncture in history.

I am sharing my story and conveying my experiences in a chronological way to inspire and offer hope to others who may feel alone sometimes on this difficult path. I do not know if I am considered a beacon of light today, but I have experienced many rare pathways into the light of God.

I have often wondered if it is because I am so unassuming that I make the right witness to what is truly available spiritually. Others tend to forget many subtle but important moments, I do not. Memories are powerful allies when the world sometimes leaves you in a ditch or views you as unimportant. Often I would keep my awareness of bigger things to myself. I came to discover that blending into the crowd can be necessary in the long run. I would eventually learn to trust the inner light would assert or advance when called to do either.

In this retelling of my life story, I will share how I traversed the cutting edge states of awakening and spiritual transformation, unlocked lifetimes of tangled karmic patterns, reached beyond heaven's gate and had astounding revelations about the universe we live in. My journey continued to find a purpose despite many setbacks. I demanded to see, feel and truly know the underlying truth of this world and with all my faculties. At times I was like a grain of sand or a drop in the river of life. I would wonder if anything knew me, yet my inner beacon was simply enough to carry me home.

Through the greatness of our creator and source, I have been allowed to see far beyond the veil and fully immerse myself in what is more real, more physically transformative, than anything I would have believed possible. Yet I do try to understand the critic in everyone. I myself benefitted from some skepticism, in this cosmic age of many teachers, but few masters. The best masters have many helpers as well that can extend aid when in a pinch.

Over the course of my life powerful teachings were unveiled for me that span the ages. The guidance from above made each step personal and relevant along the way to all that I love and hold dear. I grew to understand that something vast and intelligent was there in each moment. I had but to learn how to be a part of the mystical orchestration.

3

FIRST SIGHT OF HIM

From a young age, I wanted inner guidance and knew it was possible. As I have already stated, teasing comments from my brothers were common in my childhood. Despite being one of five children, I often felt alone and in need of a sense of connection with what truly cared about me. The semi chaos of day to day life in a large family often made me crave the peace and quiet. Once when things were really bad I cried and ran to my room like before, but this time I felt a whisper from my heart. I was drawn to look outside my window to the trees and hear the wind. As I looked out with my tear stained cheeks, I could hear the trees outside brushing up on my window. I resolved to go outside and feel the breeze. This began to happen on other occasions when my heart was heavy.

One of the many very tall eucalyptus trees had a low lying cradle where the branches spread out. It was one of my favorite spots. I would scramble up and settle into the tree branches and think of them as big loving arms. The wind, trees and I communed. I would giggle as the wind blew the forest around me. Our property had more trees than I could count. I believed the sudden gusts were in response to my request that the wind show me it had heard my wish. Then I would ask it to become very still and it would do that too. The warmth and love I received from nature was a welcome respite from the stressors of my early years. It seemed natural to speak to the wind and for it to hear my thoughts. I did not know that this was unusual.

I attended Sunday school for a few years, but it wore out my mom getting my brothers ready each week on time. We went to the First Baptist church in town. The minister was nice, but I remember usually becoming very bored. I would doodle on the little cards in the pews that people filled out for the offering plate. My sister and I would giggle and whisper silly things in each other's ears to pass the time.

My parents separated when I was nine. Around this time my

grandmother attempted to teach us kids about God and Jesus. My grandmother probably meant well checking on us kids a few times when my parents first separated. My father had moved out so his mother probably felt it was important to support her daughter-in-law with all those children.

One evening my grandmother tucked us in after insisting we read a children's story with religious over-tones. I remember it was about a little boy taking some fruit from a tree that was in the neighbor's yard. The message was that God would punish you for that sin. For my sister and me, her lectures on God came across way too strong. It was always about fearing God. "He sees everything," she would say to us. She spoke of Jesus having died for us and that we must believe in him or we would go to hell. I grew more and more determined to find out who this Jesus was and why we needed to be so afraid of God!

That night lying alone in my bed I asked silently but boldly, "If Jesus is *real* I want to see him *now*!" Before I could finish my thought, a blinding bright flash of light filled my bedroom. It penetrated my forehead. I knew instantly it was HIM. Just when I was becoming overwhelmed, the light diminished and was gone. I realized at that moment something very important had happened. Information was poured into me by that light. I could never question his existence again. I realized I needed to respect what he really is and not worry about the church and my grandmothers' version of him.

As I lay there quietly in bed I realized that Jesus would not have made me afraid of God because he was love. I knew suddenly that the Christian religion that seemed to represent him had some issues. I knew it taught some things that were not accurate like his name, but I did not yet know what his name really was. I wondered about the Bible in general, but felt grateful having been reacquainted with the real Jesus. I would eventually find the courage to approach him again many years later. At that time I chose to be silent about the whole experience, sensing that it was something special. I decided I should keep it to myself.

From a young age, I was unusually rigid in my scrutiny of those in positions of authority. I believed only in ethical use of power and privilege. I was not willing to just accept a person of authority because of some title he or she wore. I believe my parents saw me as a tad insubordinate at times even toward them. Some of my school teachers also found me not that easy to please. One of my seventh grade teachers, whom I liked, once said to our class, "I always know what Miss Henderson is thinking of my lecture by the expression on her face." He admitted that he could often tell how good his lesson for the day was by looking at me. People laughed and then he softened his stance by saying that he appreciated that I was listening and following him closely.

Some say the greatest teachers in history show us a way or a path to follow. Often the journey is not without peril and may require thoughtful choices along the way. I knew for some reason long ago that some of the best teachers are also not visible and may seem to leave us to discover what we are made of in our hour of need. I learned to pay attention to a hidden teaching behind each encounter with a visible teacher. My inner antennae would notice my heart had skipped a beat in response to the information coming at me. I would ear-mark it for later questioning of its accuracy. This allowed me to listen respectfully to a teacher in any context without being concerned that he or she were *the* authority on the topic. I had chosen to be guided to the truth of things through many levels of internal awareness.

Over the years, I kept my awareness of the real Jesus and the intelligence and spirit of nature to myself. With my parent's divorce, I was set free from all the torment my brothers were dishing out. My sister and I got to move to a new home with my mother.

At first, I felt so much peace and did not miss my brothers one bit. Over time, however, each of them ran into me at school and asked how I was doing living with just mom. I saw that they were becoming truly sorry for all they had done to me which was for the most part emotional abuse.

After many years I grew to learn possible reasons why people wound others with their words and actions. Simply put, they feel threatened. Words should be honest but not grievous and timing is important. My brothers seldom cared that their words were having a lasting effect on me. To cut down or criticize with harshness is actually to cut creation. I believed words should always bring a situation into more clarity, even if the words are initially difficult to hear or are unwelcomed. It is all about communication.

I appreciate the direct approach most of the time. It was not hard to forgive my brothers, once I saw they had a sincere desire to make amends. I secretly just wanted their love and support, as do most people. As a young person, I had to defend myself and grow tough. Eventually I learned to stop crying so easily. I knew I had to do whatever it took to face fears instead of overwhelming myself. I also learned that sometimes just being a witness to life events or being there for someone could be enough.

As I noticed others being bullied by kids in junior high, I found I could step forward and question the one involved. My words began to matter and often I could sway the situation away from insults and injury for someone else. I was thoughtful and some would say shy at first, but once thrust into the limelight, I found I had a stubborn will to survive the moment. In general I did not want to be a difficult person.

Looking back on all those formative years is still puzzling. I did not believe I was in any way unique. Despite this, I began to read and study at an early age rather advanced teachings about the mind and the universe. The concept of past lives came to me in junior high and did not seem crazy but in fact made sense. Perhaps in some other life I was interesting and unique or at least had done something remarkable. This was the mood I carried around as a teenager. I was content to observe from the back of the room unless something really forced me to the front of a situation.

When I was about fifteen, I recall staring into the bathroom mirror at my face and wondering why I looked the way I did. Our family's blood line had Scottish, English, Irish and Welsh in it. I understood it was my parent's genes. I noticed that my brown hair, blue eyes and freckled face were consistent, but I had a vague memory of something else. I closed my eyes and could imagine olive skin and brown eyes. I pulled on the sides of my eyes gently, until I looked more almond eyed. The freckles were something to adjust to internally.

Toward the end of junior high my mom, my sister and I moved to East San Diego. Six months later we moved to University City which is near La Jolla. It was in the middle of ninth grade that I began to see spirits hovering over me some nights, after I went to bed. I would scream and they would disappear. I took a class with my mom on meditation from a psychic medium. She taught me protective prayers and felt like a guardian angel.

At one of her classes she zeroed in on me and told me that she visited me the previous week. I was in disbelief wondering what she meant. She clarified that she had seen me while she traveled in spirit. She saw me in my room trying to meditate on Thursday. She added that she saw that my legs were crossed so she had whispered to me to uncross them. "Down they came and you were in the zone for a moment," she said with a smile.

I was wide eyed at the thought of this woman traveling as a spirit to visit her students! I confirmed that I had tried to meditate the previous Thursday and I did in fact uncross my legs! Because of other obligations, my mom and I could not keep attending this teacher's class on psychic development and the kind old woman passed away the following year.

My mom took me to psychic fairs on occasion. When I was about sixteen or seventeen, during a psychic reading with my best friend, the reader said we knew each other also in several past lives. One past life in particular struck me, because it seemed so impossible, but as she spoke, I remembered something about it. She said we were both young child healers and we would play with energy balls, sending them back and forth to one another. It was during a lost age, probably Atlantis.

I began playing with energy balls that night before I fell asleep and sent one off to my friend Liz. I imagined energy and light pooling in my hand until it felt full and then I sent it out. Liz was planning on doing the same from her house. I drifted off to sleep knowing something important was learned today. I would later draw from this remembered skill.

I studied the book THE NATURE OF PERSONAL REALITY, by Jane Roberts. She channeled a spirit named Seth who taught that we create our own reality, or that the universe rearranges itself to accommodate our sense of reality. My sister and I both began to read all of Jane Roberts many books. I practiced what I learned about the power of the mind and discovered that amazing miracles could happen.

For example, I had loaned a new dress to a friend one weekend. She returned it with red wine stains on it and a short apology. I stared at it, feeling such loss at first. Then I realized that if I am participating with reality, I can honestly say it would be nice if it did not have that stain on my new dress. I sighed in resigned disbelief and took it to the dry cleaners. It came back looking much the same with the stain, so I hung the dress in the back corner of my closet, unable to bring myself to throw it away.

One night that same summer I was bored and could not sleep. I began visualizing the dress in my mind. I tried to picture it without the stain. It kept showing a stain in my mind. I remembered reading in Jane Roberts's book about our emotional connection with an event. There is a need to let go of all the attachments to the event in order for the universe to change. I realized I was still angry at this friend.

I read another book called CREATIVE VISUALIZATION, by Shakti Gawain. I played more at it and thought of fun things such as visualizing myself having a better tan at the beach. Each little experiment would work. I would become fascinated with concepts like "everything is energy" and how we co-create our own reality.

One evening I tried again to picture the dress without the stain, but it still appeared in my mind's eye with the red spill. By then I had realized this new girl at our school was working hard to be liked. She had avoided me since the dress incident. I noticed she had lost other friends over the months. I felt compassion for her need to fit in. I finally let it all go and imagined that she had never even borrowed my dress. For a moment I could see the dress in my mind without the stain. I continued to do this visualization for a couple weeks, then it got boring and I forgot about the whole thing.

The following spring I was moving clothes to the front of my closet. As I grabbed the dress, I staggered backward. It had no stain! The dress looked perfect! The molecules had rearranged themselves somehow into a clean untouched dress.

The power of doing visualizations was beginning to seem almost too powerful. I soul searched what it all really meant but tried more elaborate things. For example, in one of my daydreams I would picture my senior year boyfriend, who had recently moved far away, at my front door. I missed him and saw no way to ever see him again. For a month I fell asleep picturing him at my front door. It relaxed me and I felt less concerned about heading off to college and not knowing anyone. I never imagined he would pick up on the energy of my visualization.

One afternoon, there he was standing in my doorway almost embarrassed to admit he had hitchhiked from northern California over the past three days. He said he just suddenly had to see me. He didn't really say why, but it sounded like quite an ordeal to get to my house. He was happy to be there, as was I to have him there, but it all felt strange. Was it fair? I thought for a while about free will and how the universe keeps it all straight. So I backed off doing the heavy creative visualizations.

I then headed off to college arriving in Gunnison Colorado by the end of that summer. I never saw that boyfriend again. I met a new guy named Bob my second year in college. I had dated other men, but there was chemistry with this one. He was a college dropout but with a high IQ and a charm I could not overlook. He was six years older than I was and worked as the foreman of a house painting company up at the resort town of Crested Butte. He was devoted to skiing and the great outdoors.

We fell in love and quickly moved into a place of our own. We lived together for over a year and then broke up when he got laid off and had to move back east to explore more opportunities for work. I adjusted to my first big emotional loss of a relationship pretty well and grew strong enough to do well in college, make new friends etc.

I did a certain amount of soul searching over my sense of loss regarding this man that I had loved. To gain insight I received my first Tarot deck while in college still. It arrived in the mail as a gift from my mom. Many things I pondered about life would be looked at through the lens of my card reading layout. I eventually learned to do intuitive readings for just about anything a person could inquire about.

In 1983 I graduated with a Bachelor of Arts degree in sociology with a minor in psychology. I searched for a job in some form of entry level counseling. Around that same time my mom wanted to move back to her childhood roots that were from the Midwest. She invited me to join her. Mom and I moved to Libertyville, Illinois. After reading the help wanted section of the newspaper, I prayed that I would not end up being a cocktail waitress or worse in that town. These were the only jobs available in the area. Finally an advertisement came out soliciting individuals with a minimum of a bachelor's degree in psychology or related. I had enough psychology and education credits to qualify.

I was hired and worked for over a year at a treatment facility for court ordered teenage boys with crime, substance abuse and mental health issues in Lake Forest Illinois. I was called a Group Care Worker and was assigned ten boys in ten hour shifts. These were tough kids and skilled manipulators. I learned to help them help each other and themselves through a treatment modality called "Positive Peer Culture." We were taught to ask our group questions and not to give answers if at all possible. The teaching style was designed to create an atmosphere of caring rather than aggression in the teenagers.

I remember often asking the group members to point out hurting behaviors or helping behaviors in each other. The boys were better at confronting and teaching each other how to change, than any therapy I had ever heard of. A positive peer culture would begin to form over time in the effective groups. Despite their violent backgrounds, I was not really afraid of the kids. Maybe the years of struggle with my brothers had given me some insights and a thick skin. The teenagers seemed to respond and over time I witnessed a few transforming into really caring individuals.

I got promoted then to work with females of the same age group at a smaller Girl's Group Home in Highland Park, Illinois. It followed the same Positive Peer Culture treatment modality. I remember one shift sitting at the dinner table with the ten girls. Words heated up as things escalated into an emotional explosion from one small but powerful female. She launched at another girl across the table as forks flew through the air. All the girls were afraid of this one. They fled to every door out into the street.

I jumped up from my seat at the large table and pulled her down to the floor as she spat and cussed in my face. I was not going to allow her to hurt anyone. I do not know where the insight came from, but I managed to bring her out of her rage and into tears. While pinning her down I spoke forcefully that I cared too much about her to allow her to go on like this. I said I was not afraid of her outburst.

I went on to say that I knew she could really make something of her life. But she would have to start today to be more honest and talk things out and be a good leader. The best she could be. She hugged me and apologized for making a scene. That girl made a big change after that day. Over time she began to exhibit true caring for the other girls. She also learned to confront new girls in a healthy way and motivate them to improve their lives.

I worked for less than a year more in this type of work. It made an enormous impression on me. Looking back on my younger years, I remember how I explored verbal ways to end fights. As a white girl, I was in the minority in junior high at first. Being harassed was all too common. Not getting hurt was something I had to figure out quickly.

Here it was many years later and I could feel the power of truth and how my words came from some place deep within me. I was beginning to see also that I wanted desperately to find a way out of hate and violence. I came to believe many hopeless situations could be turned around, if the person saw a better way out of the dilemma. I was discovering that something beyond my obvious awareness was quietly asking me to stay brave and allow my inner knowing to guide me.

Working with adolescents was an interesting exploration in all the behaviors that involve rebellion and aggression. I could appreciate the intelligence of these young people. They were not afraid to be different but deep down they wanted life to make sense and for people to be decent. Many had been abused and were survivors. They needed a strong person who cared and would not just let them take over. They also needed a way to be given a choice to make a change for the better. When things were forced or imposed upon them, they would rebel almost like an instinct. It was an art form to learn to help them help themselves. While working at those facilities, I learned many things from the older counselors who had worked for many years with that age group.

What a journey my life has been, and it isn't even over. As my story continues, I will describe many of my experiences with angels, energy, consciousness and dimensional doorways. First, I had to move to a new part of the country.

4

HARMONIC CONVERGENCE
WITH NATURE

My post college career had taken form. I was living with and supporting my mother in a small town in Illinois, very near her childhood roots. She was enjoying a reunion with old friends and relatives. However, I never really felt a connection to the area and had trouble meeting new people. I tried to join a gym and meet people but I could not make a single social contact outside of work. One day I received an unexpected phone call from my old boyfriend Bob from my college days. This surprised me at the time. I would eventually learn that we had a very old connection from other lifetimes.

Bob had been living in Connecticut for a few years since our breakup back in early 1982. We caught up on things and eventually it was decided he should come to Illinois for a visit. It was summer. After his visit, we began to have regular phone conversations and he invited me to come for Thanksgiving in Connecticut and meet his parents. I felt like I was finally becoming his significant other. I had a very nice holiday with his family. It was especially meaningful to meet his father. He died unexpectedly a year or so later.

Bob and I planned our new life together with more phone calls. We decided that he would come to the Midwest again with all his personal things and spend the spring with my mother and me. My mother needed a painter to paint her eleven room farm house and decided to hire him. The money he would earn could help with the next stage of the journey; relocating us to Idaho. We picked Idaho because it had great skiing, mountains, and the town of Boise and surrounding area was in a slump, so it might have affordable housing.

I flew back east to meet up with Bob and join him for the road trip.

Together we arrived in the spring with all his belongings in a rented moving van, while I followed in his truck. He worked for weeks on my mom's large house until it had a three color professionally painted exterior that everyone was happy with. It was a fun summer. We all grew closer and it was nice having him around the house for my mom.

That summer Bob left and headed further west to Boise. He wanted to secure a house with just what he could fit in his own truck. I stayed three months more in Illinois to finish out my job with the Highland Park Girls Group Home. We hired a moving company in the fall to move the rest of our things to Idaho. My mom rode with me in my car to Boise then caught a flight back to Illinois. The recommendation letter my supervisor provided for me from the Highland Park facility was very fulfilling and helped me to secure a job after I arrived in Idaho. Things were going well!

I was hired in the fall of 1985 as the director of an adolescent outpatient treatment program in an agency called the Nelson Institute. I interviewed new clients and gave alcohol/drug evaluations, ran evening adolescent treatment groups and assisted with adult groups on occasion. I was certified the following year as an associate alcohol/drug counselor. I loved having my own office and did not mind the stress of the work load.

It was time for Bob and me to get married. We would choose the Saint John's Cathedral in Boise Idaho. We were impressed with the beauty of the cathedral's intricate stained glass one morning that winter. We pulled the car over and walked in. It was Sunday and a service was starting. We found our seats. The message of the sermon was about the mystery of the faith. I liked this and the older priests' way of speaking his message. He shined for me with a soft wisdom.

As the service was ending, Bob leaned over to me and asked if I would like to have our wedding in this church? It felt right. I nodded in agreement as we headed towards the door. The Priest was greeting people as they exited the main doors. Bob asked him politely about the possibility of holding our ceremony there. Bob's Catholic background along with my willingness to take a six week class for spouses, made it official.

That spring on our wedding day we were picked up by one of Bob's groomsman in a *Rent a Dent* rental car and driven to the church. Bob found his friend's choice of car rentals humorous. I just hoped that my long white sleeveless dress remained pristine during the short ride. Before we arrived, the two men drank shots of alcohol in the car, to my dismay. It was 102 degrees that day and all the men in the wedding were in wool suits with tails. Luckily we had chosen a morning service.

We were new in town, so most everyone in attendance was from out of state. As I walked down the aisle, the organ player hit a number of wrong keys. There I was in front of all our family members and friends trying not to laugh. I was in love despite this odd omen and ready for whatever was next.

After the service, like all couples we strolled down the aisle feeling pretty good. Afterward our personal wedding photographer had us wait until everyone left to do all the wedding photos at the church. Our guests eventually headed off to the reception venue at a nearby hotel restaurant.

The wedding party photo shots were done first. The day was now very hot and we were all dripping as we were asked to pose in various ways. As I waited to be photographed, I realized I was concerned about my husband's drinking. The whiskey shots on the way to the service seemed wrong. I was lost in my thoughts of concern for my new husband. I felt a quiet invisible presence with me as I stood alone down in front near the church altar with my head down. I silently made a commitment to God to follow his guidance as I faced the unknown future. I also knew I had agreed to be with him in sickness and in health. The photographer snapped away capturing several shots.

The photographer finally finished the official wedding photos. We could now go to our reception at a nearby venue. Our reception included a band with a female lead singer that later learned I was also a singer. After we had all eaten she offered me the microphone. I asked if she knew a particular song. They knew the song so I sang it for everyone to a round of applause. That part was fun but Bob became too drunk as the night wore on.

From the time of our engagement earlier that year, I had begun to realize that my new husband was probably an alcoholic. The signs were impossible to ignore. He wasn't just drinking daily and passing out on the couch, he began to have blackouts. He would seem like a different person and remember none of it. Some days he would slur his words after staggering into the house insisting he had *not* drunk anything that day. The level of denial was profound to witness.

I found him asleep in his truck several times during work hours. He never gave a reason for his behavior and seemed oblivious to his appearance. He was becoming more unpredictable as the months rolled on. I believed it was not an accident that I was working at a treatment center for such illnesses. Everything was in place for me to have the support and insight I would need to deal with his drinking.

My employer sat me down at work one day. I admitted I had problems at home that appear to be my husband's drinking problem. My boss said that it is more common than not to discover you have a family member struggling with addiction after entering this field of work. She spoke candidly to me about my options. She said it was important to keep my husband's behavior in perspective and avoid the pitfalls of becoming co-dependent.

All my colleagues gave me a lot of gentle support over the next three years. Almost everyone at the agency was a recovering alcoholic with years of sobriety. Most of my colleagues were successful people with careers and had transformed their lives. The best advice I received from my colleagues was to pursue my own interests and avoid being overly focused on my husband's drinking behavior. If I had concerns, I was to voice them to him only when he was sober.

I was invited by colleagues from work to attend some open Alcoholics Anonymous (AA) meetings. It was so I could learn more about that program. I liked the "higher power" part. It formed an important foundation for me, as I coped with life in general and my husband's illness. As an agency, we recommended AA and NA to all of our clients. Learning about the twelve steps enhanced my insights with my clients. I knew I needed to form a strong connection with my higher power also. Anyone can benefit from a quick study of the 12 steps. Deep down I was searching for spiritual support of a more direct kind, however.

I had read books on the nature of consciousness, personal reality and intuition for years. Since I was in my twenties I had played with tarot cards to get answers and did occasional readings for people. With my husband falling into the pit of alcoholism, I had to really listen to guidance from within and discern the best path forward each day.

I became pregnant soon after Bob and I married. I remember having my first ever migraine headache at work one day while sitting in my office. I decided to visit a doctor about the sudden headaches and learned I was pregnant! Perhaps I had some inner conflict in me that created the migraine. I was very much looking forward to being a mom, but my husband did not seem as excited. Bob eventually came around to the concept of it all. I think I was realizing that my job and career would have to adjust drastically and money might be a struggle. Bob was a painting contractor always on the hunt for more work. Relying on him and his income was going to be interesting.

To prepare for the birth of our first child I did what is called a rebirthing with a new medicine woman friend. It involved a specific type of session or guided journey back to my own birth and is said to be a good way to prepare for the coming of a child. My rebirthing session took me into vivid images of a dark tunnel with twinkling lights. I felt my whole body remembering my birth. It felt like an amusement ride at night, when you cannot see much, but you feel thrown around. I was aware of a desire to come into the world when it was quiet and safe.

My father was a doctor, so he was allowed to be present at my own birth in the hospital. This was less common back in the late 50's and early 60's. The rebirthing brought up a disturbing memory of being handed around after I was born, like a specimen. I could remember not being allowed to join with my mother when I needed to. My father innocently found himself acting more like a doctor than a dad. In the memory of my birth his behavior and energy were detached. I came out of the session feeling aware of my child self being hurt and confused at that early age over my dad's clinical handling of me at first. I wanted him to just hold me and keep me safe.

I later confirmed with my mother that the night of my birth, doctors had given up on her labor progressing and left the room. It was only after this and her relaxing into the quiet of the room that I suddenly decided to be born. My mom yelled for help and remembered it was like all hell broke loose, as the hospital came to life around her to assist in the delivery. I was born sometime after midnight. I was examined by my dad and his doctor friends who delivered me and was not given to my mom right away.

One might think that doing a rebirthing is not a significant healing, but my father phoned me up soon after my experience. He said he would like to take time off and be at our child's birth if possible. I was thrilled to have my dad wanting to try and be there after our baby comes. Plans were made.

My labor with my son was long; nearly 21 hours. I was at home and the long hours did not seem hard. Once it was time for the delivery everything was ready for Bob to help out too. He had been given permission by the midwives to cut the umbilical cord. Unfortunately when the time came for it the moment was very tense. Everyone could see that the cord was wrapped around our baby's neck and his color was purple! My husband moved quickly with the guidance of the midwife. Once it was cut off Bob held baby Harry first and calmed his tears.

I had some delays in recovering from the birth because I had lost a lot of blood from a tear. I was so anemic at first; I would pass out sitting up to nurse baby Harry. I had to do it lying on my side. My dad showed up the following day. He showed uncharacteristic interest in my needs during his stay. He vacuumed and made meals for me. It was very healing to have him visiting. My mom showed up too, but a week later. With my parents being divorced I enjoyed having each of them visit separately. My mom helped out as well. I loved feeling the karmic layers lifting.

In contrast to the joy of a new baby and the comfort of being connected with new friends that appreciated spiritual interests and personal growth, I was also dealing with my husband's worsening drinking patterns. My work colleagues from our agency suggested that I try and get Bob to meet with an alcohol and drug counselor. They reminded me that there was someone formerly with our agency who now was about to open an inpatient treatment center in town. We all liked him and Bob had even met him before. After broaching the topic, my husband surprised me and agreed to meet with this man and do an alcohol and drug evaluation.

Upon his return home from the assessment, Bob stated that he learned he was probably an alcoholic. The discussion quickly became also a declaration that he was not ready to quit. I was calm and accepting of his honesty. Each small intervention into his situation delivered some relief, filled with some hope. I also knew that he was being shown an option that he could one day pursue when he was ready. He would eventually find help. I then put my attention back on what lifted my spirit and fed my heart's longing for more spiritual growth.

In Boise it was easy to find lots of interesting classes on spirituality and metaphysics. I took one workshop from a woman named Karmin. She had renamed herself after discovering that her given name had terrible numerology. She taught that ever since she changed her name, her life had become much better. I attended a weekend workshop called "Linking with your God Self" taught by Karmin. After I took her workshop, I signed up for her weekly meditation classes. She channeled and did a form of intuitive regression therapy as well.

The meditation part of Karmin's class was not easy for me at first, but I did not know why. I would relax into the music and then all of the sudden I would become startled from something. Within a week after the first class, I experienced a spontaneous past life regression. It began just after I lay down to go to sleep one evening without any warning,

I was suddenly in a different world where something awful was taking place. I was looking up at a night sky while a frightening face leaned over me. In terror I recoiled back and it brought me into the awareness of my bedroom, heaving to catch my breath. After I calmed myself, I realized that it was a past life and I had died in an unpleasant way. The travel back in time felt so real! It was compelling how even the smell of the air lingered. I prayed to Archangel Michael for protection and eventually fell asleep.

The very next day I called Karmin to ask for help with my weird spontaneous time travel. In a very matter-of-fact tone she said, "You are having a past life come to the surface of your awareness in order for it to be healed." She asked if I was free that afternoon. She said she felt certain she could assist me through a regression to address the memory. She added that her process was not hypnosis.

After she arrived, we settled into chairs in my living room. She quickly guided me into the powerful memory after calling on Jesus and the angels to watch over us. It opened up like a movie script set on an island long ago in the tropics. It was at night and the air was humid and smelled of fresh blood. Torch lights surrounded a clearing in the jungle. A tribe of Polynesian-like people all stood watching the torture and killing of a member of the tribe on a large flat stone alter. It was me and I was in a lot of pain.

Karmin asked me to rise above the scene and see if anyone else familiar was there in that life. As I peered into the scene, I could sense that I was hated by the tribe's shaman/medicine man for some reason. He stood farther back with arms folded in a cold satisfied stance. I sensed this man was connected with a dark form of power. Karmin, with the guidance of Jesus, suggested I look into the man's eyes that stood over me with his knife in my guts. I was not able to look at his face and knew he was moving a blade into my intestines.

Karmin had a calm tone and reminded me that I need not feel

anything from the images of death. It took every ounce of faith to do this. Once I did it, I instantly knew the man was one of my brothers in this life and I was no longer afraid. The person hovering over me had been forced into his role as the executioner by the chief. I somehow knew my brother was innocent and in some drug induced state. It was all part of the tribal ceremony.

Karmin guided me to see into the heart of each person involved and to unlock who they are today in my life. I discovered a different brother was the angry tribal leader back then and he had ordered my execution on that island. He was harder to see into, but with the help of Jesus I found the light underneath the powerful rage and eventually things moved toward a healing.

The method I was shown asked me to trust that there is a light, an original innocence in the person you are struggling to understand. As you drop into the heart and look for the love or light inside or behind the person's heaviness, you often discover a hidden lost child or trapped person. Love lights the way and Jesus already knew of course that it would help me and my brothers heal something very old. Because I loved my brothers and knew they were good people, I was able to release the fear and confusion of that haunting image that had left a blockage in what is known as the third eye at the center of the forehead. Love spread through the entire memory and I came out of the session feeling a great relief.

Later I learned that my ability to focus inward and meditate had been blocked by the intensity of that former death. Something now had been lifted. I could *see* colors and images more easily with my inside eyes and feel peaceful for longer periods of time in my meditations. I began to ask to really feel something in my cells from a meditation. When I meditated at Karmin's class, just the mention of Jesus' name by the instructor caused my skin to buzz or grow warm and tingly. This really impressed me. I liked a tangible tactile experience of a real being like him. It was all working and it excited me.

My husband's drinking continued to concern me. It may also have added to the heavier energy of astral souls lurking around as we slept. I went through months of battling dark energies in my sleep. I thought to myself, at least I was brave. Jesus knew better. He began to enter my dreams at night, intervening numerous times when I found myself in over my head in creepy places. He kept showing up and ending the nightmare with the lift of his hand.

One time, I recall so vividly in one dream Jesus just looked at me with a serious expression. I felt like he was saying, "Are you done yet?" I needed to stop looking for trouble and face my fears with the realization that

I would never win anything in these battles. I learned that I was hiding my fear behind anger much like a warrior does. I did not trust that love was a power that could provide answers and end a nightmare.

Karmin and I became friends. I learned that she was a sober recovering alcoholic of many years. She said that Jesus and the angels saved her from the abyss of drinking. I learned how to do her past life regression healing process. I would eventually learn to do this type of healing even in my nighttime dreams. I might have a dream of angry and murderous people. Once I realized I was dreaming, I could do the process and let love open hearts.

Other vivid past lives surfaced for me as well. This time the images came in full color dreams at night. I was thrown into a shark pond and eaten alive in one life. I woke up in a cold sweat when that memory surfaced through my dreams. My mom in that life was a terrifying dictator from the ancient world in a past life of mine. I pealed back the layers to see the patterns and forgive my part, my mother's and those of any others that were involved.

In the weekly meditation class I took from Karmin, I learned that I was a natural intuitive channel. She pointed out several times that my innocent comments in the class were the same ones she was hearing from her master guides. She said they would like to work with me more closely. I was asked to meditate before bed briefly and call on them.

I began getting awakened every morning at 3:30 a.m. for no reason. I took my teacher's advice and began writing in a journal. I wrote whatever came to me and soon I filled up several journals with messages from the Ascended Masters. Karmin recommended I also study very old books by the Ascended Masters called the LAW OF LIFE books.

One day, to my surprise, Karmin called and insisted I could heal her tooth problem. She said, "You already know how to do this, so please just help me out." I learned that she had an abscessed tooth that in all likelihood needed a dentist's care, but she had no money for one. I asked when she would have the money and she said in thirty days.

I hung up and remembered the energy balls of light and pictured light pooling in my hand, and then going to her tooth. The phone rang and she laughed and said "Thank you!" Thirty days later the pain came back. She still did not want to pay for a dentist to help her but I had done my part. I was surprised at how my momentary instinct produced physical changes in her! I did not feel confident I could do it for others so I did not go further with healing body stuff for several years.

∞

I began to make new friends in Boise. One of the women in that first meditation class taught by Karmin was named Bobbie Jo. She and her husband lived across the street from us. Since starting that class, our families had grown close. Bobbie Jo and I launched some of the first New Age Psychic Fairs in Boise. The first two were very large so other friends joined in the planning and creation. These Fairs were a fun way to meet many different practitioners. I dabbled in giving tarot readings for friends and people that asked but mostly was the main organizer of these events.

One day, Bobbie Jo and I both felt like doing an overnight camping trip up in the mountains. We planned to drive well beyond the Boise foothills. Our goal was to meditate in nature and just enjoy an evening away from kids and husbands. We asked the angels to guide us to the right spot.

After nearly two hours we found ourselves farther from Boise than we intended. Eventually we headed down an old Forest Service road, still feeling excited about the adventure of being guided to our spot for the day and night. That is until we came to the camp area at the end of the road. We saw so much trash everywhere it was shocking. There had been no cars passing us on the road for several miles back. We were alone.

With the spirit of optimism, we slowly ventured the car into an area that had a fire ring near the creek. When we got out, we just looked around in amazement. It was too late in the day to find a new camp site. Without thinking further, we did what women do; we silently began to clean the area up. Someone had hung a leaf size hefty bag full of stinking garbage in a bush. We added to it what we could and filled a few more trash bags that we had brought with us. It did not take long to improve things, but it was an eerie feeling to have been guided to this spot. We set up our tent and then just sat by the creek, which was orange and yellow in color and did not seem safe to even put our feet in.

Finally we settled on sitting ourselves down out in the open meadow. "Let's meditate," said Bobbie Jo. We closed our eyes and within a short time I felt a bear-like forceful energy. I opened my eyes briefly and looked around. Calming myself I went back to eyes closed. The energy then shifted into a strong nature spirit. I sensed he was standing nearby with arms folded in disgust.

I opened my eyes and she opened hers and we whispered to each other something like "Are you seeing/sensing a short spirit-guy, kind of angry?" She agreed and pointed to the exact spot. He was about three feet tall with a ruddy brown complexion.

We closed our eyes again and tried to ask him a question. He turned around, as if he was blowing us off. After a few more minutes, we felt a strange embarrassment and dismay. This presence clearly conveyed disapproval toward humanity in general. We were unknowingly representing humans and all their trash! I realized that the creek was probably seriously polluted. The area was without even the sound of birds or wind in the trees. Nature was really making a point to demonstrate the toxic effect humans were having on it.

We stood up and looked around for some way to remedy this dynamic further. This stretch of land seemed to be the site of much abuse. I looked across the creek and felt something sparkle farther up the hill. Then we both began to sense little energy movements coming out of hiding in a bunch of evergreens. I noticed a healthier feeling on the other side of the creek, as if people had never ventured that way. Those "sprites" or elementals across the creek were deciding on some level to give us a chance. However, I sensed we had to prove we were different from all those humans that had come and gone for so long. We both got the feeling that the nature spirits would be watching us for a while. I did not know what this meant. My friend and I sensed a subtle relief in our hearts. It became time to make dinner and settle in for the night. In the morning we drove away with three bags full of trash.

When we arrived back in Boise, I met a friend named Jan for lunch at an outdoor café near my home. I was beginning to tell her the story about the bizarre camping trip I had returned from, when I became distracted by her facial expression. She had begun to tip her head sideways and lean out, as if to see something behind me. I was in front of a planter box filled with flowers. I turned around to see what she was looking at but I saw nothing. Jan giggled and said, "I don't know how to say this, but a tiny brown skinned guy was peeking out from around your shoulder. I just couldn't figure out what to say to you." As I continued my story she laughed out loud at the incredible series of events I was describing. She wondered what these "nature spirits" wanted from me.

As I thought about it I said, "I will channel with them and find out what they have in mind." My friend laughed again and said she just saw the guy leap into a different box of flowers that lined the outdoor seating area and then disappear. We both wondered if others would see him around me and if he would show up again. After we finished our meal, she hugged me and wished me luck.

Between 1987 and 1988 I wrote a short story called "The Secret

Meadow" through channeling. This involved allowing the entire story to flow easily from my pen. It began a week or two after the camping trip. I channeled to ask the nature energies what they wanted me to do for them. Then words flowed through me onto the pages. I never had an outline or even a clue where it was all going until it was done. A friend showed up in my life that had a small editing business around this time. She said my story was great and only needed minor editing. I self published a few dozen copies for friends and relatives.

The story is about a little girl who lives in New York and visits her family's property in the Adirondack area upstate. She gets lost in the forest and begins to hear and see the nature spirits. Their messages to her were so much fun to read. The intelligence of nature was coming to life for me and my own inner child was clapping in delight. Here are two original spontaneous drawings I did from 1988-1990.

I channeled messages from the nature spirits in my garden and drew channeled images of them. These images would start as doodles, and then all sorts of complex things would pop out of the scribble. Some were so cool that I included them in the book, on its cover and inside the text in a few places to illustrate the child's experiences.

Along with the weekly channeling and writing, I began to offer sessions out of our house in past/present life regression therapy. People came about once a month on weekends for sessions. I was given referrals from a nearby metaphysical bookstore. I fit the work around being a mother and busy counselor for the chemically dependent. I was moved and humbled by the troubled people I worked with each day.

Karmin saw my gifts unfolding and invited me to join in her new business in a home she rented in the foothills. She created a new healing center called "The House of Love and Light." She did her regression healing work at the location and offered readings.

That summer Karmin and I planned to hold a community wide event as part of a world event called the Harmonic Convergence (World Meditation August 17 and 18, 1987). We both had received channeled guidance weeks before asking each of us to focus on the topic of karmic release during the Harmonic Convergence dates. I was told to put my attention on nature. I assumed this meant the animals and maybe the forests needed love and healing. I unknowingly began to leave the insects out of my preliminary meditations.

A week before the event, I experienced the spirit of a huge insect one night in my bedroom. It was praying-mantis-like, but bright yellow. It looked menacing at first, as the presence filled my bedroom. After a moment I understood what it wanted. With relief it backed off a few feet. I understood telepathically that all insects are innocent no matter how much humans feel they have hurt us.

The insect seemed to represent a collective of energies in nature. It telepathically told me that humans give out the energies of fear and harm from their emotions and this causes insects to do what they do, otherwise they would not harm us. Love could shift things, because it is an authority in nature. I admitted to my error and promised to include them.

Coincidentally Bob and I were about to go camping that night in the Trinity Lakes camping area. We could not find a campsite before dark. We had to pull off the road and throw a tarp and sleeping bags on the ground. I was uncomfortable on the ground. I focused on the love in me and around me. The pink light grew in my inner awareness, and then something made me open my eyes and look to my right shoulder.

The moonlight revealed a country mouse with big ears peering down at me. I leaped up and shoved it off with my hand in a panic. I felt so bad. I knew it was just responding to the energy of love. I admitted to Bob that I was going to have to sleep in the car or I would not get any rest. I hated being so uptight about mice, bugs and nature up close.

The important world event at House of Love and Light was this coming weekend. We hosted two guided group meditations with members of the community. One was held each day of the Harmonic Convergence. Karmin led a meditation to clear the karma on large patterns of abuse human beings have done to one another. The guided meditation I led would be themed around the karma clearance of all the harm humans have done to nature, animals and insects.

On the official day about twenty people showed up for the meditations. The people that participated gave many comments afterward. Several said that they were stunned at the depth of visuals that my guided meditation gave them. Many said they had tears during it. Some were uncomfortable and admitted to having a lot of anger at nature, but that it felt much better now. They all thanked me for the unique experience.

Karmin and I felt so appreciative of their willingness to attend our event. Our free event was advertised in the newspaper and the local news interviewed each of us and took photos for a small article. It was published that week with a picture of my son Harry in my lap. My heart was beginning to see I was part of a bigger world of unseen energy and new possibilities.

5

AWAKENING ANGELS

For years I had believed in Angels and loved reading stories about them. I had begun to recognize their presence in my personal life. What I had not considered was the possibility that I actually was one. In the summer of 1988, I had an opportunity to attend a weekend workshop that was offered in Boise. A number of friends and I went to a free talk at the local health food café on Friday evening. The woman introduced herself as Solara. She had written a book called AWAKENING TO YOUR CELESTIAL ORIGINS. She explained that she had been offering a weekend workshop all over the country that follows the information and experiences in her book. Many people decided to sign up for the two day workshop including me.

Saturday morning about forty people filled up the event hall in town. We were all told that this weekend was created to help each of us remember our connection to our original starry light and celestial sense of self. We learned we would each discover our own angel name and awaken into memories of our celestial origins.

By day two tears flowed, as many of the participants accessed a deeply moving realization of who they were before they walked on the earth. I was not sure at first if it was real, but like everyone else I was moved to tears. I was aware of an expansive angelic sense of self as it flooded my mind with light. There also was a deep feeling of humility along with it. I was aware of feeling taller as well.

Each workshop participant was also encouraged to discover a way of sharing their new angel essence through a personal *mudra* or series of silent hand gestures. Some had rather unearthly names. Each angel name when spoken by the person who received it stirred the listener. I would learn also that many names were very similar to Sanskrit words. Sound and tone were very important. The spelling of each angel name was unique as well.

During the Angelic Awakening weekend, we were told of a very old legend. It was about the origins of mankind. The legend states that long ago many souls turned away from the light and chose to head out into the great unknown, leaving behind the light and warmth of our source. It was just to see what it would be like. At the workshop we were reminded that it can look pretty dark when we are facing away from our source. We learned to practice consciously turning toward the light.

Many years later I would discover the significance of that reorientation with the light of our source in this initial awakening. It was the beginning of my own journey out of the forest of unknowing. I believe similar teachings have come and gone from our world at important times in history.

As for what to call me around town and among friends, that would take some rethinking. The new spiritual name I received at the weekend workshop was too elaborate to use publically. There was a man in town many of my spiritual friends really liked and respected. I had gotten to know him through a friend. One day he suggested that I think about my given name and look for a more accurate spiritual name. He said the name Patty did not match my energy. I had been called it for many years. Seldom was I ever called my given name of Patricia. This man explained that a name is like a phone number. He suggested I find the name that will allow me to receive the important calls in life, the ones that were meant for me. He suggested my heart would show me the way.

Eventually I settled on the name Tajalean, which was a hybrid of my new angel name. It stuck with me for a few years. It was not the name I had received at the workshop but very similar. I even added it to the cover of my book The Secret Meadow, as my pseudonym. My medicine woman friend received a new angel name at that same workshop. Afterward, she settled on a shorter version of what she received and became the name Eliah.

Eliah led a monthly *inipi* (sweat lodge) ceremony in Boise. Each sweat lodge experience brought me closer to an ancient past where the earth was my teacher and mother. Eliah was becoming a wise and skilled friend. She believed I already knew the old ways and needed only some encouragement. I went to many of the full moon sweats for several months and once even after my second pregnancy was visible. It all felt very safe and familiar to me.

One night when I was about seven months pregnant and Harry lay sleeping in his crib in the next room, I was awakened by a feeling of light coming from somewhere in my bedroom. I climbed carefully out of bed and moved toward a visible glow of light coming from our large laundry basket made from woven reeds in the corner of the room. I was not completely awake as I peered into it. I sighed in awe at a very small, naked, luminous little girl sleeping peacefully on top of the laundry.

I reached intently into the basket to the glowing miniature form, but as my hand touched the clothes I blinked awake and the light and little child vanished. I was reaching into what was now a dark basket full of laundry. Completely bewildered I thought, oh my god that was a child, wow! I climbed back into bed. I had for weeks thought I was going to have another baby boy. Now I was not so sure and wondered who this luminous being was that appeared to me tonight? My heart now sensed that the little girl was connected to the child I carried within me. How interesting! But I wanted other opinions from my spiritual friends.

It was around the time of this second pregnancy that I learned about a practice called shamanic journeying. Eliah explained that it was considered to be another way to prepare for the coming of a new child. She explained that it would involve a form of meditation to the sound of a drumbeat. I knew I wanted to do it. We set up a time that we could do the session together at my home. A tape player provided the drumming music. As we entered into the journey, I noticed her becoming a spirit animal as I became something quite different. I followed her voice at first then noticed I was dropping deep into the earth.

Eventually I was drawn into a colorful expansive inner chamber where a large exotic being was waiting for us. The tall luminous female spirit pointed to the other side of the large open space. She quietly nodded at me. There was a small very young girl hovering in the air in a lotus position and in deep meditation. I felt subtle energy coming from the little girl and later noticed the drumming music was stopping.

When we emerged from the journey, my friend's description matched my own except that Eliah had been given a bright glowing orb of light from the tall being. She said it was to be transferred to the baby once it was born. Eliah did not know what to make of it, but figured it would show up when the time was right. We both felt it was an important meditation/journeying experience and it revealed that a special soul awaited its birth as my child. My heart also informed me that this soul had not been embodied for a very long time and would need encouragement to be in our world.

My daughter's birth was planned to be another home birth, like our son's. During a meditation I saw a vision of a dolphin surrounded by light. I felt it was a sign that my child needed a water birth for this delivery. Preparations were made. The midwives were not enthusiastic but willing. I asked a couple of friends to be at the birth when it happened. Eliah of course was invited first. She was like my spiritual midwife. The other friend was

Bobbie Jo.

It was 1988 and in the month of December. The early labor was not difficult and I was appreciative that I could have a home birth again and be in my warm house for this important life event. We had contracted with certified midwives in our area. We also lived close by the hospital in case anything went wrong, allowing family members to feel at ease.

As the night wore on, Bob went to bed and the assistant midwife showed up to check on things. She remarked that the room felt so peaceful. I had felt a shift in energy after my husband went to bed. My two friends looked to me like they were in an altered state. They said little and looked rather out-of-it. The assistant midwife thoughtfully checked to see what my dilation was and then sat down. I was not that far along she said. She then sat down and seemed to zone out with the other women from then on.

After a couple of hours I wondered when the assistant midwife planned to call her supervisor. I had noticed that my contractions were picking up speed. She said it was too soon. My contractions began to increase more in intensity and I had trouble speaking before another one would hit. I began having vivid lucid dreams between contractions, as they grew closer together. In one of them, I sensed myself floating over the ocean at night with a full moon above. Then there was this burst of water coming out of the ocean. It startled me awake! I became concerned that this was a warning and that things would not be ready in time for my baby's birth.

The women calmly reassured me that everything was going to get done. Finally I convinced my girlfriend to please go to our bedroom and wake Bob up, adding that he has to fill the tub with water! I knew he would need time to become fully awake. He had agreed to the job of preparing the tub and getting the water temperature just right for the water birth.

My contractions became more and more intense. I could not wait for the midwife to check my dilation again. Loudly I said, "I am crowning right now!" I got up from the living room chair and ran to the bathroom holding my stomach. Our daughter was born not long after I sat down on the toilet to wait for the tub to be filled with water. Poor Bob was barely awake and had just started to get the water going. I was filled for a moment with frustration! My plan to have a water birth was lost. Just sitting on the toilet triggered my water to burst with great intensity, just as I foresaw in the dream. It was 3:30 a.m., and the assistant midwife barely caught the baby coming out with her hands. She quickly handed her to me. It felt like my daughter and I bonded so deeply at that second.

In a way I wanted to shut everyone else out for a moment and allow the baby and myself to catch our breath. If only I had been listened to perhaps then someone would have done as I asked sooner. We could have avoided this outcome. I began to shiver even though the bathroom heat was on high and everyone was sweating. I was sad but honestly relieved to feel her healthy pink body in my arms. She was a perfect baby girl after all. We named her Tierney. It meant, "Grandchild of the lordly."

Despite opposition, I insisted we both get into the tub of water as soon as it was full. The lead midwife arrived at that point. She was available now to supervise the afterbirth. The placenta did not come out right away and she became impatient with me. She started to pull on the umbilical cord against my wishes. Everything in me knew it was wrong to tug and not allow the uterus to expel things naturally. When it came out, a small portion was mistakenly left inside, but we did not know that at the time.

Days later I developed a fever and called the lead midwife, explaining my concerns. She came right over and removed the remaining tissue that my body had slowly worked to expel from my uterus. The fever went away after that. Another close call, but all was well in the end.

Three weeks after our daughter's birth in December of 1988, I had to ask my husband to move out. Several events had left me with no choice but to tell him that I could not live with his drinking anymore. With a new baby and a toddler to care for, I did not want all the problems that came with his drinking. I said very sincerely that I thought he needed to get help. He turned away from me and walked out to his car looking bewildered. My husband left town unhappy and in a drunken state. He decided to go south and ended up going as far as California. While he was out of town, he called me now and then with angry words and comments about nothing rational.

One evening that week, a familiar but surprising face was at my door. He was known to a few select people as a healer. He had helped me with my need for a new spiritual name. He did not advertise or really offer healing often, but when he did his thing, it was said to be something to behold. I will honor his anonymity and not say his name. He taught Aikido and had his own dojo in town at the time. He had olive skin, a brown beard and brown eyes and was very nice. Some of my friends wondered if he was one of those secret masters. It surprised me to see him at my door ten thirty at night.

After I let him in the front door he said, "Your daughter told me that you needed my help." I could see he was quite serious, as he glanced across the room at my three week old baby. All week I was becoming increasingly concerned about my husband's anger at me for telling him he had to move out. My son had been crying most of the day. Bob had left days earlier with few clothes or personal items for a destination unknown. I was definitely in need of help. Also, with the new baby, I had not been sleeping well.

This mysterious acquaintance stepped into the living room and politely asked if he could do a scan of my body first. I lay down on the floor and his hands hovered above my body. He paused over the area of my uterus, which was in really bad shape. Over the weeks since the birth I had discovered I had a third stage prolapsed uterus. It was likely caused by the midwife pulling on the umbilical cord after my daughter's birth. My doctor recommended a hysterectomy. I did not want to have one. I told none of my friends about my dilemma, but felt very unhappy about it all.

The man smiled and said, "You know your uterus really wants to go back to where it belongs." I nodded excitedly and felt a deep sensation inside my lower abdomen. I could feel it move back into place! I would notice later that all my symptoms cleared up after that night and I did not have to have a hysterectomy. My mysterious guest continued on with his intuitive scan and hovered over my kidneys. He said they had a funny shape. I silently asked for God to make them right. He paused and gave me an odd glance.

He walked over to Harry my two year old, who looked all puffy eyed and tired. After a moment the man said, "Harry will throw up three times before the night is over, so be ready and you will have less mess." I instantly realized that there was a lot of negative energy coming at me all week probably from all the chaos. Harry may have absorbed some of it and now it needed to be purged.

To my amazement Harry threw up all over the floor before the healer made it to the door to leave! I hugged the gifted soul at my door, as he made a swift departure. Our son Harry *did* throw up two more times by the wee hours of the morning. It was a long night.

My husband arrived in town to everyone's surprise a few days later and checked himself into a private treatment center for alcoholism and addiction. He had been gone for nine days. I learned that he had the good fortune of hitting bottom in California. He eventually told me the story of what brought him home.

He had been staying with a couple and they were fighting a lot. The chaos was all around him. With the drinking and drug use of other people adding to the mix, he had decided to hit the road again. He found a phone booth at a gas station and stood staring at it wondering about his next destination. Bob explained that to him the world felt like a giant storm of insanity. He remembered saying, "Dear God, I can't take it anymore I just want peace." Suddenly everything in his awareness was silent, utterly peaceful. After a moment more he felt God urging him to go back to Idaho and check himself into that treatment place called The Aerie. My husband had done his alcohol and drug evaluation there the year before. He recalled his relief after he arrived of feeling safe; he was getting help.

After the twenty eight day inpatient program was completed my husband attended daily AA meetings. Bob followed that up with 120 meetings in 120 days and got a sponsor. He said he was determined to be statistically among those that get well. Months later we both viewed the whole series of events as incredibly amazing. Bob relapsed very briefly many months later but has otherwise remained clean and sober ever since. His program and spirituality or higher power continues to be an important but private part of his recovery. He has maintained his sobriety to this day and considers his personal recovery a miracle in many ways.

Over the years people have sometimes asked me about the spiritual or energetic dynamics of child birth. I was given a rare glimpse into energy and childbirth thanks to my neighbor being pregnant that following year. She was due to deliver in the spring and we both liked the home birth option. She invited me to assist as a support person for the coming delivery of her second child.

On the day of her labor she called me over from next door. She had midwives, but I soon discovered they were not that good at the coaching part. Her labor was intense and things were moving fast. My friend was pacing the floor and in so much pain, she was becoming hysterical.

I finally shouted over her loud sobs this command, "Become a rag doll!" She heard me and collapsed into a nearby chair. Her moans began to lessen and she gave me a nod of thanks. I continued encouraging her to become limp or like water explaining that then her contractions would be the most productive and the least painful.

I had read a book that helped with my contractions when I delivered my children. I remembered also that fear creates resistance within the actual muscles as they contract. Pain then increases. It will decrease when the mom can let go and let the body dilate the cervix. I was thrilled when the baby began to crown and the contractions grew effective. The head was now visible.

Not long after this something drew my attention up to the ceiling of the room. I could see the energy of a spinning portal. It opened like a funnel cloud and came down from above. I watched in amazement, as it poured into the top of the mother and she pushed her baby girl out. What an awesome thing to witness! I also noticed a bright female energy hovering over the room for only a few minutes longer and then it was gone. This could have been a guardian of the young child.

I wondered if this energy funnel occurs every time a human being is born but we normally are not aware of it. I never had the pleasure of assisting another home birth to find out, but the vision of a funnel of energy would grow important to my understanding of new physics years later.

$$\infty$$

Our son Harry was a very sensitive child. As a baby he seemed very aware of people around him and smiled or cried in dramatic displays of emotions, depending on who was holding him. By the time he was a toddler and our daughter was born, he was known to actively engage with some people. He spoke with a sort of language that we could not make sense out of at first. He seemed to know what he was saying and his expression was very animated as he gestured and spoke. We joked about it sounding like a cross between French and some new language.

I realized one day that he could sense people that were in emotional distress. He was known to dart away from me soon after he could walk and reach up and hug the knees of total strangers out of the blue. The individual would look down at him and smile. When I caught up and apologized, they would say how sweet my son was. Then their tone would shift and they would admit they had just lost their father and were not doing well, or some other story of trauma. I began to really pay attention to our son's moment to moment awareness of things. Years later I would say he was one of my early teachers regarding emotional energy.

Harry was very engaging in general with strangers long before he could speak effectively. He also noticed energies that were astral. The astral plane is where some believe spirits of the dead linger. One day after he had seemed in distress most of the previous night, he pulled me to his room and pointed under his bed. He was trying to speak clearly but was mostly pointing at his stomach and then under the bed. I noticed a hazy ghost image of a cord around his neck. It was an after-image of his umbilical cord from birth. I remembered that it had been wrapped around his neck at birth. I instinctively reached down and uncoiled it from his neck. He suddenly blurted out perfect words with complete sentences!

He said, "Mommy there is something under my bed that keeps hurting me!" I was stunned but happy he was speaking so well. Then I became curious to understand what he was trying to explain. In truth I was not thinking anything was under his bed, but I went ahead and began to lower myself. Just as I was beginning to get a view of the underside of his bed, my body jumped back as if something had launched at me! I caught my breath for a moment.

Harry smiled and said, "See mommy." He went on to say, "It is like a baby with teeth that is not so nice." He added that they were kind of scary. Harry seemed suddenly so at peace and relieved. I now could understand him. I resolved to do an energy cleanse with prayer followed by a burning of sage to smudge the room. The house seemed OK but not really cleared. The good news was that Harry never did stop talking after that. It was really meaningful to finally learn how he viewed the world.

I was up late reading one evening later that month when suddenly I felt an eerie presence. It was across the room in the doorway of my son's bedroom. It stood between me and my sleeping child. Like a lioness protecting her cub, I turned slowly and walked directly toward my sleeping son. The dark shape vanished into the floor as I passed through the threshold of the room.

I knew at that point that this was going to take a lot more than some smudging and prayers. I decided a powerful deep cleansing of our home beginning in the basement was going to be necessary. In the morning I felt clear about my next move. A couple of spiritual friends chatted with me about it over the phone. They each said they wanted to see how I would do this. They asked if they could come over and watch. I said they could both join me that Saturday.

After they arrived I told my husband to watch Harry. Harry seemed aware that he needed to stay upstairs. My friends hovered behind me, as we stepped mindfully down the concrete stairs into the large basement of the old house. I called in Jesus and the Angels. After a few minutes a surprisingly big dark presence made itself known. I felt an authority speak through me and declare to the spirit that it had a choice to leave for good right now or be taken by the higher order to a new home. Only a moment or two passed before the energy changed dramatically. The shadow was now gone!

I was aware of many souls now coming out of the wood work. They seemed relieved. It was apparently a number of souls that had been trapped there for a long time. I began to sense them floating up the steps and out through our back door. Harry had instinctively appeared and opened the door to our back yard from the basement steps. He smiled like he understood what was happening. He then joined us in the basement, feeling safe overall. The rest of the house now also felt clean and peaceful. My friends said they were amazed at how calm I was through it all. I reported that I felt safe because I was not trying to be in charge. Higher guides, namely Jesus came when I called. It was not really me doing it. I was just willing to be a part of the process and my faith kept me calm.

∞

From the time was very young I loved to sing. My mother was a voice teacher and trained opera singer. She also played records often in the house that I would sing along with. I had a good ear and could memorize the songs by Barbra Streisand and Carol King. My mother used to say I was a natural at it. By the time I was in high school I decided to make the stretch out of my shy side and sing in my high school talent show. After it I received many compliments on my voice, but had to admit to friends that I did not play an instrument or read music beyond the rudimentary level.

Here it was years later and my newly sober and thoughtful husband decided to surprise me with a special gift one day. Inside a big box was some new electronic equipment. He said he had been at the music store and heard about a machine for vocalists. He said you can play any commercial tape and it will lift off the lead singer's voice with the switch of a button. It provided musical backup or accompaniment for amateur singers to perform, even change the key and tempo. I was so touched by Bob's generous, thoughtful actions. He said he thought I should sing more since it made me happy. So I did. I began to learn many songs and even prepared a way to sing in a church in town.

That following year I performed in two different churches, as part of their services. One was called "The Center of Peace" and was a new age non denominational church and the other was a Unity church. It was a lot of work preparing and memorizing the songs, but it felt good. Performing inspirational messages was especially satisfying.

Around this time, I also began writing and singing original songs a cappella. Having sung for myself for years, it felt natural to write a poem-like theme and just allow a melody to come through me. I did a lot of recordings with that singing machine over the years that followed. I could sense that my angel self was finding creative outlets for me.

When my daughter was about six months old, I was invited to attend a small angelic awakening workshop that my friends were presenting in a private home. Our community was all a buzz about the angelic awakenings and people wanted to experience it. This particular workshop would be only one day and a respected local awakened angel woman familiar to me was going to lead it. She received her angel name from the same teacher I did. Her angel name was NaTaZuel. She had recently partnered up with a new man from New York. He taught meditation and she wanted to introduce him to the community at this workshop.

At first I did not know what I would get out of the event, having already received my Angel name. I was also nursing my new baby. This meant I would have to bring her with me and make it work. My inner feeling was that it was important to go. I finally resolved to go and support my friends.

As the day wore on however, the seemingly important man from New York was talking on and on about himself. I watched the room of people all politely waiting for him to finish, so we could get on with the workshop, but he was dominating the floor. Our local angel presenter NaTaZuel also waited patiently to step in as the main speaker.

I grew more and more agitated, as I paced the floor in the back of the room. I did not want to be rude, but energy was building inside of me and I could find no way out of the dilemma. Finally, I just blurted out these words "I am so sorry, but we did not come here to learn about you!" I went on to say that we came to learn about ourselves. The room of people swung around very shocked, and the man blushed at the front of the room. He quickly agreed to step aside and let NaTaZuel proceed with her workshop. I felt strange, embarrassed, but *so* relieved. Soon after this we proceeded on to the guided awakening meditation.

The day was nearly over when everyone completed the guided meditation. Now each participant would claim their new name and the energy of their angel. Each one had to stand in a line, bowing first as a courtesy to the man from New York, then bowing to the assistant. The assistant was assigned the task of giving each person a quick energy clearing and wing opening. Then we were each directed to finally bow to NaTaZuel and share the spiritual name that each had received. Unfortunately as each person reached her, they admitted they had not received anything during the meditation. He or she chose to say "I am spirit" or something equally vague to everyone.

I was near the back of the line feeling sad for each of these people who had paid money for this disappointment. I was also quietly aware that it usually takes two days to do the whole process properly. Perhaps it was wrong to try and do it all in one day. Standing in the line, I planned to say my angel name, bow and call it a day. I came up beside my friend, who was assisting with opening wings on each participant. She gave me a quick combing of energy. I turned around and noticed she had mumbled something to me.

It was twilight and the sun was setting, but no lights had been turned on in the large room of the house we were in. I did not understand what was being said to me. So she said it louder, "Archangel Michael has a sword for you!" I looked at her with concern, but before I knew it, she was thrusting something into my hand that was invisible, but I could feel it.

The energy shot up through me as my hand and arm shot up into the air above me. I saw blue/white light flood my sight. A lot of energy surged through my body and out my hand which was now straight above my head. I then sobbed with heavy tears for a few moments, very humbled by it all. What on Earth is this? I thought to myself. I also knew in a flash that it was the sword of truth, as strange as that may sound. Everyone later said they saw light flash around me in the dimly lit room.

After a few moments the female event leader said, "Archangel Michael wants you to always speak the truth from your heart." She thanked me for my honesty earlier and gave me a hug. The man from New York also said as much to me, with an expression of honest humility. We all broke for a potluck dinner and I stood awkwardly wondering what to make of it all. My hands shook a bit, as I held my cup of tea. My nervous system was clearly affected. My stomach felt barely able to eat food. It was shaking.

I was never really treated the same by these friends after that day. People were nice but different. It marked a turning point for me. I sensed something new perhaps a jealousy from friends. Yet, I was amazed at the whole sword thing and did not feel at all clear about what it meant and why I was given it.

Over time I was aware that my heart was searching for deeper answers. No one I knew seemed to have any. I was in need of mountains and perhaps a new place to live away from a city the size of Boise. That same year my husband also felt ready for a change. We had started driving up to the nearby mountains a lot and looking at property or just enjoying the forests. We almost bought a house in the mountains above Boise, but other events intervened.

During one week, three different spiritual friends called and told me I needed to visit the Teton Mountains in Wyoming near the edge of Idaho. I had never been there. I asked for guidance on it and felt a huge push to go. I told my husband but he was irritated at my guidance. Bob wondered how we would afford it. He knew I felt it was where we were supposed to be moving to.

After three days, to my surprise he changed his mind. He said, "Let's just go." We put the food and hotel on a credit card. We both felt a fresh sense of adventure and quickly prepared to pack the kids in our old car and head to eastern Idaho where it borders Wyoming. It was the fall of 1990 when we traveled to Teton Valley Idaho to look at property. We found a house and cabin for sale on eight acres bordering the national forest. It still amazes me how the owners agreed to carry the loan paperwork on us, thus we did not need a loan from a bank. That was miraculous!

We moved to eastern Idaho the week after Christmas 1990. It was during record cold temps of sixty below zero on the Teton River. The property was in the foothills of the Teton Range. Soon after we arrived, we discovered that the pipes in the log house were all frozen. Our rented moving truck was stuck in the snow in the long driveway. Our money was limited at best. There I was with my exhausted husband, our two year old daughter, little Harry and we were seeing the night sky full of stars! We felt excited and hopeful about our future. Our kids seemed very adaptable and appeared to love their new home.

Within a week my husband turned to me and said, "I feel like I am finally home." We knew no one in the area and were far from the familiar city we had left behind. I felt that I was really home too. The local community encompassed three towns across a twenty- six mile long valley. Most of the people were of the Mormon faith, which we knew little about. Despite all this, within a short time we received friendly greetings from the locals all around the valley.

Our home was remote and that felt right for us. The National Forest was a short walk and we could see the peaks of the Teton mountain range through our aspen grove. We had found our place in the mystical Teton Mountains. We were ready for the next phase of our lives.

6

HIGHER GROUND

"Higher Ground is a place we sometimes seek to escape the crowded cities and clogged highways for the elevated perspective of fresh mountain air."
HIGHER GROUND (Brochure Insert)

In the spring after months of preparation, we opened Higher Ground. It was our small retreat center and it consisted of one large guest cabin that could sleep twelve people on eight acres at the edge of the national forest. After setting it up, we moved into the unfinished house higher up the hill on the property. I wrote up the information in a brochure titled Higher Ground. I offered sessions and people came for short stays to enjoy the peace and quiet and fresh mountain air.

My husband started up his painting business in the valley and was slowly getting enough work. It paid the bills but not much more. I built my first sweat lodge that first spring and held a couple of sweats for friends from out of town. I taught a class on the medicine wheel and had about eight people attend it. I also helped my husband's business at home answering calls for painting bids. We had some retreat visitors but not enough to be busy. That summer, I led my own Awakening Angel weekend workshop in the guest cabin with a dozen women from eastern Idaho and beyond. I had been prompted by my guides to offer it and knew it was a leap of faith. That previous year I had attended the one in Boise described in the previous chapter.

To my delight, by the end of the weekend all the women in my workshop had received beautiful angel names and celestial memories. Tears flowed as memories surfaced. I was so thrilled by the women's willingness to attend my workshop. We grew to be lifelong friends. Some of the highlights of the awakening process delivered that weekend included several specific meditations that align one's energy with a personal star in the heavens. It feels like looking up into the night sky and wondering where you are really from. Afterward a series of questions are asked, and each person is guided to write down the first thing that comes to his or her mind. It moves fast, so the mind is not allowed to question what comes in. It stirs deeply held memories.

In another part of the awakening weekend workshop, each participant is asked to stand in front of another participant with eyes closed at first, while soothing music plays. After aligning with the star above and letting its energy merge with your heart, eyes are opened gently. Everyone is encouraged to see past the costume or personality and into the soul light within the person he or she is looking at. Slowly each person moves around the room, facing each person present in order to see their inner light.

Often the person's face will change rapidly into many different faces, perhaps representing the different people the person has been in past lives. It is subtle but those who see many different faces are often amazed. It can be very moving to feel the love pour out of people's eyes and heart as well.

If you recall, the author and teacher known as Solara had come to Boise in 1988 and taught the workshop that initially triggered my angel memories. She had become very much in demand around the country. Solara was now the author of THE STAR BORNE: A Remembrance for the Awakened Ones. I had read her book and tried to keep up with events through her monthly newsletter. She was often referred to as the one who launched the 11:11 angelic awakening movement back then. She would write another book called 11:11 INSIDE THE DOORWAY by 1992.

All over the world people reportedly were noticing the numbers 11:11 on digital clock radios, on their watches and in all sorts of places. Often they knew it meant something important. Solara taught that this number configuration was designed to get our attention and awaken part of our DNA. The 11:11 was believed to be activating an awakening for the whole human race. Solara began to hold annual large week long awakening conferences that grew each year in size since 1988. I really hoped to be able to attend that summer in Colorado. Through a series of leaps of faith, I managed to make a plan to meet up with a friend who also now had an angel name from my workshop. She was driving from Boise, but could meet me in Utah. I could ride with her the rest of the way to Colorado. I would have to get myself to Utah first, however.

My car was old with well over a hundred thousand miles on it. For a few weeks I had been struggling with it. The mechanic had looked it over and said the transmission was shot. Even I could smell the burnt transmission fluid. Yet in my determination to get around our valley, I learned to power shift it and restart the engine whenever it stalled in traffic. My car was barely running, but I had to get myself to the Awakening Angel conference. I had little money to pay for any of it, but I knew I had to be at the Colorado conference.

I had several emotionally charged discussions with my husband about the Angel Awakening conference in Colorado. It really upset him when I said I needed to be there. He was able to handle the kids for a week, but was not happy about any money being spent on this trip. I resolved to go anyway.

With determination and a lot of trepidation about my decision, I somehow managed to get the failing car over Teton Pass and down the highway through to Utah. My husband's cousin Dave offered to let me leave my car at his home in Vernal. At least his cousin was being helpful to my situation. He would be gone, but I could sleepover there with my friend on our way back too. It was a long drive otherwise.

As I entered Vernal, Utah the air was filled with a powerful sweetness. I drove across the countryside with scribbled directions in hand. It smelled as if many flowers were in bloom nearby or something. I also realized that my car had just smoothly downshifted as I came to a stop sign. The transmission had begun to shift normally for no apparent reason as I approached each stop sign!

I parked the car at Dave's home and joined with my friend Lynda who had just arrived in her van from Boise. I rode the rest of the way to Colorado filled with a new sense of wonder. I was thinking how strange it was that my car now seemed fixed. I quietly thanked the angels for their love and demonstrations of grace.

By the way, my car drove perfectly all the way home to Idaho after that conference. My mechanic was amazed when I showed up for an oil change a few months after the trip. He asked if I had gotten a new transmission put in. I said "No, it just fixed itself mysteriously." It continued to work and I traded the car in a year later. Pretty miraculous stuff was happening more and more.

Back during the conference, several profound shifts would occur for me. My attendance at the International Angelic Awakening conference in Snowmass Colorado that year would prove to be important. I met so many amazing people. There were about three hundred in attendance from all over the world. As I registered at the front lobby, I learned I did not have to pay for the conference. I could sign a form agreeing to make payments toward the fee. My friend Lynda picked up the cost of our room and meals. Everything was working out. What a relief!

At this time in my life I wore glasses to see things better at a distance. At the beginning of the conference, I strained to see people at much of a distance. The room was too blurry to feel a part of. My distance vision was very poor. I had worn glasses ever since my first year living in Boise due to reading reports and writing assessments on a computer at that job. In all the excitement I had forgotten to bring my glasses with me, even to drive. While people were beginning to file into seats, I found one for myself. Waiting for Lynda to join me, I sat wondering if it was smart to forget my glasses, since I could not see well. With a feeling of resignation I accepted that I had done it to myself.

Suddenly I became aware of a large but invisible loving presence that was now with me. It gently spoke to my heart and invited me to let my eyes be healed. Before I knew it, my own hands were rising up and covering my eyes. A deep quiet settled over me and a trust that was deeply natural. I felt totally in the hands of God. After several minutes in stillness, I became self conscious. I realized I might look funny sitting with my hands over my eyes. Before I could pull my hands down a gentle but urgent thought moved through me. "Not yet," it said. I surrendered back into it and then a few more minutes passed before my hands came down to my lap by themselves.

When I opened my eyes everything looked incredibly clear! I could see everything in the large room in great detail. I could now read the banners behind the stage. People's expressions were so lovely. It took my breath away. I decided not to tell anyone. It felt too special to breathe a word about it. Also my friend wore glasses to see everything. I did not want her to feel bad.

Early in the week of the conference, people were allowed to come up on stage and share a song or poem in front of everyone. I loved the way that the conference welcomed everyone's contribution. I took another leap of faith and asked to go up on the stage to share something. After doing my silent mudra and stating my full angel name, I sang a song. I received a standing ovation for singing a cappella. The song I had written was called *The Seeds*. It was about the angelic awakenings and it was amazing that I had the courage to do it. After that I began to feel increasingly noticed by people attending the conference. The following are the words to the song I sang for everyone. I had written the song that summer. It goes like this:

First verse-*"A seed sent forth from a distant star. It embedded deep within the earth, where it slept and slept, awaiting stirrings from afar. But first the seed fragmented, scattering near and far. Each formed a soul essence walking unaware of its former star."*

Chorus: *"The Seeds, their emergence marks the activation of the planet, the awakening of mankind. We're the Creator's secret potential, to be revealed with the end of time. The encoded seedlings will birth heavenly beings merging matter and spirit fully aligned."*

Second verse: *"Now to embrace my parts, my collective link with the universe. Like gathering together the many thoughts of whom I am. I am expanding with each addition, blossoming with each merging. The Creations awaken revealing mysteries from beyond the beyond."*

Third verse: *"New horizons begin to beacon, as we take the challenge once more. We go where the ONE has not gone before, another playground for the life force to explore. Play more. It's a journey HOME."*

I had written several songs that summer. Each one would start with a feeling of a message. I would hum and let the words flow. Eventually a tune would form around the words. I would write the words down and then sing it fully with whatever melody matched the mood of the message.

Later in the week at the angel conference we were asked to have a day of silence and disperse so we could go deeper and meditate in private. During my own meditation in the hotel room, I felt a powerful indigo blue energy come in from way beyond our solar system. It was potent and seemed zeroed in on me. I sensed a strong ancient connection to Peru and the celestial family. I pondered the feeling in the hotel room and waited for my friend to meet back up with me.

Lynda and I met up after the silent period was over. I learned that she also seemed to have had an interesting day of silence. Just as I was beginning to tell her about my afternoon my voice changed. To her surprise and mine, I spoke with a unique accent as I introduced the Being. It called itself Raphaela. The presence spoke urgently through me. Lynda and I laughed a bit nervously. I had trouble at first trusting it was safe to allow the channelling to come through so intimately. We both decided just to wait and see if anything further was going to happen.

All of the conference attendees were asked to meet after dinner in the main hotel conference room for an evening of open sharing time. Many people had been given guidance and wanted to share their messages with the whole group. I also wanted to share, so I got in line to speak to the whole assembly on the microphone. I knew I needed to introduce the new energy.

When it was my turn, I felt a stir in the large conference hall as I introduced myself as "Raphaela." There was urgency in the message that came through next. My words formed with a distinct accent as I stated: *"You must each rise up like a mountain from deep within the earth and be who you really are! In Idaho/Wyoming, the Teton mountain peaks are visible at a great distance. They are actually young geologically. They rose up powerfully and quickly"* I stated all of this with intensity.

As I spoke I knew also somehow that areas within that range of mountains are an entry point for higher consciousness to come into our world. Then I heard myself say, *"The time is NOW for a great awakening to begin all across the planet!"* I walked to my chair and sat down. The feeling of being energized slowly subsided.

My friend and some others asked me about the experience soon after. They said they felt a powerful but beautiful presence emanating from me and wondered what it was like for me. I could not really say, but I knew one thing for sure, something was growing more and more intense and unpredictable with each day.

While the Colorado Angelic Reunion was a very moving seminar, I did not feel good about some of it. The teacher/author had behaved in a manner somewhat polarizing at times. I felt sad at the end of the conference and not sure I was a good fit for further events. Despite all the powerful people and experiences I enjoyed, I knew something else was starting to stir deep within me.

On our way home, my friend and I left Snowmass feeling ready for a side trip to the sulphur caves in Glenwood Springs. Once we arrived we quickly changed into our swim suits and even met a few conference attendees down in the caves. It was a young couple from New York. They also had enjoyed the conference.

After getting familiar with the different passage ways in the tunnels, I remember looking intently at one of the natural rock walls deeper in the caves. I could make out patterns in the rock surface that appeared to reveal a scene of people in a large room and a woman being tortured. Lynda looked at where I pointed and agreed it was vivid and strange. I experienced a growing awareness that there were trapped energies there that could be set free.

I decided spontaneously to sing my song *The Seeds* to awaken and set free the energies. As my voice echoed out, the stone's shape shifted right in front of my friend and me causing us to step back in awe! Something definitely released. Wow, I thought, could it get any wilder? The subterranean wet heat and natural sauna felt great too after that. Lynda and I headed on to Utah and then went our separate ways on home.

Over the months I had felt a need for a new spiritual name. The name Raphaela was interesting but I was still using the name Tajalean that summer. My given name of Patricia was just a name on my driver's license. As with everything else, I trusted that a new name would come to me if it was meant to be. For many years since then people have asked me how I came to have the name SoLaMeé. The following is how it all came about.

I received my new spiritual name one day without any warning. Some friends had phoned to inform me of a special celestial event. It was the Solar Eclipse of 1991 in Baja. Bob was at work and the kids had a play date that day. I was free to take in some quiet time. I was urged by my guides to climb to a nearby rock outcropping and meditate during the eclipse event even though it was over a thousand miles away. The eclipse's path of totality was far south in Baja but I felt it was important to meditate during it anyway.

After hiking a mile up a hill, I was drawn to a rocky knoll that had a nice view of the valley below. I felt a lightness come over me and then heard a creek flowing far below the ridge. I settled onto the large rock and opened my senses to nature's rhythm. Tingling sensations moved through me like waves, as I allowed the stream of thoughts to unfold. I could see shimmering golden light around the image of a temple-like dwelling. My thoughts wandered to a place of healing that others could come to. My inner voice began to repeat the name "Tajalliyat."

I was prompted to pull out my spiritual journal. First I was urged to look for the notes I had made from the Colorado conference. I found a page that jogged my memory. At the conference I had met a man sitting near the lobby entrance who was waiting in line near us. He asked what my angel name was like many people were doing. I told him the long version of my angel name and then revealed that I had a shorter more comfortable name of Tajalean. I said I preferred to be called it.

I recall that he looked amazed for a moment and then said his daughter was named Tajallia. He said he named her that after learning about the translation. He said it had to do with an interesting person in the 1800's in Persia. This person was considered an avatar. He had revealed a teaching called the "Tablet of Tajalliyat," which represented the laws of the new age. Each Tajallia is said to be one of the Laws of Truth.

The full translation of the term "Tajalliyat" reportedly means "the effulgence of the Sun of Truth." The man suggested I think about why I was given the name. He believed it was not an accident that my name Tajalean was so similar to this other name. After thanking him for the insights, I had jotted down the information in my conference journal.

I sat on the rock and looked over those older notes for a moment. I was unsure what to think. I asked myself, how do these important names pertain to me? I had been curious about the possibility of a new project more like a place of healing or renewal. My meditative vision had been of a temple, but it seemed so otherworldly.

After a few minutes of peaceful introspection, I sensed my heart warming. I then heard "listen, listen." I pulled my journal back out and allowed the flow of information to come through. I heard the name "So-la-meé," slowly sounded out. Then I heard it again. Finally I was told, "This is you, my child." The spelling looked weird and I admit I did not like the name. After a pause, I opened my heart bigger and just spoke it. "I am So-la-meé." I felt something. A hawk flew right above me and circled.

I stood up and said the name again. I pronounced it like this: So-la-meé, with an emphasis on the "So" I heard from the spiritual guidance coming into me that the name loosely meant "river of the sun" or "life force." I could see in my mind's eye a far distant galaxy much larger than our own. I sensed that I was in alignment with it.

I jotted down the following statement: *"The Central Sun of Truth will flow like a river to you at times."* The solar eclipse seemed to allow this energetic alignment to occur. I pondered this and thought of a stream of water as I listened to the creek far down below. My name felt like a stream of the sun! I also felt a musical quality to it, simple and yet like the first notes in a song. I was still unsure but pleased at the *feel* and sound of it.

I headed back to my house and decided to let things settle for the time being. I sat down in my living room to meditate some more. The music triggered waves of energy to flow through me, as something quickened inside. After about an hour, I opened my eyes and felt refreshed and curious about the music I had selected. I glanced at the new meditation tape that I had popped in just after I sat down. It read on the cover, *"Raphael-Music to Disappear Into."* It matched a feeling deep down inside me that was beginning to gel. I then picked up a pen and wrote the following message:

"I am the Keeper of the Keys to the New, the new laws of reality. You must now open your sealed orders and fully step into your appointed role as Keeper of the Keys. These keys unlock new universes of possibility, realities previously veiled from this dimensional universe. Go within to the keyhole that was placed within your ethereal body."

Back in May, a healer friend of mine had discovered an invisible energetic object in my leg during my massage that seemed intriguing to both of us. It appeared to be in the shape of a geometric object. I sensed that it was waiting for some event or person to activate it. I had almost forgotten about it.

I closed my eyes and went within, instinctively knowing how to go towards the odd shape. I saw that the tiny keyhole in the middle was in the shape of a rectangle or doorway. I instinctively made my sense of self very small and flew through the rectangle opening. Immediately upon passing through it, everything in my awareness became illuminated. Bright colours danced everywhere! I was floating inter-dimensionally. Then a large golden book came into view. My anxiety rose, as the importance of what I might see came to me. It opened to the middle. I scanned the golden intricate words on the page, and a voice spoke them out loud. I cannot remember what I heard. It took me deeper into a meditative state.

I do remember I was viewing the earth from out in space. I could see each key holder spread across the planet. Each was like a golden pillar of light. I somehow knew that once each pillar had assumed his or her position, they would each become activated. I watched as energy shot out of each of them toward all the other key holders, linking everyone together in a beautiful golden grid-work of energy surrounding the planet. I was aware that I was one of seven specific souls selected to play some part in all this. I opened my eyes feeling slightly dizzy, but made myself write everything down. As I wrote my notes more information flowed. I heard the following:

"The pillars are all the carriers of the keys to the new. From many far corners we have come. Our inner dwelling place will activate these dormant keys, automatically awakening the bearer to their purpose in creation, the new creation."

I was awestruck and nervous about the messages and visions. Something deep within sensed that the energy is like fire and will flow like a river of truth to everything on earth, but from the Central Sun. It will purify and burn away the old, while allowing in the new laws of freedom.

The next night I was awakened for the third time that week and drawn to a bright star out my window. It appeared with a very light green ring around it. This time I resolved to close my eyes and connect with my higher self. I shot toward the star in my light body. The message I recorded after I came back was this:

"We have called you here to prepare you for what is to come. I am the keeper of the doorway to the new. We have been preparing you for this

important point of transition for some time. The incoming frequencies lay the framework for the New by altering the air, water and earth molecules through the flow of cosmic fire. Many people will begin to migrate to places of spiritual rest and renewal when their heavily left sided brains begin to feel overwhelmed with these new fiery energies."

I sat for a while and then pushed the journal aside and went back to sleep. I buried the notes in a deep file that would surface many years later, around the time I began writing this book. Looking back on these notes recently has been revealing. My old notes sound an awful lot like the description of solar flares from the sun. Maybe even a distant much larger sun.

In recent years, much has been documented about changes in our earth's magnetic energy as well. It was bizarre, but interesting that these channelled messages and notes would reappear after all these years, just as I was first publishing this book in 2015. Also a total solar eclipse would be passing directly over our valley floor in August of 2017. Does this have a connection with events back then? I did not know, but it felt important.

My sense of being linked with the 11:11 movement of awakening angels had peaked and then faded by the end of the summer of 1991. I knew the deeper truth of awakening was out there, but realized I might need more advanced teachings. Too many things with the awakening angel methods seemed focused on fancy names and titles. External appearances and complicated rituals were more often the practice with the angel stuff. It had good aspects to it, but I felt drawn more toward focusing on the underlying reality of things. I was ready to learn the deeper truth about the reality of our world. To do it, I would need a more advanced teacher, a Master Teacher.

By the end of the summer it felt increasingly more right to introduce myself as So-la-meé. People generally responded to it with a smile and a nod. My husband said he was good with the new name, as long as I promised not to change it again. I had released the name Tajalean and began to introduce myself around town with my new name.

In the meantime, I was beginning to seriously question many things about my identity. I began to question the nature of reality itself and how we all wear costumes or identities, but seldom discover who we really are. A name that you wear can affect many things. I was feeling better about sharing my new spiritual name and letting it begin to anchor within me. I believed it provided a stabilizing point that would prove very necessary in the weeks to come.

I began to struggle with thoughts about God. Why would a whole loving God create a world made up of so much suffering and ever present death? I felt I was at a turning point away from easy answers from teachers and authors of books. I was determined to find the underlying truth, whatever it was. This was not unlike what I did when I was nine years old and needed answers. The questions came from somewhere deep inside me, as if I was setting my life on an important new course.

Around this time I received a new very long channelled message. It was early September 1991. The message spoke of my future and a need to prepare for what was to come. Much of the message seemed so potent and impossible to imagine. It spoke of an important purpose that would alter everything in my sense of self and the world as I knew it. I was being asked to be ready to leave everything--friends, family, my home and step into the unknown. The message said I would be letting go of everything even my children.

Tears flowed for a few minutes, and then I buried the journal and notes out of sight. Soon after this I forgot most of what I had written, other than the importance of getting ready. I think I was overwhelmed by it all and wanted to keep some amnesia in place.

Over the weeks, I noticed myself organizing many spiritual tools and personal items. I seemed to realize that I was going to be giving away many things that no longer felt real to me. The actual messages and notes had faded from my conscious mind, yet I could not shake the feeling that I was lightening my load and assessing what had value. I made piles of crystals, jewellery, healing stones of all kinds.

Most importantly I had to find a home for the vision quest staff, drum and medicine bag that I had received in a giveaway from my medicine woman/angel friend Eliah a couple years before. These things had to be given away with some care. I had received them unexpectedly. The tall, hand carved vision quest staff had chosen me in a private give away ceremony back in Boise over two years earlier. I sat down to recall that amazing experience again.

My friend Eliah had placed everything in her bedroom for her ceremonial Indian give-away. It was a private gathering at her home that she had been guided to set up. Each person was to go into her bedroom alone and emerge with whatever called to him or her. It felt strange, like someone had died. I was ushered in near the front of the line, so I felt honoured.

After entering the private room, I looked at the beautiful things and wondered what to think about it all. Something then nudged at me to just touch the wooden vision quest staff leaning in the corner of the room. I chuckled under my breath yeah right, what do I know about vision quests.

I circled the room picking up items and holding them in my hand, as I was told to do, sensing whether they were supposed to go home with me. The spiritual nudge pushed harder. I felt something insisting that since I had touched everything else, I should just hold the staff for a moment as well. I relented and stepped up to it and pulled it up right with my hand.

Instantly I was in a totally different world, way up on a mountain. The wind was howling and there was a powerful rain storm. Lightning was flashing all over the sky. I was holding a tall wooden staff like this one. I was the owner of it and understood its power and purpose.

The next thing I knew I was back in my friend's bedroom with a jolt. My friend's nine year old daughter's face startled me when she burst through the doorway which was now open. She asked loudly "What are you doing?" I felt so odd and uncomfortable, but there I was holding her mother's hand carved wooden staff. I might have not admitted to touching it, had she not walked in and seen me holding it.

I was carrying her amazing tall hand carved staff when I walked out into the living room. My friend looked speechless as the room went silent. After a moment she said, "The drum and medicine bag must go with the vision quest staff." She bowed to me and said it was right that I take them all home. I returned to her room and located the hand drum and the medicine bag my friend had created. I knew so little about the three items, but had to fulfil the agreement.

I experienced time travel one other time with the tall wooden staff. It was brief and took place when alone in my own home. In that journey, which lasted only for a few seconds, I was in England near a cave. It never felt truly comfortable to be a holder of the medicine bag and drum, but by then I was certain they had chosen me. I also knew that the reason for having them would eventually be made clear.

That day came a year later as I recall. I received a call from a desperate woman asking for spiritual healing. She was visiting from out of town and had tried many healers but was still struggling from daily psychic attacks. She said a psychic reader told her to come to Boise for her healing. She admitted she had moved all over the country to be free of whatever it was that was affecting her.

I met her at her hotel room first and sensed her tough nature but fatigue from all her failed attempts and receiving affective help. My initial session with her was only adequate, but she did begin to see me as the right person to work with. I realized she needed big medicine, as we used to call it. It turned into a three day ordeal.

I reluctantly admitted on day two that I was also a medicine woman and we could do a ceremony. Perhaps this would finally shift her situation. I grabbed all three items and we headed into the foothills outside of Boise. As the car climbed up in elevation I started looking for a place to pull over. A spot of sunlight seemed to highlight an area walking distance from a bend and turnout up the mountain road.

After parking my car the woman followed me to the spot I had seen at a distance. I made an energetic circle around us and then my instincts took over. Layers and layers of misplaced and unwanted spirits left the woman and were directed into the light. Finally it all gave way and the woman was set free from dark energies that had plagued her for years.

She looked like a different person as we drove back to town. The following day she thanked me with all her heart. She said she had experienced her first full night of rest in years. She added that even the air in her hotel room smelled sweet. I remember we hugged and she headed down the highway out of sight.

I thought how interesting that years later, I now need to do my own version of a give-away to disperse my personal spiritual things. It was my turn to do something similar. I looked at all my spiritual stuff spread out in our extra bedroom. I decided to give most of my stones and crystals to some close friends in Idaho Falls. I then remembered that a friend of mine from Boise named Rene was going to be in my area soon. After a quick phone call to her, she confirmed that she would be visiting Fort Hall Indian reservation that week. She said she could pass on all of the medicine items maybe to her native friends in that area.

I learned much later from Rene' that the three items were brought out during one of their annual gatherings and offered up to anyone. Most of the tribal members showed no interest in them at first. Then to everyone's surprise one of the younger members, a girl about age nine, walked up and claimed all three. The sacred drum said to be blessed by Brooke Medicine Eagle, the attractive leather medicine bag with feathers, stones and bones inside and the tall handsome carved wooden staff with owl medicine had been claimed. Hearing this made everything feel good. They were able to find a new owner.

During that summer of 1991, a few people who had met me at the Colorado conference had shown up at our place. Some stayed at our guest lodge. My husband did not like these strangers showing up to see me and felt under pressure to be part of this new age movement. He had a difficult time with many aspects of what I was involved with spiritually speaking.

In the meantime my husband was working to keep the painting business productive and felt alone with the burden of supporting our family.

All of this I understood and it weighed heavily on me. My marriage began to unravel as the weeks passed. I had a number of difficult verbal fights with my husband over money.

A month later I awoke with a severe case of asthma. In the past whenever something felt oppressive, I would manifest a mild asthmatic condition. That night it felt like I was unable to get much air at all. I sat up and continued to struggle to get air. I felt as if my whole life was not working and my marriage was straining.

For weeks I had also been nursing along an infected toe that had popped up out of nowhere. I knew that the condition was reflecting something unresolved in me. I was dragging my feet as they say. I felt afraid to step forward and trust the new energies coming in. I struggled to believe I would not be led astray. In contrast I also felt that if I stayed in that rut, I would die or something!

That night a powerful loving presence filled the room and suggested I get up from my bed. I moved into the living room. It was lit by moonlight and I began to slowly breathe better. With each thought of needing to breathe I realized I had to go away and get some clarity. My airway began to open fully. Finally a message came in and reminded me I could spend the week with my friend Carrie. She was heading out the next day for Boise to do training for her job. The guidance surprised me, but I silently agreed. I packed a week's worth of clothes and then went back to bed breathing easily.

In the morning I called Carrie and she cheerfully agreed that I could ride along with her and another friend. I would however, have to find a place to stay in Boise once we were there. She assured me I could ride back with her as well. After that call I announced to my husband that I needed to go on a little trip and figure things out. I explained that I would be going to Boise for a week to clear my head. The news was a major shock for my husband. His work had slowed down. He was able to watch the kids for a few days without too much difficulty. Suffice it to say my leaving began one of the most challenging periods of his life with me.

For five days I kicked around Boise, visited old friends and felt rather unsure what to do next. Events fell into place after my return to our valley. Looking back over this period of my life, I can see that the stage was being set for me to really leave behind everything. I was heading into a void. I would step through a doorway far more difficult to experience than any journey of awakening I had previously gone on. I would be journeying to the end of time itself.

I would soon learn how our physical bodies are made to be part of the transformation in consciousness. This is not just a journey of the mind. At times, I was invited into the instrumentation of vast orchestrations in light and sound. It was beyond words to experience the music of a universal creation and feel we are all intricately woven into it. My journey was only just beginning to spiral inward towards the center, where all our potential lies.

7

AWAKENING INTO NOW

All existence constitutes the one organism of the entire cosmos, emanating love as the brightest manifestation of its vital energy and having consciousness as the center of the spiritual galaxy. To comprehend this, the heart of man need simply be transformed to enable it to discover the harmony in the universe. Then it will spontaneously attune itself to the music of the spheres and will find peace on this earth.

Swami Rama, *Love Whispers*

It was the fall of 1991 and I was heading toward a literal unravelling of my inner and outer worlds. The night before I left Boise, I realized I was still not ready to return home to my family. I called up a new friend named Carole. Carole and her husband lived near the town of Victor on a property with a main house and a couple of cabins. The location was nestled up against the Big Hole Mountains. They had moved to the valley the previous year with their nineteen year old daughter.

Over the phone, Carole said she could accommodate a temporary stay. She spoke of a Master Teacher in Wisconsin that she was very excited about. They had all recently spent time at this Master Teachers retreat community and were already making arrangements to return, perhaps permanently this time. It was welcome news to have a place to go, but who was this Master Teacher? I would soon find out.

After arriving back in the valley, I headed over to my friends place. I called my husband and said I would be coming by to see him and the kids. After a pause I said that I would be staying at Carole's for a while and be away from home longer. It was a difficult phone call to make. Once I arrived at the house to get clean clothes, the visit with my children grew particularly hard. I remember my daughter suddenly saying to me, "I want to go with you to see the angels!" It was all I could do to reassure them both, as well as myself that this was a temporary move. I was taking everything one day, even one hour at a time to keep my head straight.

Carole spoke at length over dinner that night of the amazing Master Teacher in Wisconsin. She said he was teaching resurrection of the body, also known as physical transformation. He taught first and foremost that what mankind called reality was really a dream or holographic drama. He stressed the importance of studying the profound writings in the book A COURSE IN MIRACLES and of waking up spiritually. I was familiar with that book, but had never studied it.

Carole described this Master as "a whole light insertion" she said. He was from outside of time, adding that the information in the A Course In Miracles (ACIM) book was also from outside of time. The intense high energy of the daily sessions that were led by Master Teacher were triggering revelations or Kundalini awakening for some people studying under him. Carole believed this was facilitating a process of metamorphosis into bodies of light for many community members.

I followed her words, but honestly did not know for certain what to make of it all. She had a cassette tape of one of the Master's talks and wanted me to listen to it. Two other guests were visiting for dinner, so she waited until they left before putting the tape on. Just sitting and listening allowed me to experience this rare teacher's message. It was like nothing on earth. His words really cut right through the core of my minds deeper questions. He really made sense.

I grew quiet with my thoughts. Suddenly in a twinkling my whole perception of reality shifted. In the blink of an eye everything appeared undeniably dreamlike! My friend and her daughter talking across the room were images in a dream. I could not distinguish if I was at that moment asleep in bed somewhere in a night-time dream. I was stunned! I was dreaming a dream. This whole world was truly just a dream! Something began to tingle on the top of my head. I reached up with my hand absentmindedly.

My mind exploded with a million questions all at once. After a few minutes I found myself repeatedly looking up at the ceiling for no apparent reason. At first I saw only the cabin's ceiling. Then a different vision began to reveal an intense shaft of light streaming in. It was almost like a crack was opening up in the fabric of space/time! I felt light touching the top of my head to better understand. The most incredible longing grew inside me. I kept looking up, knowing something incredible was right above me, ready to open, like a portal. I had the feeling this doorway had been with me my entire life. I thought that maybe everyone has this same potential access to the light. A very deep singular endeavour took shape within me. I understood I had to choose to go *up* to my true home, but I did not know how.

Over the next couple of days, waves of intense disorientation moved through me. All my old beliefs about angels, spiritual guidance, people, life, truth, all seemed hugely questionable now. I felt very alone some moments. I looked back on what I thought had been bright spiritual experiences of awakening. Hierarchical spiritual structures like archangels, priesthoods, or the secret order or council of this or that seemed less relevant now.

The new teaching being presented was that all identities are false. I had never heard anyone say that the very concept of having an identity was a big cosmic oops. As in a domino effect, my previous beliefs fell away. I began to release all that the world had taught me. All that really mattered now was connecting with that light that was shining down upon me. Deep within grew a longing so strong I could not resist its pull. I needed to return to the light of my Source.

I could see now I had only dreamed of waking up. Maybe the celestial angelic energies were like an incubator that prepared my soul for a way out of my shell. I decided to not judge any of what led me to this point in time. Yet I knew for certain I was really not awake but aware of something quite profound. I would later understand this to be a state of being that is somewhere between asleep and awake or in "The Borderland," as described in the book ACIM. I knew I needed to stabilize around those who understood what was happening to me. I asked to stay longer at my friends place in Victor.

I made arrangements with my husband to be gone for a few weeks this time. I set up the childcare with a local woman the kids liked and made some other arrangements that would allow Bob to handle our affairs without me. I met with my children and expressed that I needed to be away, but I would be back. It was the hardest conversation I have ever had with my children.

I packed up enough clothes for a few weeks only. It all had to fit in one bag. Everything felt like right now. There was no tomorrow to plan for, but I did think I needed to go to Wisconsin next. It was difficult emotionally. I returned to my little cabin and really looked at what I was considering. After a few days of stewing about all the possibilities opening up before me, I determined to go with Carole to the retreat community in the Midwest where this teacher was. She agreed to support me in whatever way she could.

Carole said she and some others would first be travelling to Salt Lake City for a weekend event led by students of this Master Teacher. She said many people were already awakening through this energy. With literally no money and no expectation of needing it, thanks to my friend, I headed south to Salt Lake City with Carole and her daughter Janelle. The event was in a hotel conference room. The Friday evening presentation had almost 150 people packed into the room. A donation was suggested at the door.

In the front were about half a dozen people sitting on the floor, but behind the speaker facing the audience. I was told this was the Light Team. As the main woman spoke, I knew this was not like anything I had ever encountered! Some people from the audience were clearly upset and asked difficult, almost hostile questions while she began to teach.

With each moment of difficulty from an audience member the energy in the room would shift momentarily and the speaker would pause. Then a flood of light energy would seem to pour in and lift things up. She could then continue sharing the message of awakening. I witnessed to the fact that truth is either liberating or it is very upsetting, even threatening, depending on who is hearing it. I felt a powerful sense of liberation coming towards me, but could admit I was scared too. The main speaker was so bright my whole body buzzed as she spoke. The speaker said things like "I am a reflection of you from the end of time."

By day two of the event, fewer people were attending it. I was told this always happens as the energy sorts out those who are able to *hear* the message. I was very alert in my seat and could not deny the intensity of what I was going through. My hands began to shake at times and it felt good. I noticed that many of the people with the Light Team also showed shaking movement in their bodies. They shook and moved like electrical energy flowed through them. They had smiles on their faces and looked pretty happy.

By day three of the event in Salt Lake City, I experienced something that would change my life forever. The woman giving the talks was called Dee Dee by everyone. Her real name was Diana. She had an effect on my body as I sat in my chair. The energy affected me more each day. It grew inside me and my hands began to shake as the speaker walked down the aisle toward me. She taught that she was an expression of a mechanism of illumination designed to shorten time. She referred to herself as the new species of man-spiritual man and said to everyone, "You called me through time to wake you up." I realized I was hearing my future self speaking to me through this woman.

I whispered to myself, yes, yes. If everyone is a projected self somewhere in time, it makes sense that coming in contact with a reflection of the healed and whole me, means I can now leap into the final dream association. These were new words to me but I understood them. There was a reservoir of knowledge splashing over me.

Dee Dee and another woman from the team moved towards me and hovered next to my chair as she spoke to everyone. This bright person seemed to be activating an incredible acceleration in me. Like a magnet, I was being speeded through time toward a moment in space/time that she was emanating from. Something exhilarating was taking over.

I stood up and before long my arms had to stretch above me as the energy shot up my arms. I remember wanting with such passion to return to what is real, alive and awake! I became aware of the most incredible golden light as it poured down into me. Everything surged with intensity as the potent hand of God reached down into me from above. Then a sudden thrust of incredible magnitude seemed to fold me inside out and up into the blinding lights of Reality. My consciousness turned inside out! I was thrust into the brightest state of being I could ever imagine! I yelled from the intensity of it and then sobbed in gratitude to God for a while. It was the most overwhelming sense of relief. I was so energized I could see into a thousand directions at once. My awareness was utterly beyond words.

I was only barely aware of the place I had left behind. My heart exploded with joy that I was back to being really alive! Joyous laughter rippled out from me. I had a sense that wherever I had been a moment ago was so reduced, dim and dense that I did not want to think about it. My heart could not contain itself. It remembered how to expand and flow with the teeming, explosive life energy! I was aware of infinite fields of living patterns and souls so luminous and welcoming words do not do it justice!

After what seemed to be a long, yet timeless expansion into the infinite, I slipped back down into an awareness of the room. My attention had returned to being a body in a physical world. I could not understand human language at first. The sounds around me of people moving chairs and talking were so odd. My friend spoke and touched my arm. Her words to me were like funny sounds only. Then suddenly it all decoded and I was back in this world of separate people places and things. My physical cells were on fire and buzzed for several hours with a strange ache.

That evening at a potluck dinner party given by the visiting teachers, some of the Wisconsin people came up and invited me to come and join them there. I learned from others at the weekend event that this Master Teacher understood the power and difficulty that comes during an awakening. He had created a community in Wisconsin that allowed things to unfold naturally but with the support of others. People were moving there from all over the world to learn from the Master Teacher and awaken. I now knew even more clearly that I had to go there. Some of the others who attended the event also chose to suddenly pack their cars and head there.

We now caravanned with two cars packed full, heading to Wisconsin. Regarding hotels and meals along the way, every time I mentioned I had no money, someone paid for me with no comment, just a warm smile. Living in the moment with no plans each day seemed to be the way.

The community encouraged everyone to study many books but especially The Course In Miracles (ACIM.) It was the main source of insight all the teaching was centered around. I would just open any page of that book and my heart and mind would leap into states of realization and revelation! It became my daily dose to open the book and experience what the words were saying.

I kept myself on the razors edge of life and awareness each day. I had left my family for this opportunity to learn. Nothing was casual when interacting with others. Everyone there agreed to not consume animal meat or fish. I made a commitment to be a vegetarian and it has stayed with me ever since. The Master Teacher also asked that everyone abstain from consuming drugs and alcohol while living in the retreat community. Many people voluntarily went off medications too, once they were there for a while.

I saw many miraculous healings in people who were both visiting and living there as residents. Most every day, the Master Teacher led four hour nonstop sessions in the big room of the Main House. He appeared to be an older man, but it was difficult to guess his age. His voice sounded like that of the old Hollywood actor Jimmy Stewart. It was a gentle voice, but his presence was potent.

I found a seat on the floor like many others and listened to his talks. During what they called "quiet time" music from the movie sound track *Field of Dreams* would play. After that it would become anything but quiet! There were many people having spontaneous emotional and physical outbursts from the energy.

My initial days there were very difficult. I was unable at first to access the energy. The doorway out of the dream was eluding me. I began to understand that this energy was not something in my control. It came in more like an invitation from above that allowed for it to unfold. How strange it was to now sit in each session led by the Master Teacher, while all around me people were leaping into revelatory states, crying, gasping, and laughing with great joy. My psychic pain and sense of utter defeat grew each day.

I awoke on the third night in my small windowless room, but the imagery around me was that of a coffin. I thought to myself, oh no, I have died! Oh my God, I can't die! I believed I had been abandoned, left behind somehow. In my hysteria I pounded my fists on what seemed to be the ceiling of my coffin. Then in an instant the shadowy imagery of my dark bedroom reappeared. The dormer ceiling angled right over my bed was not far from my face. My hands had been hitting it in my sleep.

I collapsed back down on my bed in relief. I grew concerned that I was going a bit crazy. I also knew that physical death would never get me anywhere, but back into a dream and probably a worse one than this. I wanted to go all the way home and really *be* awake, but this would take time to unfold.

The next day I went through my fourth tortuous session with no relief. I prayed for help from the universe, from God. After the session I went for a short walk in the woods of the countryside. The cold fall air could maybe clear my head. I decided I should reach out and ask for help from one of the resident Brothers who were part of the Light Team. Soon after I thought of this, a car pulled into the main house parking lot. I saw a woman I recognized from the Salt Lake City event. She walked up and asked if any of us newcomers had any questions.

Wow, that was a quick response and I had never even opened my mouth! After a few others spoke up, I admitted I was not doing well at all. When I finished telling her of my coffin experience, the woman burst out laughing and said, "That is so perfect." She explained that my "pain" was just energy and should be used or directed up to God. "Give it to God!" she said. I pondered this and thanked her, but I still felt lost and concerned.

In the next room of the house I could hear a piano playing a beautiful song. Someone was singing an original song about waking up. The words were like open ended questions beginning with "Did you ever." The songs beautiful melody drew me into the room along with a few others. The man playing and singing was a recently endowed composer of new music. This energy was opening many people up to creative gifts or abilities they had never experienced before. He sang well and was gentle and compelling.

I decided to stop fighting off the energy pushing down on me. At some point it occurred to me that I was feeling the pain of this world and it was overwhelming! I had never felt so separate and alone. The contrast with the joy and love as it was being demonstrated in the daily sessions was excruciating. Since I'd arrived, all I knew each day was the magnified pain of separation from God and everything!

For an instant I quit holding it off and let it flow. A wave of acute energy swept through me. With a rush of emotion I surrendered it all up to God then everything sort of imploded. At first dark energy surged through me with such a rush. I nervously directed it all up to some place above me. It was ready to go to Light! I cried tears of such relief, as everything blasted up and out.

I was high as a kite the rest of the day. From that point on, I was able to spontaneously go "out of time" as they called it. In one session in particular, just after Master Teacher passed by me, I felt like the fireworks on the Fourth of July during the grand finale. So much light was showering outward. It was very fiery and elemental. He said, "well, well would you look at this one."

On other days after the session was over, I would be carried by the energy into subatomic states of matter. I remember I became first the essence of water. Everything in form became watery. I swayed gently and peacefully for several minutes. A resident Brother was drawn toward me like a magnet. My eyes were closed but I felt a shift in the room's energy. He moved backward toward me as our back sides touched. Suddenly I became pure fire energy. Everything lit up for a moment. We both screamed out loud from the joyous intensity.

We were taught to make each moment total and all inclusive. Dissolving into each fluid state became a useful practice. This session like others sometimes continued on after Master Teacher had left. Eventually people would get up and join the others making lunch in the kitchen or elsewhere. I offered myself to do chores whenever possible, in order to contribute to the community. I think it also helped to integrate the high energy by doing something simple but physical to ground yourself.

While I was in the Wisconsin community, we sometimes were taught about biblical passages that inspired spiritual awakening along with many other classic books. Even quantum physics, as applied to revelatory experiences, were woven into many of the sessions with Master Teacher. Someone recommended a book for me to read called the HOLOGRAPHIC UNIVERSE by Michael Talbot in order to keep up with some of the science behind all the phenomena.

I spent about twenty eight days in Wisconsin. I slept in two different residences, while attending the daily sessions with the Master Teacher. About 150 people were in residence from all across the planet. We were put up in motels, homes and apartments in Baraboo and the surrounding towns. Food was plentiful and I never had a need for money. Those who had it gave it generously, while those like me that did not, humbly received the bounty.

My gratitude was strong, but my desire to make full use of this opportunity was equally strong.

After a couple of weeks, I was invited to meet in a semiprivate session with the Master Teacher. I thought about the invitation for a moment and then said "yes" to the meeting. Anna-Anna, the woman who handled some of his affairs, added that the Master saw four people at a time in his little house across the street from the main house. He was affectionately referred to as Dear One by most of the residents. Actually everyone was called Dear One if not some new name Master Teacher gave him or her. I was never given a name.

I arrived the next day at the Master Teachers little house. At the assigned time I noticed I was walking in with three other women who had not been there long but had many questions. The Master Teacher always had a very intense effect on me. I waited quietly and noticed energy building within me. As the he finally turned to speak to me, he started by asking my biological age. He then smiled when I answered I was thirty years old. He asked if I was staying at the community long. I said I did not know and that everything was unfolding moment to moment.

Then before I knew it, the whole room disappeared! So much fell away all at once I gasped. Master Teacher and I were in a void-like space that was timeless. I began to panic almost as if I had been stripped naked or unveiled. I was exposed somehow and very vulnerable. I stood shaking. He said "It's alright my dear you are safe...do not be afraid." I was only aware of myself looking at his face with its dark brown eyes as we hovered in soft dull light absent of all form.

The next thing I knew, the room with the other women had reappeared. They immediately began asking, "What just happened?" I felt stirred to my core and needed to leave this room. The Teacher smiled warmly and nodded understanding, but the women tried to get me to talk. I apologized and said I felt fine but needed to get going.

As I walked across the street, my whole body went into full body systemic shaking movements. I wanted to shake off the density of the world so bad. Tears rolled down my cheeks. Everything in me knew I was not from here. In fact, it took a lot for me to be in this world. I knew it to my deepest core. The density of those women's pushy fearful questions really affected me. I was aware I needed peace and quiet for a while. I was grateful for the private room I had been given. I sensed I would really need to keep my energy "up" above the conflicted energies and get through this weird time of transition.

Toward the end of my stay, I remember an evening at the residence they called the Mountain House. Each residence had a nick name. One of the resident brothers ran inside to tell everyone to go out onto the roof deck and see the night sky. There was an incredible aurora borealis above us. It arched up toward the apex of the night sky. At the center we all could make out a triangle area set by the stars. The center of it was pulling me up into it.

Many of us were out on the deck jumping up and down joyously. I gave into it and that last jump had me collapsing down onto the deck. Then I went back to my bed and lay down. As I let go completely, I heard and sensed my young son Harry calling to me from the other side of the sky. I heard so clearly him yelling, "Mommy, I love you so much!" For the first time in weeks I knew without any doubt that it was time to go home. It was time to remember I had a life and a family.

The next morning I went to the vespers session at a church someone had recently purchased for the community. Dee Dee was leading this session and she seemed to be speaking directly to me at one point when she said, "Thank you for your faith in God." I was swept inward. I shut my eyes and saw my young daughter strolling in the tall wild flowers in front of our mountain property back in Idaho. I gushed with tears and felt given back to my life and my loved ones.

After the service I called home and my husband agreed to pay for a train ticket. Flights were harder to get on short notice. Many people in the Wisconsin community thought I was crazy to leave Master Teacher and lose all I had gained spiritually. I had some concerns, but my heart spoke of the importance of keeping my energy up and not indulging in fear based thinking. I felt certain that if this transformation was real, it would go with me. I also believed that it had begun before I arrived in Wisconsin and would continue, if I listened carefully for God's guidance.

I knew that I needed to continue my journey of transformation and awakening but with my family in Idaho. How I was able to be away from my children for those weeks amazes me to this day. I have a very strong maternal nature and I now ached to see my kids.

When I returned home to Idaho, everything seemed different. For about nine days I saw the light of Creation shining out from things and felt wonderfully in the fold of God's love. This wave I left Wisconsin on however, began to fade and I dropped into a wildly chaotic state of being. For two months I felt like an energetic yoyo. Each day I fluctuated between the intense pains of being part of this world of separation or in contrast up with the joy and light of a Holy Instant. The Holy Instant is our purest true state of being. I knew I would either make it through the changes unfolding or I would not. I might then feel forced to return to the supportive energy of the Midwest community at great cost to me personally.

My husband could see I was having a rough time. He didn't understand any of what I was going through. To his credit, he let me know he wanted to support me in whatever way he could. He offered to take the kids out some afternoons so I could have quiet time to stabilize and raise my energy. My biggest problem was shifting from having daily energy sessions at a regular time, to fitting them in around being a mom and wife. The more random and spontaneous mode for accessing energy would eventually win out and become a powerfully useful skill to integrate into my life.

The critical turning point came in early January 1992. I was acutely aware that everything was about faith or fear. After an argument with my husband I hit the wall of doubt; I began to panic and believe I had to go back to Wisconsin and soon. Simultaneously I knew I could not leave my children again without severe guilt and a sense of extreme loss. I paused in my escalation of emotion long enough to feel the truth of the matter.

With a certainty that could only come from my source, I suddenly understood several things about my life and journey. I was placed in this exact location geographically, in a marriage and with children, for a reason. Every aspect of my story would have to be the perfect ingredient for my completion and purification process, or I would easily be able to return to the Wisconsin community.

I let go and exhaled, then faith rushed in. From then on I decided to trust this holy process and give full value to everything happening to me, no matter what the appearance. I experienced a profound overall shift in my energy that day. I also came to learn that some of my most uncomfortable moments would produce my biggest breakthroughs in life.

By March of that year I seemed to pass through an invisible threshold. The roller coaster energy swings between being deep in the conflict of the world and then back up into the fresh air of truth, had dissolved behind me. Memories had fewer sequential references, but a calm certainty was there.

At night I remember being awakened a few times in the dark at night by a moth flying repeatedly at the top of my head. My heart smiled at the thought that there was so bright a light coming out of the top of my head, it attracted a moth. One night in particular I completely merged with so much light that I began to reference my sense of self as truly back in the light of reality. I felt like a visitor here on earth, beaming up and out at times. I remember finding myself suddenly standing in the corner of my bedroom in the dark and knowing I had just returned from the light beyond the veil.

The spring brought with it an incredible wave of universal love. The days of warm sunshine, blooming flowers and my children playing happily, nearly overwhelmed me with joy. God's light shined so brightly from everything. The very air felt energized and intelligent as it blew around the hills. I saw my daughter walking happily through the tall wild flowers near our home just as I had months before in a vision.

I remember being guided at that moment to open my A Course In Miracles book to a particular page. What I read reminded me that *"Once all blamefulness or guilt has been lifted from the world as you project it, the imagery can become a sign of life, a promise of redemption and a breath of immortality."*

I was aware of the struggle to survive and thrive all through nature. I could now see that this was the guilt of separation from truth and from our wholeness with God. I wanted to set us all free by witnessing to the unity instead of the guilt. The vicious cycle of death and guilt was a burden to behold all of the sudden. I wanted to witness to an eternal reflection always and with everyone.

Everything we consider solid or made of matter began to look very much like consciousness, made dense for a moment in time. I could not separate out the trees, dirt or even the air around me. It was all one sweep of live energy in an agreement for a moment. The light of creation was behind all the denser images or particle mass, crying out for a witness to set it free. Much of my energy activity was about an opening for that possibility.

I returned to the Wisconsin community only once after the initial month long experience. It was about nine months later. I had received a letter from a friend who had decided to stay in Wisconsin and become a resident. She mentioned in the letter that Master Teacher had spoken of me in session that day. I paused and remembered I had written him a letter a while back thanking him. Perhaps I had said something that invited his attention.

According to my friend's letter, he seemed to want to make an example of me. He played a song during one of the group sessions that I made of songs I had sung and recorded. I had mailed it to one of the residents. My friend said that in the session with Dear One he had said to everyone, "Can you all hear this?" to the group. My friend did not know what he meant, but she thought I was a fool to be so far away in Idaho and not there with everyone else. When I asked for inner direction, I heard, "Go, it is fine to be there for a moment."

Over the months I had begun to learn to access through my awareness the Wisconsin daily sessions from my own living room. I would decide that Wisconsin was two steps forward from where I stood in energy. Time/space seemed to collapse into a possibility of non-locality. I decided to trust the theoretical physics that taught me that there is really no distance between two points. On several occasions, I began to hear the sounds and feel the energy of the daily sessions in Wisconsin, while standing in my living room in Idaho. Now I had an opportunity to physically return and see how it all felt in person.

I was spiritually guided to go and stay for only eight days this time. Arranging the trip was effortless, as all the usual necessities of money and childcare fell neatly into place. While I was there I experienced new explosive expansions in consciousness and understood that this journey I was in was not necessarily typical. I was in a greater awakening now that included people and patterns beyond anything I could describe.

On the last day of my visit and just after the Sunday service in the church, I entered a rare confluence of energetic potential. It began when my energy started rippling upward. First I felt at peace as all the months of difficulty and joy released. My sense of self shot up energetically, racing up the corridors of light. I can still remember the feeling of being lifted up to that holiest of states. Tears poured out for a moment, as the gratitude and relief swept through me.

Then just as suddenly, spirit seemed to expand my being almost as in a silent nuclear explosion. At the peak of it I experienced an intense state of clarity as to what I am. Instinctively I then linked with the energy of all the brothers or community members in the church and out in the world at large. A spinning glorious golden cyclone of light energy formed through me as an extension of my heart or core. Nothing can describe how good it felt to step for a moment into this sense of purpose! I was for a moment an instrument of transformation at a magnified level.

After it completed itself, I heard many people panting for air, as we all caught our breath. Wow! It was an experience of expanded creative capacity that very well may have caused a huge shift of some kind that Sunday. I know it shot me to a whole new pitch. As I walked out, I saw people experiencing ripples of energy as I passed them. I left Wisconsin truly *high* on God and very hopeful about further opportunities to expand in such a way.

Back in Idaho and with my family, I underwent two continuous years of daily light episodes in multidimensional states of consciousness. I held small gatherings at our home where I would share the energy and insights as they flowed through me. My life was a daily unfolding of harmony that addressed the needs of everyone all in the moment.

Every chance I could get I would sit and enter into the upward arching energy. First I would make sure that the kids were busy playing a game or watching cartoons. Each day I got the chores done, fed the kids snacks and meals and did whatever was needed so that I could find a moment or thirty moments to enter into the light. I would be interrupted often by the phone ringing or my child needing help with something. The ease with which I could slip in and out of high states in consciousness was slowly becoming apparent and essential.

I met up with community members a few times over the next two years when they were in my area travelling to teach. I liked to go if possible and join with the energy. At times strangers at their events asked me what I was! Letting go into the energy sometimes could look like a genie coming out of a bottle with a lot of intensity.

Some people from the Wisconsin community were not comfortable with my explosive ecstatic self expression and would pull me aside later to scold me. "You are going to scare people!" they would say. I remember being shocked and speechless for a moment. How could so much light and joy coming from someone be bad? The concept would bounce around my heart for a few years.

Looking back on that experience, I know now that it stayed with me and may have harmed my willingness to share publically what is possible. I returned to my concept of a private joy in the safety of my own home to avoid overwhelming anyone. Energetically it was a powerful journey of being that revealed many hidden truths about the spirit of life and what physical forms really are.

Each moment that I let go into the upward ascending currents, everything physical would fall away. I would be aware of a vertical alignment shooting me through layer upon layer of consciousness, until I would pop through to an entirely new state of being. For a time I would acclimate and enjoy playing expansively in all directions with the patterns of light and sound.

My sense of time became very fluid and singular. Like an accordion, my perception would stretch and contract, depending on certain factors. As the energy would fade, I discovered myself back in sync with the needs of my family. Holy Spirit was in charge of *time* itself. I could accomplish a lot of manual things in the moments when I was associating with my body and family. Time would compress and expand to meet our needs. Many days after slipping into brighter and more timeless states, I realized it was helpful to put notes on the calendar to track time. If I went for too long without an energy release vertically, I would become nervous that I was falling too far back into the chaos. The calendar reassured me that it was often more than once a day to my surprise. So much of my world, the universe itself, was aligning with this upper re-association in consciousness.

I knew I also needed to integrate every level of my energetic experience back into the personal life as a mother, wife and friend. Throughout this phase of my life, I would call on the Holy Spirit for direction. I felt a constant inner connection with a loving inner Director of sorts. I was reading the book A Course In Miracles daily and often opened it randomly for in the moment insight. It always paid off and sent me into joyous energetic ripples of realization. Often the energy of the moment would pull me into an opportunity to expand or join with the higher octaves.

On one occasion I felt energy pressing in on me, but I had the morning chores demanding my attention. Odd headaches were not uncommon during some of the significant energetic upgrades. My husband thankfully decided to take the kids sledding and I agreed to stay behind. Almost as soon as they drove away, energy started building within me. As soon as I closed my eyes and surrendered into it, I witnessed the acceleration in consciousness I had grown so familiar with.

My mind and heart instinctively stretched to several dimensions of space/time on the hunt for something. I remember I passed through what can only be described as an energy envelope. I heard the words "whole light being" and enthusiastically leaped into this association.

I recall that all the patterns of life as we know it were like different instruments, yet also whole orchestras. I was an orchestra, yet I was also able to act as a conductor activating the incredible sounds of all the patterns of light within form. It was awesome and wondrous. Unfortunately my kids sledding activity finished too early and my kids burst through the door. I had to force myself to come back down in vibration too fast which was difficult. My head throbbed soon after, so I took a forced long nap to reset everything.

In other matters, my perception of places and people everywhere shifted so distinctly that I had to ask for additional assistance from the Holy Spirit. I was in the moment to moment awareness of NOW. One time I was driving my car and had just pulled up to a stop sign. I realized I did not know where I was. In a calm neutral way I asked for help. I wondered about this lovely country road.

A moment passed. I suddenly felt a simple truth spread through me. It made me smile, as I realized I lived here and drove this country road to town everyday! This is Teton Valley Idaho. Wow, this really is what the NOW can demonstrate. I made a mental note to adjust my vibration a tad so I could continue to access some of my important space/time memories. Linear time had a place in the day to day routine. I also knew the fresh and clean moment to moment awareness was a gift filled with light.

On another day, I noticed I was observing a person with a beard and gray hair whom I was calling a child. For a moment, I really viewed this individual as a child. I was very neutral about all of this as well. As I examined the feeling in my heart, the inner guidance said, "They are all truly just children." I suddenly remembered what gray hair meant and blushed to myself. I realized I was looking at an older man.

In contrast I met a very small child one day when visiting a home. This child came eagerly down the hall to see who was at the door. We practically bowed to each other respectfully. Spiritual age became what mattered and biological age disappeared from relevance. The child's mother was shocked. She said her daughter is usually so shy toward strangers.

My perceptions of many things were purely innocent and unassuming. I felt much taller too on many occasions. I could *see* from a higher point of reference, as if the homes were tiny and the buildings with the people in them were cute. My human self was there in the mix and was aware, but it had a quiet contentment in those days. My human small self felt safe and trusting of a higher order. I had very little fear. I learned that innocence is what I was being shown energetically by those moments and that innocence is really in everyone.

I eventually worked as my husband's painting helper. His painting company had a big job going and he needed some extra hands. I met a new friend who was one of his fulltime painter's helper. Before I knew it, I was sharing insights into awakening with her, while we sanded each window casing. She became a student of mine along with her husband and a few others in the valley. We would meet at the house for sessions once a week.

Nature was enlivened and intelligent in my daily interactions around our mountain home. One day during a lightning storm, my husband was on a couch reading and I was standing in the kitchen. Heat or white lightning rippled through the air and passed right into my forehead and third eye with a jolt. With a groan, my husband felt it pass through his gut at the same moment. He sat up and we both looked at each other stunned! The loud thunder followed instantly! There were many lightning storms that were spectacular to witness according to our neighbours across the road. They said our house would often appear to be getting hit multiple times. Energy in many forms was a daily experience in that home up on the hill.

On another occasion, Bob and I decided to hike up to the top of Table Mountain. It was a popular, yet arduous climb to a mountain crest from which you could look right up at the Teton peaks to the east or see the whole valley to the west. My energy was growing so sensitive to everything around me that I began to become startled as hikers were passing us. I could really see for a moment their entire skeletons all lit up in golden light! It floored me and sent my body into momentary shakes all over, as the energy revelation passed through me as well.

It got really strange later when we started to scramble up the summit block. The mountain was giving off so much energy that it hurt my hands to lean on the rocks. Bob just laughed, as my body would shake and arch. I quickly decided I could not summit because something magnetic was really affecting me. I felt like a lightning rod and did not want to find out what that would look like on the summit. The magnetism subsided as we hiked down.

"The sun shines not on us but in us. The rivers flow not past, but through us. Thrilling, tingling, vibrating every fiber and cell of the substance of our bodies, making them glide and sing. The trees wave and the flowers bloom in our bodies as well as our souls, and every bird song, wind song, and tremendous storm song of the rocks in the heart of the mountains is our song, our very own and sings our love." John Muir

Over the next few years, I read countless books on spiritual awakening, across many mystical and religious lines. Since then I have discovered my experiences were in many ways universal and matched many other disciplines. In the East I might be referred to as a "householder yogi" or one who maintains a home while seeking further union with the divine.

In February of 1993, I was filled with a desire to attempt to describe my incredible journey in consciousness to ever brighter states. I began a long article that I titled *The Big Bang Mess*. It flowed and took shape over the weeks and delighted me with the new insights it revealed through the process of putting things in written form. By 1994 it felt pretty complete. I would end up rereading it many times over the years and experience the original excitement of many breakthrough revelations. I changed the name to *The Big Bang – A Miraculous Event* in 1998.

Around this time I also wrote a new original song. I called my new song *Spirit Fire* because I was so aware of the heat I felt in my body as energy surged through me. It felt so purifying. I learned that the dross had to be burned away in order for the truth, light and innocence to be revealed. The song goes like this:

> *"Spirit fire...oh spirit fire, spirit fire. It's a spirit fire, and it burns deep within. It's a spirit fire; it can't be quenched only dimmed, But then it burns brighter hotter still again.*
> *It's a spirit fire that consumes the fear and pain. It's a spirit fire. It's a spirit fire. Spirit fire; invite the torch into the mind cave. Spirit fire; cleansing in light heart's deep stains. Spirit fire... hum.*
>
> *Spirit fires bubble and spark, always flowing, never dark. Spirit fire, giggles with freedoms delight. It's a revolution. It's the end of night. Spirit fire... spirit fire. Can you feel the joy? Can you feel the light it's soaring, exploding?*
>
> *Spirit fire... spirit fire. I am a spirit fire burning bright.*
> *Ignite all minds with God's grace and light.*
> *It's the time for reunion, remembrance of LIFE.*
> *It's your turn to enter the freedom's flame and sunlight.*
> *It's time to awaken in the dawn. It's time to draw the first breath of a Christ. You're a spirit fire, you're a spirit fire.*
> *It's time, it's your turn, and it's time to awaken.*
> *It's time to enter the freedom flame and sunlight."*

I sang the song *Spirit Fire* without any music, just my voice. It began to flow and take shape as a recorded piece still with no accompaniment just like I had in the past. My singing machine doubled as a recording studio. I did several takes until I got it right. Several cover songs that inspired me were included in the recordings along with my other original ones. I called the cassette demo "Songs to Awaken" and shared it with students and friends. It would evolve and change as more songs were recorded and added to the cassette.

My husband awoke on Groundhog Day in 1993 with his own epiphany about his life and purpose. He decided to go back to school and become an architect. He stirred me awake on that Groundhog Day as I lay next to him one morning. He explained his original desire as a young man to attend the University of Idaho and how his parents had forbidden it. To his immense disappointment at the time, they wanted an East Coast university, preferably an Ivy League School, for their son.

Now many years later, he could fulfil his heart's desire and many factors would lean in towards his achievement of that desire. Bob's new college plans led to a change in my life as well as our kids. It also brought my years of awakening to a close around August of that following summer as we prepared for our new life in a college town.

By that summer of 1993, I had discovered also that I had reached an energetic ceiling spiritually. After two years of continuous infusions of light, I was not being allowed to go any higher. I realized with some concern at first, that from now on, I was to find the light, to find God, in everyone I met. I knew Jesus held the blueprint for all that was transpiring and his lessons were now etched into my heart and soul. This was emotionally difficult, but a necessary redirection away from further energetic vertical access. To find the connection horizontally would be new. It was a horizontal re-association with all life. I had to reach out to people all around me and find meaning and even a pulse of God's presence behind all the appearances of separation. *He* was there, but it also meant a gentle falling in vibration was beginning to take place and become apparent to me.

With a sigh, I began to mingle more with the masses. I attended more community events, at first feeling timid but willing and curious. I knew to balance this new social directive with regular energy time. I would reach back in and up and expand momentarily into the vitality beyond the veil. It always felt so good and refreshing to go up and access the light. I would tap in often for a few more years wanting to take more time to secure the connection.

Even years later I would reach back to be sure that the doorway was still opening for me. It was reassuring to find God's eternal light was and is accessible. Somewhere along the way I realized I was also tracking an important pathway home. It was like going up to a high pitch joyfully but then falling down further each time in vibration.

Having said all this, I should clarify that I sought to develop connectivity with all of life in its natural rhythms as well as the exalted ones.

I noticed that a change within my heart space was unfolding that would allow for more emotional connections to develop again. I was trusting that I would remember the way back to the heights and beyond. I felt reminded that love is the unifying spark that binds us all, even in our dimmer states of being.

The yearning for connection with the greater light and love of our source had fanned into a fiery passion for years now. It resulted in sensations that are energetic, jumpy and tingly at times. For some time now I knew to welcome the electrical energy and allow it to move my body until it became an electrical baptism or rapture of love. I also knew to revisit it as often as I could and to enjoy the cleansing renewal that it delivered.

Eventually I grew to be not as concerned with coming back down in vibration. It was becoming the new norm. I understood that I had been rising to new spiritual heights for years. I now had to ease myself back down from the mountain top and remember to love and embrace this very human world.

8

INTEGRATING
INTO THIS WORLD

For a few years now I had been given many opportunities to explore consciousness and immerse myself in daily energetic upgrades. I understood that gears were shifting underneath me and it was time to integrate all that had been learned and received. I needed to re-engage in the world of work. I was also about to be dealt one worldly challenge after another, but I would discover a way through it.

We sold our mountain home by ourselves and moved to Moscow, Idaho the summer of 1993. It took thirteen hours to drive the rental truck to the college town in northern Idaho. Our new home would be in a campus family housing unit. My husband was enrolled in the University of Idaho's architecture program. Bob was very excited to finally achieve a career that matched his intelligence and talent for art.

I was excited at first, but the stress of the professional program took its toll on our marriage. This was in large part due to the stress of living with a husband needing to get a five year degree in three and a half years. That first year only a small number of students would make gain entrance into the upper division studies and studios of that department. Bob seemed under tremendous pressure to excel. Being an older student and having to support a family added to the need to graduate as fast as possible and prevail against all odds.

Our son was in first grade that year. This was a larger town with a crowded school system. Within a short time we discovered he was getting bullied on the playground by older kids. I even discovered him being harassed by kids around the apartment complex. I learned he was getting into some trouble at school as well. He argued about everything and was fighting a lot with his sister. The kids seemed to be feeling overwhelmed by it all. I struggled to find a job in the college town and often wondered if this was all going to work.

After about three weeks, my intuition led me to a job. The position had just opened up. I worked with elementary age children in a private school in town and enjoyed the work. The kids were very intelligent, but many had attention deficit issues. I noticed a lot of aggression in the interactions of kids at the school and even around our campus housing.

I was promoted quickly to a paraprofessional teacher. This allowed me to write a lesson plan on emotions or feelings. I introduced the concept of energy to teach healthy emotional expression and that feelings are energy. I had the students draw free flowing pictures to identify different emotions. The husband and wife instructors and school owners had PhD's in education and loved my input. We saw immediate improvements in the overall behaviour of the students in the school. As my ideas grew, and were shared with parents, it became the "Be a Bright Heart Campaign for Caring" slogan.

To my surprise one day, I was laid off. It had been less than four months. My employer's father had become suddenly ill and was in the hospital back East. She would be leaving someone in charge. She gave me notice to my surprise stating that she had to reduce her staff to cut costs. The job had grown quite meaningful and I was very surprised by the decision.

After deep soul searching and a flood of guidance, I looked at my home situation as well and made some bold moves. I decided to move back to Teton Valley and leave my husband to his studies. It was a bombshell of an announcement for him. The mood was intense and he was not happy, but he understood my resolve.

The kids seemed relieved and even excited when I gave them the news that we would be moving back to Teton Valley. I left with the children just before Bob's second semester of college started. I was not offered any money, but I left just the same. He had his own challenges to secure financial aid for school tuition and other monthly expenses.

The kids and I packed what could fit in the car; our clothes, toys, kitchen things and linens not to mention our cat we called Angel. We had no furniture and not much time was spent planning on what to bring. The kids showed the spirit of adventure in their expressions, as we headed down the highway out of town. I think they too had had enough with being there in all the tension and harsh predicaments.

Once back in Teton Valley, I struggled to find a place to rent. I had very little money to get us there and had to dip into our savings to secure a rental. A sweet little house became available in the tiny town of Tetonia. It turned out to be the only thing on the market available at the price I needed. An old friend in the area donated bunk beds for the kids. I slept on the floor and thanked God for a roof over our heads. In a moment of joy, we all celebrated the added touch from the universe. The house had a cute built-in kitchen table with booth seats! Anyone with young children to feed and no furniture can appreciate how helpful this was. Overall, I celebrated the lack of any intense emotional energy. I experienced a deep respect for what we were receiving. We all did very well together and my son and daughter seemed surprisingly at ease.

I did not blame my husband for things turning out this way and really hoped he would excel as a student. I just could not live another day in that energy. I wondered about the other women out there in the world who had to leave husbands and make it by themselves while caring for their children. I struggled to find odd jobs and very little money came in at first. There were no professional jobs from my former career as an addictions counsellor in that area without a long commute out of town.

At one point I had to go to the county courthouse and ask for canned food. We were a month behind in rent. I had been guided to do this by my angels. I watched as one thing led to another and I ended up being approved for a rare housing gift. First I was handed a phone by the county clerk and asked some questions by a woman at an agency in Idaho Falls. After telling her about the different odd jobs I had been doing to make it, she said, "You must have angels watching over you to have lived the past five months on so little money." The housing program paid a one-time check for the rent or mortgage for people with children who were on the edge of becoming homeless.

One check caught us up. It was not long before other challenges took its place. My car engine blew a rod and could no longer work for transportation. We had to hitch-hike from Tetonia to Driggs to get groceries. Bob eventually helped by co-signing a very small loan on a used car. He was there for us when he could be.

Soon after this the kids and I moved to Driggs and found a rental house with three bedrooms. A friend moved in with us which helped with the rent. I went from working as a gardener to being a cleaning person and eventually worked for a professional cleaning company in Jackson Hole, Wyoming. The money was finally stable. Bob visited a few times and we continued to hope for the best, but the separation more or less continued because he had school.

One summer Bob lived with the kids and me during his break from school. He designed his first house remodel for a local contractor and made some money. Things were still not great between us. I could not seem to remedy the situation. In general he did not appear to have anything in common with my friends. That summer I had been offering a weekly study group using the book A Course In Miracles and making more new friends. Things were rather tense as he headed back to Moscow for his fall semester that year.

As dumb luck would have it, I was unfairly evicted from the rental in Driggs around the same time. At first we were told we did not have written permission to have a dog. We had been given verbal permission the pervious spring. I eventually learned that the landlord just wanted to sell the house to a business developer and the dog was the excuse to get us out. We ended up bringing it to the local animal shelter.

Once we were evicted we had to float from place to place. A friend offered a room at first. After a few days she realized she had never lived around small children. She had to ask us to leave. It was very stressful, but I kept a good attitude. Finally I found a four bedroom house for rent in Driggs that had an option to buy. It seemed like a pipe dream at first, but I immediately loved the funky two story house.

One night, while I was waiting to get approval from the landlord, I dreamed of going up the stairs and seeing a brick wall blocking me from the large master bedroom with windows facing the Teton peak. I felt myself pausing and then something in me just knew I needed to walk right through the wall. As soon as I stepped confidently toward the bricks, the wall melted away into stairs, allowing me to climb on up. I then woke up. I decided that this was a vision of guidance for me to not lose hope, to persevere no matter how blocked things appeared to be. We moved in as renters at first. A girl friend and then a guy friend became housemates to help us pay the rent, but it was not easy.

My husband was not comfortable with me living with new friends and us so far apart in more ways than one. He began divorce proceedings at a distance and we settled on a simple mediator. Things were not all going wrong however. I received a surprise phone call from my dad. He said he was sitting with his father, my aging grandfather, at his retirement home. My grand daddy wanted to hear how I was doing. He had heard I was having trouble securing a place to live for the kids and me. I admitted that I had found a rental finally but was hoping to buy it. I did not want to get evicted unfairly again. I needed a down payment however.

Granddaddy chuckled and said, "You know at my age you realize that you can't take it with you. How much do you need?" This was a big change coming from him! He had never just given money to anyone. With it I made an offer with the low down payment. I then watched three months pass before the broker could secure a lender for a mortgage. The money had to just sit in the account and not be spent. Against so many odds that most women of low income face, I closed on the property right after the New Year. Bob and I completed our divorce soon after. It became official on February 29, 1996, leap year no less.

The following year was a hard one for many reasons. There was still no child support and we had only a few things to split up. Around the time of the divorce, our son had been struggling with his third grade teacher. He did not get along with her and was very upset one day when I picked him up from the winter sports ski program. I saw he sincerely needed a way out of further confusing power struggles with that teacher. I thought of the school I had worked at back in Moscow. Through the generosity of my mother-in-law, we were able to enrol him in the same private school I had worked at in Moscow. Bob was happy with the new arrangement. Harry moved back to Moscow and lived with his dad.

We then each had a child to care for and lived a twelve hour drive apart. I missed Harry so much. Tierney missed him too, but we made it work together, mother and daughter. My sister Joanna moved in with me in the spring. She helped with babysitting, so I could work longer days and save on childcare. That summer Harry came back to town, while Bob went abroad to Italy to complete a senior year semester of college in Rome. Harry said he was doing well at the private school. He said he enjoyed writing stories and getting more attention from the teachers. I worked my heavier summer hours for my clients and the kids got to spend some time with each other.

By the following fall I sensed subtle energetic changes just beneath the surface of things. My spiritual self was still alert and watchful. I even sat in energy when I could find time. It had to fit it in around my busy schedule. I gave free intuitive readings with Tarot cards for some of my new young friends.

I remember mentioning to one woman that I believed something new was affecting people across the planet. I explained that I had been shown intuitively that a strange metal-like dust was being sprinkled secretly into the atmosphere. I sensed it would affect the brains function. It could rob many people of their memories of uplifting spiritual truth for some reason. Admittedly, I did not know how this could be possible, but I wanted to remember the insight. She looked amazed and seemed concerned. Years later I would learn about "chem. trails" or dust cloud lines in the sky left by low flying aircraft.

Other things were beginning to trouble me. At first being a single woman was not a big deal. Over the months I noticed there was a prejudice applied to women more than men when they are single. It felt like a growing vulnerability. With regard to dating, I was not sure where my heart belonged. I had met a few new men and I had several very nice guy friends, but I sensed they were not right for me. My prayers were answered one day when the energy lifted. I was advised to look back at my former husband and think about restoring that connection. I made the difficult phone call the following November and Bob said yes by the end of the phone call.

We got back together just after he graduated early in December of that same year with a professional degree in architecture. He graduated summa cum laude and was also awarded a gold medal for excellence from the architecture department. He was older than most of his peers and was determined to make up for the years since he first dropped out of college.

Bob moved in with the kids and I just after Christmas 1996. In late 1996 having the whole family back under one roof in my Driggs home was meaningful to us both. (For the record, Bob and I remarried just a few years later in a small legal ceremony after we moved to a new home in the foothills.)

My husband was hired by an architecture firm in Jackson Hole Wyoming doing commercial and institutional scale projects like banks, hospitals, law enforcement and schools. He was excited to be moving away from his earlier work as a painting contractor doing high end homes and private residences. We were both commuting to work each day. I was now self employed and making much better money with my own cleaning company.

I inherited many well-to-do clients from my previous job with a cleaning service. My tips grew each year along with my connection with each client. They learned about each of my children, while I cleaned their homes and got to know about them. Some of the clients learned I had a college education and that I used be a certified alcohol and drug counsellor, but I was not able to find work in this area. So cleaning their homes was my job for now. I believe I was appreciated for my having a good background and education.

I decided one day to tell one of my clients about my background with healing and intuitive skills. She was a retired Episcopal priest who was suddenly very eager to talk with me about a practice called "the laying on of hands." I supported this topic with great interest of my own. Before too long

I had learned that she sponsored a monthly open group in the evenings at her church. She also learned about my singing in a Unity church years ago in Boise. I became a guest singer-healer for her next group. At first it felt nice to be around people that loved God and were interested in the Holy Spirit and healing.

Each month I sang one song with my singing machine and the group grew in numbers. I loved the part when we circled around and laid hands on a person asking for help. I noticed my energy waiting for the Holy Spirit to guide me, while others just pushed up to the person. I felt the heat flow through my hands and would sense the group shifting its position. This allowed me to come closer to the person in the chair.

At the end of each group, as we were getting our things to head home, someone would discreetly come up to me and whisper words of gratitude for my gifts. Some even described the feeling of energy coming from me and how remarkable it seemed. I enjoyed the outlet of singing a song each time. In general the group members gave me much praise as an uplifting singer and individual.

The change came when after a few months I noticed some church members overtly insisting on making my friend the priest the central figure in the healing effects. She was admittedly new to the practice, but would smile when they complimented her. I felt it was the Holy Spirit *doing* the healing. I also loved all those who showed up with simple heartfelt intentions. The undercurrent behind some of the women's comments were likely something to do with me not being a member of their church. The gossipy energy swirling behind my back felt uncomfortable. I could see that I was becoming a threat over time to some of these people. I was not a member of their church or any church really. I believed in the membership of God's kingdom and in the human race being under its care.

By the fifth month I was growing weary of the group dynamic. I knew that my time was probably nearing its end with that group of people. My friend the retired priest sensed something was changing in the group and perhaps did not want to lose me. She invited me to sing at the Chapel of Transfiguration near the entrance to Grand Teton National Park for the Sunday service. She was going to be leading the service as a guest priest.

Bob, my daughter and my son came to the service to see me sing that following Sunday. I was asked to sing two songs. A busload of tourists along with some of my friends and the locals, poured into the small chapel. After my first song, the priest walked to the front to give her sermon.

Harry stood up confidently and introduced himself and his family to everyone in the church. He explained that we were from Driggs Idaho.

People chuckled and the Priest managed to go with it, before returning to give her sermon. By the time the sermon was done Harry had become restless and moved to the back of the room. I then proceeded to sing my other song with passion and poise.

I was flooded with smiles and hugs from many people afterward, as we all walked outside. My son told me that he saw many people crying when I sang my songs. A friend chimed in that a lot of them were men. She thought the song I sang was very moving. Harry paused and then said he knew that his mom was like Jesus, really bright. I shook my head in disagreement but hugged him warmly. I knew that Harry believed being a bright heart was really important. He once told me he wished he could be a person who helps the world a lot.

The following Tuesday evening I reluctantly agreed to attend the healing circle. It was being held at the smaller chapel in town. I had already decided it would be my last healing circle in Jackson with that church. I was aware they had some guest minister who did some form of "healing of the spirit" as he called it. I was encouraged by the retired priest to come.

I arrived with a strange feeling of dread. After a brief introduction by this man, everyone in the small chapel formed a line. One at a time each of the group members went up before the man and got on his or her knees, as requested. Something in me sensed things were not what they appeared to be. I asked for the Holy Spirit to be with me, as I took my turn. As his hands came down on my head, he said some statements and then I felt myself being enveloped by a sort of dark heavy energy. I was not in fear but knew to not be in conflict with this man. When he seemed satisfied, he lifted his hands off my head.

An instinct for survival surged up from deep within me as my body shook off the heavy weird energies, like a dog that has stepped out of a muddy pond. Light from above reached down and lifted me up higher than I had been in a while. The man's eyes widened and he stepped back quickly from me. One more person went after my turn. I politely waited till we were all done, then went to get my coat.

Not long afterward, I was approached by the minister. He had the strangest expression of bewilderment and almost seemed to apologize to me. I guessed that someone early on had led him to believe I was a problem or something, but he now knew I wasn't. He almost bowed to me as I nodded acceptance of his mistake and calmly left.

Tears welled up on the way home. The memory of it all still lingered. How could such creepy energy be what that minister was inadvertently working with? He was so focused on dark energies needing to be cleansed, that the reverse was taking place. He was unknowingly calling them into each person as he laid his hands on them. It was so shocking. I recalled that important old teaching "What you put your attention on you will increase or magnify." I tried to always put my attention on the light and the innocence within a situation. At least then there was a chance for the inner light to grow or find renewal and restoration.

So many things seemed so dark and corrupt in the world at that time. I thought about all the bullying going on at my son's new middle school. It had grown much worse since his younger years and was a big problem. But nothing was simple. Perhaps offering loving energy at a nearby church might not be the best use of my time. But I already knew this and had said my goodbyes. I could not shake the feeling that events were in motion that could not be reset and that the river of life was about to flow over a waterfall.

9

HARRY

Our son Harry was a special child. He was outgoing but sensitive and loved life in general. He wrote stories about angels when he was six with amazing original coloured drawings. He loved telling stories and imagining that he could make a difference in this world. He could not make sense out of many of the kids in his own age group. The boys wanted to play by shoving and wrestling each other. He used to say, "Mom, why do boys like to hit and push each other around?" His good friends were often kids much older or much younger.

The bullying began during his first years in school and never really let up. His transition into middle school was particularly difficult. He was ganged up on in the basketball gym at our local school by several boys. They threw basketballs at his head hard enough to knock him down flat. He reported the kids to the principal and said his head really hurt. I was not told about this from any school official for about ten days.

He came home very sad that day and said he was tired and that some kids threw balls at him and his head hurt. He went to his room in a gloomy mood. He seemed resigned to being bullied. We had talked about the bullying and spoken with teachers to no avail. I was very aware that the victim is constantly the focus instead of the maladjusted aggressive child.

Because of my years of experience working with teenagers with many behaviour issues, I was very frustrated with the lack of intervention in general. I had grown disappointed in the school system's inability to keep kids safe from bullying. I was also just sad and so tired from my own workload that I felt somewhat powerless. My job, the bills, everything was taking its toll on me.

Bob was an intern architect with his own stressors of very low pay and slow upward mobility. I earned more than he did. He could not contribute much to my monthly bills. After a little over a year working in Jackson, he decided to seek an advanced degree in architecture out of state in a specialized field. He also liked the option of being able to teach architecture at the college level some day. This had set up a whole new situation for our family. His decision to go back to school again was not a happy feeling for me. I felt like I was on my own with everything.

In the meantime Bob was growing excited about his plans. He was making the final preparations to move to Oregon and get a degree in a special advanced program on green architecture. He would be leaving soon and I would be carrying the whole load. Our kids were not thrilled with him moving away to complete this masters program. Bob had planned to visit as often as possible, but we all knew the drill. It would be a long wait.

Harry saw me crying one evening around that time. I was too tired to make dinner for everyone. I think Harry was aware of my own sense of giving up. The general current picture of both of our lives seemed pretty bleak. I was feeling heavily burdened and unhappy about it. Harry also may have had a strange sense of confused loyalty about where he should live at that point in time. Bob presented options for Harry to join him, if he wanted to, but it would be pursued later on, after he got settled in Oregon.

The night before Bob's planned departure out of town, Harry invited a new friend over to spend the night. He had just started middle school like Harry. We took them both out for pizza and Harry seemed happy to have a new friend. The following morning the little friend yelled from the bedroom saying that Harry did not seem right.

When I walked into the room the visiting kid looked scared. As I glanced at or son I noticed Harry was face down in his pillow and all curled up. I screamed to my husband to come help us. I reached down and pulled him upright and his body was stiff. His eyes were shut and he weighed a lot. Suddenly I knew I was holding a corpse. Harry was dead. I remember crying out, oh my God, oh my God! For a moment an image of a smiling face flashed across my awareness. It was Harry looking happy. This so shocked me I felt angry for a moment at him, like he was playing a game with me. It was very freaky, all of it!

Bob came running into the room and then called 911. After a few minutes we decided to get him to the hospital ourselves. It was a few blocks away. We had only a pickup truck at the time. Nothing could have prevented us from at least trying to get medical help. When we arrived, the ER medical staff looked at his blood pooled complexion and zero vital signs with compassion. Bob left quickly to go back for the kids.

I was surprisingly welcomed right into the ER room to the foot of the exam table they had put Harry's body on. That moment I felt energy rippled through me and then flow out of my hands toward his two feet. Harry's cheeks seemed to become pink all of the sudden. The nurses and doctor suddenly chose to do CPR on him with tremendous passion.

After a few minutes we were all aware that it was no good. The doctor had known our family and gave me a hug. I walked out and saw Bob had arrived with our daughter and the young boy who stayed the night. We as a family were forced to do what everyone must do when there is a death. You find a way to cope with it.

Harry died in his sleep on September 19, 1998. He was eleven years old. All day that Saturday my husband drove around with our daughter, my sister and one of his friends from work, looking at the different cemeteries in our valley. I chose to stay home in order to catch the long distance phone calls coming in from relatives. I also knew I needed to greet friends showing up at our house, desperate for news.

After many hours my friends realized I had not eaten all day. They would try to get me something. When I looked at the food it made me sob uncontrollably. Something about nourishment seemed so strange when so many more important things have happened like death.

Later that afternoon Bob called the house to firm up a decision on the choice of a cemetery. He described each place they had visited. I agreed that the Cedron Cemetery was the best place for Harry's burial. It was on the west side of the valley, set against the foothills on a grassy slope facing the west facing side of the Teton mountain range. Bob and our daughter thought it felt peaceful and had a nice view.

An informal service was put together for friends and neighbours at the fairgrounds for the next evening. People poured into the old building with letters, cards, flowers and photos of our son. For many it was a place to grieve and to try to make sense out of the confusing information surrounding his death. There were a lot of potluck dishes available and many hugs, but I believe I was rather numb to it all.

More family arrived in town the next day as the formal service began to take shape. We decided to hold it in a nearby church. We met with the priest of the local Episcopal Church in Alta, Wyoming and agreed on Tuesday afternoon for the service. I was empty inside after having spent so many hours of crying off and on. People had arrived from across the country over the previous two days.

I pondered the plans and message for the service and my head cleared a bit. My heart began to feel the importance of Harry's funeral being done right. I knew I did not want a typical religious sermon or service. I thought maybe I would even sing at the funeral. This idea surprised me for a moment. Then I decided I could just go along with the idea of singing and opt out when the time comes, if it did not feel right. I also became inspired to include a children's story that my son and I liked a lot into the service.

As we drove toward Alta on the day of the funeral, I felt energy draining out of me and then I went literally limp in my seat. Apparently being emptied out energetically was necessary. I quietly said a prayer to the Holy Spirit. The car pulled up to the church and then everything shifted inside of me. Energy now was pouring in. I felt strong enough to walk in with the conviction of fulfilling my part in the service. The kids who had bullied Harry showed up at the service looking pale and lost. A couple of parents said their sons were seen crying for the first time in years. So many people showed up at the service that they crowded in with standing room only.

I read out loud the book ALL I SEE IS PART OF ME written by Chara M. Curtis with illustrations by Cynthia Aldrich, to the packed church. I held up each full colour illustration for all to take in. I felt the hearts of many people were swept up in the wonder of our son and his similarity to the little boy in the story. Harry often asked such unusual questions and pondered life's big mysteries. We all used to say, "Harry has big thoughts."

When it was time for me to sing, I somehow managed to do it well. Not everyone understood that I had grown up singing a cappella and had learned many songs by ear. Some knew I had performed recently in the churches over the hill in Jackson. I sang a song that I loved and had learned many years earlier. It was on a cassette tape and my singing machine was able to reduce the voice of the singer, so I could sing the song myself with the accompaniment.

The song was called *"At the Same Time"* but I do not know who wrote it. I had already performed it in Jackson Hole, at the monthly healing circle. It is all about the heart beating in everyone across the planet and how we all march on through thick and thin, despite the confusion of these times.

Ultimately the song lyrics go like this: *"Think of the all the hearts beating in the world at the same time. Think of all the faces and the stories they could tell, at the same time. Think of all the eyes looking out into this world, trying to make some sense of what we see. Think of all the ways there are of seeing. Think of all the ways there are of being. Think of all the children being born into this world, at the same time. Feel your love surround them through the years they'll need to grow, at the same time. Think of all the hands that will be reaching for a dream. Think of all the dreams that could come true...we need to build a world that loves and understands."* I finished the song and felt my heart bursting as my tears rolled down my cheeks. I knew I was ready to sit down and just allow the grief to take over.

People had responded to our request to wear colours of the rainbow. Our son loved bright colours. We opened up the microphone to anyone wishing to speak or tell a story about Harry. Many people spoke and we ran way over our time allotment at the church, but it did not seem to matter. So many people had met our son over the years at the grocery store, at the local diner, at the park with their kids etc.

In each story, our son had made a huge impression on the person. It seemed they could not find words big enough to express their gratitude for having met him. All agreed that Harry was a unique child. My heart was so touched by these people. I later decided to gift some of them with a copy of his little handmade book called *"The Angels"* by Harry Robert Heneage IV. He'd created it when he was just six.

I remembered for a moment the joy and wonder I'd felt when he created the book with me. It was back when we lived in Moscow Idaho. He had been getting in trouble at school. He was in first grade and we were living in on-campus housing. I was called by the school administrator and asked to come pick Harry up at the school office. I decided to keep him home the next day to sort his behaviour out.

Harry had cried at bedtime and pounded his little head with his fists saying, "I don't know what my mind is doing Mommy." The next morning he nudged me awake very early to show me a picture he had drawn. Harry was smiling and happy again but wanted to tell me about a story he needed to write down. He asked if I would help him with it. I made coffee and settled into a chair next to him at the kitchen table.

I watched as he drew picture after picture with great speed. I asked questions and jotted down his narration at the bottom of each image as he nodded approval of it. This was the month before the kids and I moved back to Teton Valley. Harry made a few other books as well. They were priceless to our family, but we had not shared them with many people. Now it felt right to reveal his creative side and desire to inspire people to believe in angels and other magical things.

After six weeks and many tests on Harry's cause of death, it was pronounced as "unknown" on the death certificate. Our grief was profound. Our young daughter had lost her brother and best friend. Bob decided to stay with us and continue at his job in Jackson Hole. I could not be more relieved. His plans to move were all cancelled.

As I look back on things from that time period, the world felt like it was heading into a darker energy or passing into a strange orbit. Light and hope were harder to find for many, not just our family. That first winter was particularly long. Grief is a personal process different for everyone.

Two weeks before Christmas we were shopping for our daughter in Rexburg and noticed a box full of puppies in front of Wal-Mart. A smart young woman asked if I would just hold one of the puppies while I shopped. I agreed and before long we both realized we needed to bring this puppy home. We made it a surprise for our daughter but it really became the family pet that we named Cashew. She was part cocker-spaniel and part golden retriever. She was treasured for many years.

As we continued to mourn the loss of Harry, our daughter suffered from several physical challenges in addition to her grief. First she had a ski accident and broke her leg at our local ski resort. The second set of X-rays, done as a follow-up in Jackson Hole, revealed a growth plate fracture to the knee.

Within a few days she had also broken her arm while trying to walk in the front door of her elementary school with crutches. The floor of the school lobby was wet from the heavy snows the previous night. It made for a dangerous surface, since it had virtually no mats to soak up melting snow from boots. She went down hard onto the floor even with me right next to her. Off to the hospital ER we went to get yet another X-ray and cast this time.

In the next two months or so after those issues healed, Tierney appeared to have lumps forming on her arm and shinbone. The Wyoming doctor was very distraught, knowing what our family had already endured. He did not want to cut on her to get a biopsy. Instead he quickly decided the lumps were probably benign cysts and likely not cancerous. He cautioned me to call him immediately if I saw any change in their appearance.

When we got home, I decided to tell our daughter my spiritual thoughts on tumours or growths in the body. I said that I believed that the heart, when it is very sad and cannot fully express some emotions, will compartmentalize them to an area of the body and a cyst or tumour will form. I asked her, "Do you have any feelings about Harry's death that you are not allowing yourself to share or feel?"

She burst into tears and vented about God taking away her brother. "It was not fair!" she said. She was also mad that in every picture of Jesus she had ever seen, he is never smiling! "Why is that?" she asked in disgust. I could not answer her, but supported her honest expression and inquiry. The lumps disappeared within a few days to our family's relief. I understood that potent authentic expression is so important in the restoration of harmony in the mind and body. I later found a sketch of Jesus smiling that someone had made and gave it to her.

A few weeks or so later we had an even bigger scare. Our daughter came into our bedroom one day and appeared to be having a stroke. She tried repeatedly to speak to us, but her words did not make sense. My body froze as she kept attempting to form words in front of us! I believe I may have thought she was about to drop dead right before our eyes.

Finally she smiled at the strangeness of her situation and I stood up and walked her to a chair. I think I asked if she needed a glass of water or something. After about twenty minutes the symptoms went away. She said she thought the sensations of not being able to talk had happened before, but this time was worse.

Within a few days we had an appointment in Idaho Falls with a neurologist. After the test results came back, the doctor decided our daughter's condition was full blown epilepsy. We had never seen anything like a seizure happen in our daughter only the strange loss of speech. We felt we had to go along with the doctor's diagnosis. This local doctor put her on strong medication that unfortunately changed her personality. Her grades began to plummet. So many things did not seem right. I felt like teachers and doctors were ignoring our input on our daughter. The doctor continued to insist that the strong medication was necessary.

After several months we finally tracked down a Paediatric neurology center in Boise. We took a trip to see a specialist there and learned quickly that the first doctor had completely misread the EEG report. It turned out to be a seizure disorder affecting speech only. The Boise neurologist said our daughter actually had a form of epilepsy called benign rollandic epilepsy. It was named after the rollandic area of the brain. He emphasized that our daughter would grow out of it by the time she was 16 with or without minimal medication.

I cried with relief and hugged the doctor. I was amazed that my daughter's accurate diagnosis took all year to sort out. I was very disappointed in the first neurologist. My motto ever since then is to get a second opinion when you have any doubts about the accuracy of a diagnosis.

I had a few health crises too that winter. One nearly killed me from an infection in my uterus. It took months to fully develop and when I was high with fever and giving up on life, my daughter was the only one who noticed. She brought me water and suggested I might need to go to the hospital or doctor. Instead I reassured her and sent her away. I quietly gave into what I thought would be a likely death.

Jesus came vividly to me and up close. He reminded me to look at what I was really doing. I felt him whisper to me very gently but firmly. He said, "If you die, you will have died of despair, nothing more." I felt ashamed and pathetic. He knew me well. He smiled with relief and then guided me to visualize water inside my uterus. I did as he directed and suddenly water burst out of my loins.

Over the next few weeks I discharged many very black bloody clots and began to realize that my connection with motherhood had started to die after my son's death. My body had simply acted out my inner sense of loss. I became determined to pull myself out of my despair. I needed more support. Bob and our daughter and I agreed to talk more to each other. We grew closer as a family, while our grief sorted itself out.

I dreamed of my son Harry at times that first year and knew the messages were for me to not view him as dead, just doing his part in a different kind of life, as it were. I also sensed his spirit on some days with other souls around him. He wanted me to meet his new friends. I instead urged him to join with the light or go to a higher place. I prayed for help to lead him to a safer state of consciousness away from the astral plane and its confusing layers of souls.

I even felt at one point like Harry wanted to come back into a new body and be a baby again. His spirit seemed very close by and wanting me to know. He then paused in his sharing this with me. We both suddenly knew it would have to be with a new mother. He said, "I will find a mom who knows you so I can still see you." All of this caused me to sigh and tear up at the ramifications of it all. I wondered if I would be made aware of the family that would receive Harry as a new baby. I decided not to think too much more about it. Ten years later he did show up and remembered who he was before. It was quite a shock to me and his new mother. He was someone else's child and I was grateful to know he was doing well, but as a girl this time.

I had another encounter with Jesus unexpectedly within the same year of 1999. I was driving from a job to get to another home I had a contract to clean. A dump truck stopped suddenly in front of me causing me to slam on the breaks. A sports car behind me slammed into my king cab truck. The owner was very angry as he approached the driver side window. All I could think was what next? The man calmed down once he saw my frightened face looking out my driver side window. The impact had jammed my knee into the steering wheel and thrown my back out of alignment.

A few weeks passed and my car was repaired by the other driver. My back seemed a little off and hurt a bit. I had been to an orthopaedic physician for my knee and he noticed I was walking funny. I was not in a lot of pain and decided to not pursue any further doctor visits. The driver that hit me was hot tempered and maybe I felt unwilling to fight over further medical costs. More than likely I was just emotionally numb and did not care enough to fight about anything.

That night Jesus came into my awareness. He whispered something like, "You are going to need that spine." After a moment something adjusted in the area of my spine. My eyes welled up in gratitude to him for his help. Soon after that he was gone. I cannot express the utter gratitude and humility I experienced every time Jesus showed up for me like this.

Over the next few weeks I thought about the energy that used to flow so powerfully through my spine and out the top of my head. I thought that perhaps I should try my energy work to get something moving for the first time in quite a while. Finally one day when the mood felt right, I sat down and did energy. It helped, but it felt so diminished compared to what I knew was possible.

Not long after this I received an urgent psychic message on my way to work. It was strong and insistent, so I pulled over the car. I realized with great clarity that I was being asked to fulfil an important mission and it would require me to really trust that God would bring me back from it. I sensed almost a high level of sensitivity surrounding my part in it.

I cancelled my day of work and went to a spiritual friend's home for support. She saw energy swirling around my heart area. Something was being deeply encoded and all of the sensations seemed to indicate it was altering aspects of my consciousness in some way. It looked like I would be in need of that spine after all and everything else.

10

BLACK HOLE - WHITE FOUNTAIN

In 1999 there was a mass murder shooting in Littleton Colorado, at Columbine High School. It had affected me deeply at the time. I felt it marked the beginning of the coming era of violence in our country at the hands of young people. For me it was a new pattern rippling across our country. As 1999 came to a close, I could really feel bigger changes coming for the earth and its people. With a heavy heart I felt drawn to assist the cosmic churning of events, while I continued to process my child's death and his intuitive link with me. I felt a deep foreboding that I was being drawn toward a dark whirlpool of energy that nothing can escape.

I felt Jesus speaking to my heart, telling me to not be afraid and to always know light and love were in me and with me. Yet he also added that it was time to "batten down the hatches" so to speak, as if I were about to embark on a very unusual voyage and it would not be easy or simple. On Christmas Eve Jesus left me with a promise that he would see me on the other side of this when I came out. Out of what, I was not sure.

Beginning in February 2000, and for many months afterward, I felt the world passed through an energetic eclipse or phase of darkness. I will never forget the drop in vibration as though I had entered an elevator going only down and then sideways. It was an awareness that could not be compared to anything I had ever known, but it unfolded for about thirteen months.

It felt like I was at the center point of a compass as it spun around unable to get a fix on true north. I grew unsure about the whole experience as it took hold. I felt lost and adrift in a spinning field of dimensional states. I seemed to descend into each sort of "hell" place as the darkness increased around me. My heart was quiet and clear even as very odd, weird beings became aware of me. Simultaneously I was aware of the physical world of my life and family. I had to cope and interact with a layered type of reality. Over time it grew steadily clearer that with regard to these other worlds, non-doing was all that kept me from becoming entangled in the different patterns and spirit worlds. It is very hard to be neutral about such intense experiences, but I tried. Multidimensional journeying had to be mastered. I sensed that multiple futures were being revealed somehow and our collective future potential, as members of mankind, needed to be sorted out.

I witnessed many unpleasant futures. I learned to let go and allow each story line to unfold with minimal intervention other than holding space for a universal higher field to assess. The universal overseer seemed to loosen through me each pattern or layer of destructive potential, as I became aware of it. My regular world needed my attention also, but it was hard to focus on both. I can only describe it as walking in more than one world at once. My heart discovered it had a point of light or inner connection with our Creator/Source that was undiminished. It was all that felt true and I could almost rest in it. Nothing else was as real. Yet everything was dim energetically.

People in town seemed to look at me with a quiet inner understanding. Perhaps they just thought of my son's death and the grief I was in. I felt that they too sensed that something was seriously *off* for everyone. I wondered if our town was the epicentre of something profound and unique. Did it go far beyond our region of the country? If so, then many people were in a strange state of consciousness all across the world, not just me. My sensitivity to the unusual reality unfolding was very difficult to explain. Most moments I decided it was not useful to talk about it with anyone.

Some days I would ponder much of what I felt, as layers of human consciousness flooded my senses. The veil between so many realities was thin. It was like finding yourself thrust into many different complicated worlds with people very engaged in survival and not knowing or understanding why I was there.

I noticed one pattern that was consistent in many of the groups of souls I encountered. They did not know God. They thought everything depended on them to be solved. Faith in a higher order was a foreign concept. This was the dream of separation at a depth I could not fathom.

Many souls asked me how I came to be in their world. To them I did not fit in. I was just odd. In my heart I knew God was the light within me, yet that included everything around me as well. Quietly I understood I could not possibly be alone. I shared this with them in my own quiet way, but it only sank in sometimes. At a certain point in the encounter there would be this awakening. The soul entangled with me would realize the inner true light and then it would disappear. I would soon find myself with a new group of souls. It felt like it would go on forever, layer after layer.

Often I had to drag myself to work each day and struggle to keep my wits. Really being able to complete a meal and sleep was growing more and more difficult. The Master once said "Be in this world, but not of it." I was in many worlds but definitely not *of* them. They seemed foreign, unfamiliar. Some worlds I entered had entities that would try to hurt me or affect me in some way that was unpleasant. As in all dreams that are nightmares they would eventually end. But some nights I just had to endure the test and be as simple as a point of light in darkness. Over time I learned more clearly than ever that I had God's light at my core. If I kept my certainty on this eternal truth, I would not be made into something dead or worse. I trusted that it would all eventually fade over time but probably not for awhile.

One weekend after speaking with a long time intuitive friend over the phone, I decided to go to Boise and see if anyone there had ideas on what might help me. My friend let me stay with her for the weekend. She said she knew a psychic in Sun Valley and called her on the phone for me. The woman asked to speak with me after hearing a brief description of my situation. I spoke to her about what I was experiencing on a lot of days. She asked for my birth date and then paused.

After a few more minutes she seemed to be receiving a download of information. She started saying something like, "Oh my god!" She then said I had somehow taken someone's place. "You are doing someone else's job," she said! She went on to caution that I was not really designed to fulfil this type of purpose, but I must succeed. I could feel her fear for the first time.

I agreed with the feel of her words and in some ways it was a relief to have someone else understanding my problem. She paused and then said something about my basic nature makes this a tough one to get through, but she believed I would eventually be okay. I was not sure what she meant but stuck with the faith that I had a quality that matched the other soul or I would not have been asked to do this. I went home feeling trapped but more aware. I would have to find my own way through this.

I returned to my daily grind of cleaning homes and trying to keep myself on task. One day I was cleaning a home while the owner was home. He was a retired medical doctor. We had chatted with me at first when I arrived about the usual things and I felt fine. An hour or so later I was very aware that I was slowly losing a sense of clarity. I felt very light headed. The owner asked if I was all right. He brought me a glass of water and without warning I keeled over on his couch. I could barely find the strength to mouth the words to call my husband for help. He did so with great concern. At that moment I felt so thinly connected to my body I was unable to explain it to the home owner, let alone myself. He checked my wrist and said my pulse was very weak.

When my husband arrived, I could barely walk. When we got home, I tried to eat soup and could barely hold my spoon. I told my husband that this light-headedness had been coming on to me out of nowhere, but so far I had been able to keep myself okay. I apologized for the embarrassment of having to come and retrieve me at a job. I told him that something was happening to me that I could not explain, but it might fit into one of his science fiction books. In fact several intense Hollywood movies came out over the next few years that had uncanny plot lines similar to what I had experienced at times.

So many souls came and went over a period of thirteen months. I witnessed some very unpleasant futures for our world that appeared to be a potential for great losses in all aspects of society. These worlds had potent dramas taking place and it kept me up many nights. It was so dark and unfulfilling some moments. So many layers of humanity were steeped in confusion about who we really are.

Power in any form was the theme and it continually corrupted in each story line if it was source-less or ego driven. I would track the corruption in my consciousness for a period of time like an unhappy witness. At some point, I was allowed to fall away from it just as a new one would emerge.

Diseases were another pattern of humanity that I came upon and processed. I could see and feel that fear and judgment or hate was the energy that manifested most illnesses. Projection of the responsibility was a polarity that sustained the pattern of illness. Love set it free and forgiveness undid all remnants of it. The cells could only reflect diseases or the tangle with pathogens until a better choice was made. Each disease was like a mob of people, angry and confused and not able to remember that love is what we are.

I had to walk between all these worlds, knowing this was very dangerous work. I sensed the future was simultaneously tracking backward into this time in history through intuitive people like me. There was a desire to "get it right," or something. Time was like a spinning compass that seemed to be deciding the fate of our human journey through this important juncture of history. I knew many other intuitive people had been sent into these patterns across the planet and never emerged whole again. I ended up being given gifts from it all, but it would take years to fully understand them.

Because I worked each day cleaning homes for the affluent, I had to travel over the mountain pass adjoining our valley. I began to notice subtle energy shifts as I travelled back and forth. I could feel a change in my consciousness every time my car entered Wyoming. It would shift back every time I headed back home over the mountains and into Idaho. It was all very surreal. I wanted the twilight zone thing to end as soon as possible but I had to wait on things to align with a way out.

On many days I could feel souls or rather sense invisible people with very distinct personalities hovering near me somehow aware of me not being from their world. Some of the spirits seemed concerned that it was taking a toll on me. I was given guidance on several occasions to imagine I was already driving home. Just picturing it in my mind would allow my head to clear for a while. But the guidance was not always useful and could even add a strain on my situation. I was learning to navigate at the level of consciousness no matter what was unfolding.

One day as I drove over Teton Pass to work, I could sense I would have to go in deeper to find my way all the way back. The dimensional patterns overlaying my day to day existence were not something I could just turn off. I saw the future in my mind's eye and knew it would be a trust fall and I might end up in the hospital. I sighed with a tired feeling of resignation and relief.

I worked that morning doing my weekly cleaning at one of my high end homes. I began to feel the call to surrender completely into what would come next. I could see that my body was growing numb as I wiped the shower down in the bathroom I was cleaning. Eventually my body was being left in a motionless state all crumpled over.

I became aware that my sense of self was expanding way beyond a size I could measure. I could see inside the Earth and was aware of a bright group of beings trapped in our earth that needed some sort of shuttle up and out of the area. I discovered I was a huge vessel in consciousness that could link with lost beings displaced by the same layered condition I was in. I somehow knew how to ferry them back to a place beyond our world. I swelled with compassion upon seeing their luminous, gentle but fragile smiles as they were set free. They nodded in gratitude to me. It reminded me of an old movie called *Cocoon* that had beings of light inside coral encrusted rocky cocoons left at the bottom of the ocean. In the movie they were not from here and needed to return to their own home world.

I later wondered if all the dimensional states/worlds were in some sort of confused cosmic jumble for some reason and I was more awake than most people to the situation. As I tracked all of this through my consciousness, the owner of the home had found my body in a nonresponsive state. I was still holding the rag I had been cleaning with. He called 911. My point of awareness felt very detached as I hovered over the efforts of the EMTs after they arrived. I believe they gave my body smelling salts, but it did not respond. I was rushed to the hospital in Jackson and put through many medical tests aimed at figuring out what was going on.

I became somewhat conscious as I was removed from the ambulance and we arrived at the ER. From my perspective it was like seeing through a mirror but from the other side, everything was reversed. It was puzzling but consistent. Speech was very difficult. I understood everything I was being asked, but could not respond normally. Everything was being experienced energetically and minimal interaction was easier. I could read the thoughts of the physicians and nurses. Some were more attentive and aware of the anomaly of my situation than others.

Through it all, I felt a gentle presence was with me. Angels are quite tall and this one was about eight feet tall. I sensed it was overlayed on my person for protection. One nurse said I appeared to her to be very tall, like well over six feet! I could not respond to her statement but thought, I am about five foot eight. I decided that the nurse's comment was validation that the angels were with me. The staff looked guardedly fearful and confused most of the time when interacting with me.

To follow-up on the tests that were done that day they discovered that there was no foreign or toxic substances found in my system. The EEG tests were negative as well. The medical staff decided I should be put in the paediatric wing, because the staff observed each room all night. I barely fit in the bed I was assigned to. All night I could hear the sounds of children beyond the walls crying and whimpering in their hospital beds. I sensed massive but gentle whales swimming by and through the walls. I knew these were ocean spirits and they were calming the children and providing general protection for me.

The next day late in the morning, the doctor came in to my room to speak to me. Bob had arrived a little earlier. We were all surprised when I suddenly began to form words! The doctor asked me several questions. I was now able to respond easily. I explained that over the months I had felt like I was holding onto this world with all my wits. On many days I felt I could barely stay in my body. I mentioned that I had a lot of spiritual and metaphysical experience and so what I was saying might not make sense to a doctor. The doctor smiled warmly and said not to worry; he thought he knew what I meant. I knew not to say too much about the multidimensional travel I had grown accustomed to.

I did tell the doctor and my husband that I was scared and unsure if I would come out of what had taken hold of me, the day before. I added that I wanted a long rest away from my cleaning business. I explained how I had not been allowed any real break since the death of our son in 1998, less than two years earlier. The doctor supported my need to quit my job if necessary. Money was still a big concern for us both and my income was significant. My husband eventually went along with it, realizing I needed to take a break, a real break this time.

Changes in many aspects of our culture unfolded over the next several years. I could see into the layers or patterns of ignorance, and yet I had a deep sense of faith that it was happening according to a bigger plan. I felt hope and possibility behind each problem that came into view year after year.

After you've been to the depth of the darkness and endured, everything looks pretty bright and full of promise. People around me would worry about certain world events and disasters. I would think to myself oh, but it could be so much worse, I assure you. My mind would drift for a moment and recall some of the memories. I knew that some unseen elements hung in the balance.

I would need a long rest to even accurately evaluate what everything meant. My contribution to the bigger world events were not for me to know about. It was time to blend in and normalize all aspects of my life in order to survive the next phase. I kept my memories and insights to myself for several years. Writing this book has been a way to finally share more of the full story of what happened to me and who I am.

Over the years I would notice some of the inter-dimensional chaos manifesting in cycles, but now it was going on in other people's lives and in different parts of the world. I sensed the cosmic waves crashing onto other shores and quietly prayed that they would all get through it. My unique sensitivity or ability to track such patterns meant I had to begin to relearn to keep my attention on basic patterns in my immediate environment, i.e. be here now!

About six weeks later, I remember feeling that I had passed through the eye of the needle in some way. I began to notice the dawn's sunlight was a living field again and I felt more and more of the light from the universe shining out from everything. I received an intuitive promise that some new possibilities for mankind would be coming into view, but the larger patterns were still being sorted out. I was assured that the worst of mankind's patterning was cleared from any future potential. My role would gratefully subside now. I learned that I had been more like an understudy stepping onto the stage for a few shows because the lead actor could not show up.

I began to remember that at one point in it all, I had to dive deep down to retrieve a sort of key that was buried at the bottom of something. I sensed that this key was needed in order to bring hope back and transformation for a struggling humanity. I understood that the rest of it would repair with time. The strain on my body's heart and soul would require a number of elements to come together over the next few years for me to experience a full return from all that took place during those thirteen months in multidimensional consciousness. Back then I thought, bummer for me. Would I ever be the same? It would take some time to shed all that came with that spiritual assignment. The bottom of the ocean can look pretty scary and feel very dark if you have to hang out in it for a few years. I also knew it was an ocean full of living things that all deserved a chance to be part of this great unfolding.

We as a human race often wonder about forgotten souls or fallen idols throughout time and space. I learned that when energy drops in vibration and substance, it can be lost and unrecognizable even to itself. I had a task assigned to my energetic field that brought home what is lost. Never doubt that you are missed by god when feeling in exile. A place setting is laid at the table of life awaiting the return of all the lost fragments.

11

FRAGMENTS

For a few weeks I did very little. I sat in the sunlight and soaked up the rays of simplicity on my back porch. My heart processed so many questions about what I had been catapulted into the previous thirteen months. My mind and heart needed a rest. My body especially craved the stillness of the moment, but the energetic waves of information and awareness of people elsewhere would waft like a breeze through me in and out of the days that followed.

I felt physically quite weak, even numb, so movement was slow as I did laundry, cleaned my own home and made meals for the family. My heart was exhausted from the demands of all those months of having to respond to wave after wave of energetic challenges in consciousness. Tracking the pattern in consciousness to its singularity so it could collapse was usually the mode. To relax and stare into space while feeling the breeze was beyond just good for my soul. It was grace.

Within a month, I discovered that an old colleague of mine named Kim lived in Driggs. I had known her years before during my time in Illinois when my mother and I lived in that big farm house. Kim and I both worked back then with court ordered adolescents at the Highland Park Girl's Group Home. Back then we had become friends, but I had not seen her since I moved to Idaho with Bob. She was now the owner/director of a mental health agency right here in my town. What a coincidence! I saw her name in an advertisement in the "Help Wanted" section of our local paper.

I called the number from the advertisement and immediately recognized Kim's voice. She remembered me right away. Kim was impressed to hear of my work in the field of alcohol and drug treatment soon after I last saw her. I added that back then I became a certified alcohol/drug counsellor. Apparently her agency here in town included mental health clients that had substance abuse issues. She thought I would be a great addition to the team of people at her agency. She remembered how well I worked years before at the group home. My years of training as the director of the Adolescent Treatment Center in Boise would also come in handy now.

I was interviewed barely two months after my ER visit. Kim seemed more than happy to hire me. She was not concerned about my earlier difficulties. She agreed that there had been a sort of cosmic weirdness going on all around the year 2000. She then changed the subject and began to bring me up to speed with the job requirements. I needed this job, but was a little worried at first about full- time hours. She said I could start part-time. We exchanged stories regarding how we had come to live in Teton Valley and the years that had passed since we had last seen each other in Illinois. It felt good to be treated like a professional again.

Over the years my tiresome house cleaning business had really taken its toll on my self esteem. I felt the signature of God behind these events, gifting me with this opportunity to work as a professional again helping people in need. The job involved being a Para Professional with a minimum four year college degree in a related field. Many psychology credits were required. You did not need a license to do this work. I was now looking forward to teaching and problem solving but this time with individuals struggling with severe mental health challenges.

For the next few weeks I eased myself into the lives of these individuals that were assigned to me and approved through the Idaho Department of Health and Welfare, Adult Mental Health Division. I eventually branched into working also with children. I learned all the administrative aspects to the job as well and began helping in the office.

I became knowledgeable about the Medicaid quality assurance requirements of each document or log note. Before long I was also asked to proof all the annual Task Plans and required documents for each client before they were sent in by the other case workers and rehab specialists. I enjoyed the paperwork side of the work as well as the client contact hours.

My life became buried in stressful but rewarding mental health work. As a case manager, rehabilitation specialist and eventually business owner, I poured my heart into my work. I was sensitive to the complexity of these people's plights. We were all assigned the task of keeping things simple and structured for each client. A lot of what the job required involved teaching the clients skills to cope with all the aspects of their situation or condition. The diagnoses were given by their doctors and clinicians. I sometimes did not agree with the diagnosis. I would allow my description of symptoms to sometimes redirect their care in my annual comprehensive assessments.

As a case manager and psychiatric rehabilitation specialist, I found it to be a time of deep service and modest rewards. The money was similar to cleaning houses, but the hours eventually grew to be too long. Crisis line phone work and seven day work weeks became the norm.

∞

Years earlier, I had met a local man named Charlie through some spiritual friends from Wisconsin who rented his home that winter. I had been invited to stay with them at Charlie's house with my kids for a week when we were looking for housing. Charlie had met me only briefly at the time. Around this time in the summer of 2001, I ran into him at the post office. We exchanged thoughts about the year 2000 predictions and how the world seemed to have made it through.

Charlie told me he had stored many boxes of spiritual books of wisdom for safekeeping. He now felt he could let them go to a new home. I liked his unique character and was intrigued that he now wanted me to come and pick up as many of the boxes as I could. He laughed and said, "I guess they can be donated to a library or something."

The next day I went out to his place. He lived in a remodelled home made from a Quonset hut. It was off the grid and received its electricity from solar panels. I believe he had a greenhouse too. All the boxes were left on his porch and he was not home. First I pawed through four or five large boxes. It was an enormous number of books, so I sorted quickly and then just began moving them to my car. I brought them home and spent a few hours lost in all the titles. Some were quite rare. There was something from every spiritual tradition on the planet.

Eventually I dropped two boxes of books off at our local yoga center anonymously. I had begun to attend classes there after Harry's death and enjoyed the steady stretches and strengthening that yoga offered. In one stack, I came upon THE ESSENE GOSPEL OF PEACE: Book One. I was spellbound by the writing of the Essenes, quoting Jesus. I saw that several other books were listed on the back page but likely out of print. I vowed to find time to order all four books from the Essene Gospel of Peace for study and contemplation, but it would be a few years.

Most of my energy was still occupied by my job. In my off time I read several books on Eastern mystics and yogis and then thumbed through some of other old books on metaphysics. The content eventually began to make me tired for some reason. I then decided to shelve the old books.

On the morning of September 11, 2001 I was getting ready to take my daughter to school. The television news was interrupted with footage of an airplane crashing into one of the Twin Towers in downtown Manhattan. We both just stared in disbelief and horror for the next hour, making my daughter very late to school. My husband called from work and said everyone had stopped working and was watching the news also. I thought back on the year previous and how many times I sensed underlying premonitions of events that could still take place. It was very intense to have live footage of an attack on our country with such detail.

When I finally got back on track with my day, I was surprised at how unimportant it all was to the mental health clients in my care. They just shrugged their shoulders and we took care of business as usual. My heart was very affected by the energy of the day. I was glad when I had finished with my last client and could head home.

It felt as if the hearts of many people had been blown open with compassion in the aftermath of 911. The stories on the news flooded in over the next few days. The news matched what I sensed was taking place at ground zero that first day. At night I sensed many souls were displaced and lost at first by their sudden deaths. I felt countless souls were helping with the chaos.

Within a few weeks I learned of one flight that crashed before hitting its target. I was so moved by the heroism of the people on Flight 93 over Pennsylvania. The brave willingness to rush at the terrorists and cause the plane to crash before it could reach its target, which by all accounts was the White House, was nothing short of a miracle. I said to myself, now that is what makes us Americans. We have a little rebel in many of us coupled with a desire to take back what is ours. Americans are known to come together and be spontaneous in a crisis.

Internationally, as bad as it all looked on the news, there was an outpouring of compassion sweeping across the globe for our country and all those who had died or been impacted. Months later I grew very concerned when our government moved our country toward war with Iraq. Something felt very conflicted about the gearing up to go to a full scale war when that country had no part in 911. It was very unsettling and seemed to foretell a path we would all have to live with.

In the mean time I was becoming physically stronger. That spring I attended a week long yoga "boot camp" in the mountains of Utah with a popular yoga instructor from Los Angeles. The retreat center was set in the mountains near Zion National Park. I camped in my tent on the grounds and received all my meals through the centre's dining hall.

The first day I wandered into the large empty meditation hall to get my bearings. Lining the walls of the yoga retreat center were the framed faces of the masters of the old yogic tradition. I became reacquainted with each face for a moment and felt a smile grow within my heart. I sensed that they understood what I had been through. I felt like I was part of something very old, as strange as that may sound.

On the first day as we began the morning asana workout, I noticed that the yoga teacher was familiar to me. After a few minutes to my surprise, I recognized that this man was from a past life. I even remembered in a way that he had renounced almost everything in an attempt to gain enlightenment. I was intuitively aware that he had starved to death in that life. I did not know if this vision was true, but it was compelling. The awareness came to me in such a clear way. There he was now looking quite fit, well off and perhaps a bit body obsessed, but I also saw his heart was good. I enjoyed the days of workouts, but preferred the meditation time most.

One evening we were called together for a special presentation. Our teacher said he was a student of a teacher from India and he had a video to show of him. We all watched a short video of the noble scholar Pandit Rajmani Tigunait, a devotee of the late Swami Rama. Our yoga teacher promised everyone attending the yoga retreat a signed copy of the biography of Swami Rama. It would be coming out soon.

I had brought with me some of the rare old books that I had pulled from the donated boxes months before. One book was called *A Visit to Saints of India* by Swami Kriyananda. The association with India felt comforting and familiar. During my week long yoga retreat, I enjoyed reading the intimate but relatively brief stories around the American swami's encounters with six remarkable people. I loaned the book to a couple of retreat attendees to read and they returned Kriyananda's book by the end of the week. I was happy being given a little time away from home to be myself and connect with traditional yoga practices.

The yoga retreat overall experience was good. Months later in 2002, that yoga teacher came through on his promise, when a free signed copy came in the mail. The book was titled *AT THE ELEVENTH HOUR-Biography of Swami Rama* by Pandit Rajmani Tigunait, PhD. Tigunait had been a very close devotee of the swami for 30 years. Swami Rama worked closely with Tigunait to record his life story. It is an interesting one. I read it with great interest and laughed out loud at a number of the detailed stories of the young swami and his travels. In some ways it reminded me of *Autobiography of a Yogi,* which I loved and had read in 1992.

As I read *At The Eleventh Hour,* I felt such a familiarity with India and the old ways. I read of Swami Rama's encounters with many different Masters. It was as if I was there or knew some of the teachers personally from that era in India. Perhaps I was just feeling the deeper truth behind the real life individuals described. In chapter four of Swami Rama's memoirs he states, *"Those who seek God within are blessed with divine creativity long before they experience their oneness with God."*

Swami Rama's main teacher was a master at demonstrating his connection with the divine in all types of settings. Swami Rama's life was full of leaps of faith and obedience to his teacher. Rama eventually becomes a master of many things but appears over time to settle down into a conventional role as a teacher with only rare demonstrations of his level of awareness as a master. Still I wondered about Rama's Himalayan Institute retreat campus on the east coast and if it was still functioning. It was established by Rama in the 1970's. The book invited me back into my hearts longing for the divine as a daily practice beyond the asana and the ritual.

I introduced the concept of starting a weekly Sunday open meditation time at the yoga center. I sold the idea to the instructors as a weekly sit that is not meant to be led by anyone. It took a little while for it to become attended by many but it did anchor the group theme. For me it was nice to be able to sit with others and meditate.

While at one of the sits I learned about a retreat coming up in April. It was a nine day Buddhist retreat, led by a teacher my friends liked. They called it a *Vipassana* or "insight meditation" retreat. I decided to attend it. I worked in the kitchen as part of my donation. It was so fulfilling to be undisturbed for a time in deep meditation. I became familiar with the Buddhist practice of forty five minute intervals of meditation in a sitting pose followed by what Buddhists call a walking meditation. It all worked for me.

On day four I remember my sense of self dissolving into the ethers and felt delicate snowflakes landing on my face. I opened my eyes and saw out the window that it had begun to snow. I was indoors but could feel the atmosphere outside. I was grateful and encouraged, but unfortunately, I could only enjoy five days of silence, because I had to get back to my town. I was doing a business start-up.

Since my son's death my yoga asana practice was an important physical aspect to my over all wellbeing. I had been hitting a class each week and doing a home practice for a few years now. However around this time I was developing painful arthritis mostly in my wrists. By about 2002, I had to quit my active yoga practice and do just the stretches and sitting postures. I went to a rheumatologist MD to learn more about my symptoms.

A blood test ruled out a genetic marker for rheumatoid arthritis. Instead I learned I had reactive arthritis. All the doctor could offer me was anti-inflammatory medication and a bleak prognosis. I knew the arthritis was a deep pattern and not a random occurrence. It started from an infection in one of my fingers in late 1998. Back then I had a day surgery to cut open the infected finger and drain it. I had weeks of painful physical therapy to restore the flexibility in my finger. Antibiotics and water therapy were supposed to clean out the infection. The medication never successfully killed off the bacteria. Instead, the infection lay dormant for a few years before coming back and spreading especially to my wrists. The body had reacted with swelling and tenderness, eventually calcifying my wrists. I knew I had to learn what the trigger for the condition was.

After some soul searching I decided the arthritis was giving me an opportunity for others to carry the heavier loads in my life. My daughter and my husband had to help with lifting heavy objects and contribute more with chores. I had to learn to ask for help with things and it was very hard. I did not like feeling so weak.

It was in September of 2002 when we put our home in town on the market and moved back to the north end of the valley. We rented the Driggs house out until it eventually sold. Our new home was nice. It was on a private 4.44 acre lot in a subdivision that had a beautiful view of the Teton mountain range. I felt such a quiet joy living in the country again with very few neighbours.

My guidance quickly began directing me back to the old ways of earth medicine. I sensed it would provide some much needed healing for my body. I was leaving behind most of the yoga asana and becoming reacquainted with native practices. With the help of friends, my husband and I decided to create a large medicine wheel on our property that fall. I made small alters of rocks at each of the four cardinal directions. Smaller stones followed the boundary of the large circle in a flat meadow below the house.

Through some friends in town, I discovered that some Seneca tribal elders were coming to our area to do a long dance ceremony just before the summer solstice. I learned it was open to anyone to participate. I signed up and met a whole group of people from across the country that arrived to do their annual "Harmony Dance." It was led by Bob Nitsch, the grandson of Seneca Wolfclan Grandmother Twylah Hurd Nitsch. He was from New York. Bob's wife Lee Nitsch was a medicine woman in her own right, but from Canada. Together, they were resurrecting this very old tradition through the guidance and insights of Grandmother Twylah.

The medicine wheel Bob Nitsch had created in Teton Canyon was very large and had smaller stones marking out twelve sections within the four directions. Each wedge or vector was assigned specific qualities. The dancer moved into each space and worked with the energies therein. Everyone in the dance was moving slowly clockwise around the circle. The Harmony Dance takes eight years or cycles to complete. This particular annual dance lasted about twelve hours and I loved the freedom to move and commune with nature to nothing but the beat of a huge drum. I received a special feather for participating along with some ashes from the ceremonial fire.

I later passed the ashes on to a man who passed through our valley with his wife. His name was Antonio and he spoke fluent Lakota. He invited me to help build a sweat lodge on his property one summer so a few of us locals could participate in sweat lodge with him. When I got home I jotted down notes so I could remember how it was done. It had been a few years. It was nice also to attend a sweat when his lodge was up and running. After the sweat I realized I needed to think about my own lodge coming together on my property. I would wait until the following spring.

Back in January of 2003 I had quit my job working at the mental health agency that my friend owned. I was not happy with her management of things and knew it was time for me to step away from it and regroup. I quit along with another co-worker who was also unhappy there. Within a few weeks this colleague invited me to join with her and start our own agency. For a few months we made plans.

At first it was fun creating a LLC new business with my colleague. Some of our former clients chose to join us from the previous agency that we had worked at. The workload grew from there. I had more experience with Medicaid billing and all the administrative aspects of the mental health or psychiatric rehabilitation and case management business than my business partner did.

At first she appreciated my setting the files up and establishing all the office systems. A few months after she and I had the business up and running, money was finally coming in. To my surprise she now wanted to end the LLC partnership. Lawyers had to split the business up and officially dissolve it, in order for me to get my seed money back out of the assets. I quickly started my own agency after this, but with a slightly bruised sense of trust in people.

Running my own business however turned out to be the best thing for me. Within a short time I was feeling pretty content having established myself in the community as the newest mental health agency. I hired a PhD clinician to supervise the client's weekly care and an employee or two at times to help with the increasing billable hours that were approved for service.

The following spring I decided that it was time to build my own sweat lodge for further healing of my body and heart. I was still struggling with the reactive arthritis condition that had now spread throughout my body by then. The arthritis symptoms had begun to plague me with periodic overall fatigue. Despite this, it felt right to be bold and follow my heart with attempting to build my own sweat lodge on my property.

With a few purchased tools I began to create the lodge by myself over the course of a few days, beginning with the harvesting of some mature willow bushes near our home. The building of the sweat lodge was like making it to the moon! After it was done all my joints swelled up and I ended up on our couch for a few days, but then things began to improve a little.

I waited a week and then made another bold decision to do a solo sweat. I cleared the ground and filled an area for the bon fire that would heat the volcanic rock. After carrying all the heated rocks into the pit at the center of the lodge I settle in, wrapped only in a cotton sheet. A gentle healing came from my efforts to give it all to the earth.

I went on to offer three more sweats for a few different friends that summer. It felt so empowering to sing and *be* with the smells of the earth. My husband helped out as the "fire keeper" for one of the sweats. Bob preferred to be on the outside of the lodge tending the hot rocks and passing them to me.

Around 2002 I was invited to go with a couple of friends to a hot springs for a soak. Earlier they had met an interesting healer who frequented there once a month and believed he would be there that weekend. He was a big man, over seven feet tall! He had long curly dark hair and a long beard.

He reminded them of the character called Hagrid from the Harry Potter series of books and movies. My friends said, "You have to meet him!"

Harry Potter was a popular series to read and the books and movies came out not long after our son Harry died. Our son Harry loved playing a wizard as a child. Many aspects of that Harry Potter story almost haunted me because it matched so many parts of our son's magical life. Even the strange wizard hat in the story that each student had to wear for a moment to identify the "house" they were to join with, intrigued me in real life. I felt like I was like that hat in some ways during the 13 months traveling between worlds. It was nice to just let it all be a curious puzzle to figure out. I was more than curious to meet this Harry Potter character at the hot springs.

After we got to the hot spring I was introduced to this healer man named Louis. He really was quite tall and big, yet clearly a gentle soul. My friend asked for him to give her one of his water healing sessions. My other friend and I watched as she swam over to him and then floated onto her back. We noticed his method of moving a person's body slowly through the water, bending them gently while always keeping their head above the water like a skilled practitioner. I decided to go next and experience his healing work. I floated on my back and was initially moved gently through the water cradled in his arms in a form of physical therapy.

At one point he asked if he could do something that might seem odd at first, but his face was quite serious. He asked me if he could blow his breath on my lower spine. I agreed cautiously. We moved to the steps so I would be sitting upright. He then breathed and gave a very low tone from his throat close to the skin on my lower back.

At that moment a very distinct live young dragon face appeared right in my mind's eye. It was looking directly at me, inches from my face! I was stunned but felt it was asking if I was really the ONE! I looked openly back into its eyes and the intensity diminished. The dragon disappeared after that. The session was complete. I thanked the man, admitting that it was not what I expected. I knew it was important, however. He spoke of his work with disabled kids to my friends. I listened then chose eventually to swim off by myself for a little while, still feeling some of the energy.

In one of the larger hot pools I began to feel whale spirits moving near me. They were in a pod and they conveyed a warm acceptance of me. I felt safe. I recalled a similar vivid experience at a hot springs in Wyoming during my difficult thirteen months in 2000. The whales showed up there as well for me. These vivid encounters with species like dragons and whales made no sense to me. I was lost in thought the rest of the day.

The next day I found a need to go to the local rock shop in that town by myself. I noticed I was being drawn to a stone statue of Quan Yin, the famous Japanese female Buddha. I remembered she was often depicted with a dragon. I found a nice one carved out of marble. The figurine was pouring watery fluid out of a bottle, representing compassion, while she stood with one foot on this dragon below her.

I felt that my dragon vision represented an experience in powerful energy that had come literally to the surface. I sensed it respected me but otherwise had disappeared. I understood also that I had never felt so feminine or "yin" in my life in regards to my own energy. I was mostly just allowing things to flow or come together each day. I was deeply connected to the divine and knew somehow I was safe. I think I appeared meek and unassuming to those around me. Like many experiences in my life after that weekend, I filed this one away.

I would like to revisit my life as a parent and mother since my son's death. Thanks to an increase in income through my husband's work, we were able to eventually finance our daughter's alpine ski racing career, beginning in middle school. Some people that have lost a child can become overly protective of the remaining child. We did not want to do that, but I did have my scares. Some moments it seemed crazy supporting her desire to fly down a mountain on skis at high speeds. I can still remember watching her in a Super-G race at Bogus Basin near Boise. A few girls before her had lost control when encountering a bump and turn in the race course. I stood watching as she approached, pre-jumped the bump successfully and looked generally awesome as she flew by.

When she was a freshman in our local high school, she asked if she could attend a private school and race with a better team. She was still coping with a sense of loss from her brother's death, but wanted to keep working on her own goals as an athlete. We found such a place in Steamboat Springs Colorado. Our daughter was accepted for her sophomore year onto the Steamboat Springs Winter Sports Club alpine racing team.

Our daughter attended a private academy nearby where she lived in a dorm with other girls. The school gave her a good education. I was not always sure about our decision to move our daughter to Colorado. She called home a lot and I was more than good with it. I needed to hear from her. All of this took money and we were disciplined enough to put it aside for college as well as provide for all her needs.

Tierney decided to transfer back into our local high school in the middle of her eleventh grade year. She would graduate from Teton High with honors letting ski racing go. She was accepted at a top university in Colorado. She eventually graduated after four years from the University of Colorado with a degree in history. Our daughter was and is a very impressive young woman and continues to work hard in all she does.

Having a family is often a very important journey of its own in life. I felt a sense of honest commitment to our daughter's needs as well as the needs of my husband, as he climbed up the ladder of success as an architect and business owner. Women often make sacrifices so others can achieve a measure of happiness while putting their personal goals on hold.

I kept my deeper spirituality for the most part hidden from my professional mental health work. Friendships were harder to maintain around this time in my life. I had long hours with clients and paperwork. It was difficult to socialize when I was carrying around a crisis line phone linked to my clients. I had to keep pace with all the demands of my workload. I was pretty certain I was not meant to be doing mental health work forever. I viewed it as my assignment for the moment. In the back of my mind I was aware that it was important to also keep nourishing my soul with books filled with wise teachings whenever I had the time.

Ever since my awakening in 1991 I had read several books linked with A Course In Miracles. Other books I read had a similar link to Jesus as the source of the teachings presented. Most of them were just good. For the most part I enjoyed seeing that Jesus was inspiring and teaching in many ways and to multiple authorships, especially through the 1990's.

Around the year 2004, an old friend handed me a book she had come across. She said she had been carrying it in her car for a couple of years. She added that she had never read it, but just knew it should be given to me. She said that she still is not comfortable with Jesus and most religions that are based on him, but something told her this book was different. The book was LOVE WITHOUT END: Jesus Speaks, by Glenda Green.

The book begins with a physical encounter with Jesus in 1992. The author was a portrait artist reportedly of high regard at the time. Jesus chose her to paint him for his people. In the process of months of him showing up physically in her studio, he passed on profound teachings ready for the modern age. The book covers aspects of some of the mysteries surrounding his life as well.

A powerful now famous portrait came into being by this painter Glenda Green. It is called "The Lamb and the Lion." I was truly comforted to discover I had been taught many of the same broad teachings over the years from my contact with Jesus. In the book, the author reports that she learned that his name in Hebrew was really Yeshua. Today it would be spelled with the letter J, but pronounced as if it still is a Y.

I thought back to a book of channeled conversations with Jesus called THE JESHUA LETTERS, published around the same time as Green's book. Back then I had dog-eared the pages to find important quotes within it. After the death of our son, I liked to look at that book cover which had an artist's rendition of only Jesus' soft wise eyes across a gold and magenta back drop. I had many pages marked and passages underlined.

I now had this new book, LOVE WITHOUT END: Jesus Speaks by Glenda Green to explore, even if it was many years after its initial publication in 1998. As soon as I had any time to myself, I would read it. Once it was done, I told all my friends to read it. The book is a refreshingly intelligent, deeply reassuring message that is full of the real Jesus.

I marked many pages for quick retrieval of my favorite quotes. I noticed the year he revealed himself to the author. It was 1991 and the same year so many things happened to me as well. The book has truly unique signature teachings of Jesus/Jeshua. Thanks to my friend, the first edition copy had eventually found its way to me. There was even a chapter on advanced scientific studies! I was thrilled.

After four years plus I was increasingly more unfulfilled working in the field of mental health as a career. I was still working long hours, except that now Medicaid audits were the new stressor. The stress peaked one day when I was on a much needed vacation with my husband and daughter. My cell phone went off while I was in New York City.

The caller was a representative from the Department of Social Services Mental Health Division and she was standing outside my office back in Driggs Idaho. She said she had faxed my office the audit date and time. I apologized and informed her that I was in New York and could not possibly make the appointment that day. I made a call to my employee and learned that she had not been in the office recently or noticed any faxes had come in. My employee went on to say she was unavailable right then and did not see it as her job to read my incoming faxes.

I changed my flight departure to the next day and flew home. The auditor had thankfully agreed to a new meeting time after my return. The employee quit soon after I returned. I passed through the audit successfully, but it was growing easy to imagine myself moving on from this line of work.

One day when I had some free time, I found myself searching online for the authentic original name of Jesus. I enjoyed seeing books that had come out identifying the name Jeshua, but I wanted to research it myself. If you recall, my connection with *him* was awakened when I was nine years old. I had never resolved why so many things about his life were hard to confirm and controversial.

I went online a lot after this. One web search around that time linked up many lost teachings and found relics. I ordered some out of print "lost" books from the Bible. They were powerful but difficult reading. His childhood was documented in great detail. It puzzled me that so many of the stories were left out of the Bible.

In AD 325, the Council of Nicaea had decided the fate of thousands of ancient manuscripts. For instance, one chapter in THE LOST BOOKS revealed that Mary, mother of Jesus, hung his cloth diapers up to dry like any mother, while they were traveling in Egypt. People liked to touch the swaddling clothes because the contact with the fabric reportedly healed people of many ailments. Several chapters speak of the stories of healings that followed in the wake of their travels. Jesus' mother understood this and so took it in stride. She was described as a teacher and mentor to the people who began to follow them as they traveled.

In another chapter of the old book, Jesus reportedly turns a mud carved dove into a real dove that flies away. By then he was a young boy and was living in Jerusalem at the time. One chapter even states that Judas was a childhood friend of Jesus. Those interested in this information can order a copy of William Hone's collection of 1820. It is slow reading, but compelling.

I also found and read a book called THE UNKNOWN LIFE OF JESUS CHRIST. It was written in 1858 by Nicolas Notovitch and later published in 1907 and translated into English by Virchand R. Gandhi. Notovitch had the privilege of seeing a preserved ancient manuscript from the monastery of Himis in Tibet. It revealed a number of things about Jesus. He learned that the Buddhists encountered Jesus when he was around the age of twenty. They called him Issa. He lived with them for four years and studied all their ancient books. Issa's manner was reportedly so advanced and unique that they, for a time, thought he was their Dalai Lama and Buddha.

The Himis manuscript is in the Pali language. It describes the early Jesus as Issa, meaning "Master" or "Lord, "and recounts his travels beginning at the age of thirteen when he went to India and then traveled all over the region for many years. Jesus reportedly challenged the India caste system, teaching slaves as well as any others who sought him out as a teacher. He reportedly attracted much curiosity and awe as he went. I appreciated that there was evidence of Jesus/Yeshua or "Issa" and that he was intimately connected with Tibetan Buddhism two thousand years ago.

When I reviewed all the documents I had on Jesus I noticed that original ancient Greek copies of the early Bible called him "Iesous." You can see how this name could have evolved two thousand years later as Iesous became Jesus. Scholars can agree now that his true Hebrew name was Yehoshua and Yeshua for short, as I had already learned.

His name can be translated a few ways. Each name when translated could imply that God cares deeply about humanity and is offering us, through Jeshua, a way back to our source by remembering who we are. My study of his true name settled well in my heart. Now it was time to explore what he really looked like.

In the 1990's, I had come across a small image of Jesus (Yeshua) near the back of a yoga magazine. It looked compelling enough to tear out and save for later. I wanted to now send away for it. I sent in my twelve dollars plus postage to the United Kingdom. When the life size picture arrived, it had a written accounting of where it came from. When I opened the package, it was so powerful I had to look away for a moment. I could barely hold the gaze of Jesus face for long without so much emotional grief rising up. The paper insert called the image "The Sai Baba Jesus." After a few days, I realized I felt him really looking back at me through it. The picture would grow to be a significant image for me. I looked upon it with deep love, respect and care.

The story goes that the Jesus photo came into being when a Christian woman from England went to see Sai Baba. She was an avid student of Sai this India guru. Sai Baba would sometimes comment to the many westerners flocking to his teachings that Jesus was their true guru. In honor of this, the British woman brought a paper copy of the facial image of the famous relic called *The Shroud of Turin* to a large gathering of devotees of Sai Baba. She, like many others believed that the rare relic is the shroud or cloth that was laid over Jesus body in the tomb after his death.

Images of the face of the relic were circulating in the 1980's and she had found a paper copy for herself. The life size image was like looking at a film negative of a full body somehow embossed onto the fabric. The face of the shroud, in particular was very compelling to see. The mysterious image came about when Sai Baba walked directly up to the woman from England.

Sai Baba asked what she had in her hand. He then asked if she would like to see what Jesus really looked like. She nodded in approval.

With one touch of his hand the black and white image of the mysterious relic transformed before everyone's eyes into a full color image. It was now a developed image of Jesus face, bringing color and depth to the image. The crowd was amazed, as was the woman!

It is said that many people now regard the transforming of the black and white negative into a color photo of the face of the shroud, as one of Sai Baba's important miracles. When the woman came back to England, she had many visitors wanting to see this face of Jesus. She eventually made it available to the public for just the cost of the printing. A foundation was eventually set up that continues to this day to distribute it. Anyone can now easily get a copy on the Internet.

I later read about the face's origin and learned of the mysterious relic or Shroud of Turin. Carbon date analysis done on the shroud would become controversial when dated years later to the Middle Ages. I found out from a different article that during the Middle Ages a fire had burned the building down around the box that protected the shroud at that point in time. I began to wonder if perhaps the smoke from the fire reset the carbon dates in the fibers. I believe it is important to do further studies on the relic.

I had recovered a few lost fragments of myself through first my connection with yoga. Along the way I began to work again with the earth traditions and native teachings as well. I had retrieved lost sources of knowledge about Jesus in ancient times on up to the present. They were each in one way or another assisting my slow restoration in body mind and spirit, but mostly heart. I knew there was more to uncover and study. I was hungry for more ancient wisdom. I could see I was trying to find my way back to a brighter sense of self and purpose. It would take a few more years.

∞

By 2006 I began to have more time to look into the unfinished business of my heart. Years had passed since I had any contact with teachers and friends from that Wisconsin spiritual community. Actually I had been in contact with a few in our valley but we never discussed how that group had dispersed and things had changed in Wisconsin.

One day I visited with an old friend and former Course in Miracles Wisconsin community member that I had known from my time there years before. She was a teacher/student of Master Teacher. We agreed to go for a walk together and catch up. I carefully mentioned that I had heard over the years some troubling news regarding Master Teacher and his community in Wisconsin. I told her that I wondered what had happened to everyone, especially those that became teachers. First she informed me that Master Teacher had died earlier that year, reportedly from a heart attack. I felt a strange mix of emotions at hearing this news. I said I was aware of some important change in his community, but I wanted it confirmed. With knowledge of his passing confirmed it now felt resolved.

Years before, the tone and energy of many of the Wisconsin Course in Miracles teachers had grown quite difficult and confrontational to some students and other teachers. Over the years, even when I was no longer teaching the messages from A Course in Miracles, I struggled to make sense out of how the Wisconsin community, under Master Teacher, could go from something so bright and liberating, to something oppressive and rigid.

My friend honestly had no answers for me. I learned from her how some of the familiar Wisconsin community residents were doing. I had lost touch with most everyone. My friend appreciated my interest in everyone's wellbeing from the old days but seemed less motivated to explore the topic further. As we walked and enjoyed the gentle breeze of summer, we agreed to move on from the topic and enjoy our walk. I shared what I had learned about the healing qualities of the earth and how much joy I experienced connecting with the energies of nature. She agreed with me that connecting with nature was really nice even helpful to the development of expanded consciousness.

After nearly five years working as a mental health provider for Medicaid approved clients, I knew it was time to make a change. It would have to be one that allowed for days off, even weekends and actual vacation time. I closed my agency when events provided a natural transition for the clients and me to move on.

I then took a couple of months off to regroup. I got bored at a certain point and wanted some spending cash so I looked for a job. Financing our daughter's ski racing career and saving for college tuition took precedence over everything else. Bob was thankfully earning much better money now, but very little was available at that point for anything else.

At first I did not care what job I got. I took a job working as a preschool teacher for three and four year olds at a preschool/daycare center just outside of town. The curriculum was fun to teach. Because of aggressive behavior patterns in the children, I introduced a "feelings chart" that I had created as additional instruction. Over time my students showed an interest in the authentic expression of emotions minus any hurtful activity. However, the job was limited in many ways and the school/daycare was not being managed with integrity, so I quit after about nine months.

I was thrilled one day when my father called to invite Bob and me on a vacation with him to the island of Saint Lucia in early spring. When the time arrived we all enjoyed ourselves with snorkeling and beachcombing, not to mention elegant meals at the five star restaurants in the resort villa we were in for a week. It was a very generous gift from my father. How nice to be able to easily jump at this opportunity to travel. As the years progressed, Bob and I would do our own trips to different places, even abroad to England, Scotland and Nova Scotia.

After I returned from our vacation with my dad, I decided to visit a business called Teton Temp. It offered short term work through their agency. First I was assigned to a job working for the county as a building permit administrator. The permanent position had not been filled yet, so I was asked to step in.

This all took place during a time when our county was backlogged with subdivision proposals. The small two office suite had literally stacks of files of proposals for new subdivisions and developments spread everywhere even on the floor. We were so backed up that the timeline required for each proposal to be reviewed was not being met. Things grew to the level of a crisis. A moratorium on any further development submittals was instituted by the county commissioners. Tempers got heated when landowners felt blocked from cashing in on new potential developments.

A high profile court case settled the matter within weeks when a judge forced the county commissioners to lift the ban on new submittals overturning the moratorium. I received an education in the emotional intensity of people who believe that their rights demand action over everyone else's. The overdevelopment at that time of new subdivisions fed into the collapse of our local land and housing market. Our county became flooded with empty subdivisions from that era of high stakes development.

My next temp job was working as an administrative assistant and bookkeeper at a large landscaping company and retail store in town. It worked into a permanent position. I really enjoyed my job there. As the months went by I slowly began to get bored with payables and receivables and the busy world of commerce. After less than two years I was again ready for a change. With the collapse of our local economy and world markets starting to slide, I believed my hours were going to be cut. I gave my notice and did not look back.

My mother and most of my siblings were born with polycystic kidney disease. Our mother learned she had it at the age of forty-two. A psychic reader had told my mom that because her disease was congenital or from birth, her condition was considered a karmic agreement. My mother eventually died from the disease in 2003 after twenty-two years of dialysis. My mom devoted her life to finding a way to rise above her condition. She was a strong woman who defied her odds. In 2008 just after I gave my notice at the landscaping company and store, I traveled to California in September to be with my family.

We were all supporting my brother David through his kidney transplant surgery that fall. He was able to receive his wife's donated kidney. With my brother and sister-in-law facing a serious operation, it felt nice to be able to just hop on a plane and be there with everyone. My previous jobs over the years had prevented me from showing up for my brother Peter during his kidney transplant surgery. His kidney had come from his twin brother Mark.

A few years later I would be able to also travel to be with my sister and support her soon after she received a donated kidney. I respected each of my family member's personal struggles with having to do dialysis, followed by successful transplant surgeries. They were all brave souls and deserve a lot of credit for the healthy lives they have created for themselves. My standard of living was growing high enough that it felt reasonable now to explore being fully supported by my husband's income and explore a more spiritual vocation.

12

FINDING THE ESSENE WAY

When you support, enhance, and magnify life, healing will follow.
Life is not only in you, but all around you in abundant supply.
(Jeshua speaking)
Glenda Green, THE KEYS OF JESHUA

It was 2008 and I was finally able to find time to dig out some of my old spiritual books. I soon felt spurred on by a gentle nudging, to find that old fifty nine page book called The Essene Gospel of Peace and read it again. Soon after I read it I was compelled to find the other out of print books online. Once the other books arrived I read the 130 page book called *The Essene Gospel of Peace: Book Two* and it stirred something deep within me. It was distant at first but warmly familiar terrain. When I finished the book, a wave of energy began to sweep over me.

I eventually read *The Essene Gospel of Peace: Book Three, Lost Scrolls of the Essene Brotherhood* and *Book Four: The Teachings of the Elect*. I found several other books on the Essenes by the same translator, Edmond Bordeaux Szekely. Each of Szekely's books was translated before World War II. I poured through each and felt my heart surge with a deep sense of connection to it all. Perhaps I was long ago in a past life connected to the Essene community. I wanted to immerse myself in the ancient practices that flowed across the pages. Each book revealed hints and insights into an ancient way of life that I now wanted for myself.

I read the book THE ESSENE WAY-Biogenic Living, authored by Edmond Bordeaux Szekely PhD. In The Essene Way, he states the following: "Essenes meditated on the Sun as a great living force in terrestrial nature. It was an ever present source of energy without which there would be no life on earth, in the ocean or in the atmosphere. By becoming receptive to the solar energies, one can establish a perfect unity between the self and the sun and distribute its energy throughout the body."

I discovered that in my own practice, I preferred to try standing and meditating, as well as sitting. With eyes closed, I would open my hands and heart to the energy around me and let a spontaneous flow occur. I knew to become at one with each element of life; air, water, fire and earth. It was refreshing to rediscover lost wisdom from ancient manuscripts!

The fourteen daily communions were further analyzed by Dr. Szekely in The Essene Way-Biogenic Living. He says all forms of water are contemplated such as rivers, creeks, rain, the sap in trees, plants and so on. Szekely sates that this will establish, *"As a living reality, the unity between the waters of the body and the waters of the planet."* I loved that everything is so connected to everything else. He went on to say that *"The Essenes considered the circulation of water in nature to correspond to the circulation of the blood in the body."*

To continue, the purpose of communion with the Angel of Air, according to Szekely, *"Is to make man conscious of the dynamic unity between air and life."* He also stated that *"our body's respiration is the link between the organism and the cosmos."*

I loved that I could now have time to soak in the silences of nature with long periods of deep meditation. These Essene communions were the perfect launching pad for my heart to begin again seeking the pathway back. I was shedding many years of stressful employment. Tragedy and trials of the spirit had left me still quite depleted. I could now return to a rhythm or pace that honored my spirit and soul's yearning to reconnect with the energy of life and come up in vibration.

The Essenes written record of these teachings are astoundingly rich with wisdom and detail not found in Biblical sources. A pattern of the real Jeshua/Jesus emerges as *"He speaks to the weary and afflicted"* about communion with the Angels of the Earthly Mother and Heavenly Father. I believe anyone could benefit from practicing these communions and for old timers to the path of meditation and contemplation, these teachings could ignite your practice.

My daily work with the communions continued to unfold like a rich tapestry of intricate texture and beauty. I returned to my notes each morning and evening for months. The practice warmed and inspired my daily meditations and walks near my home through the energetic communion with the sunlight and other elements.

The complete set of all four books of The Essene Gospel of Peace originated from an ancient manuscript made up of many parts that were copied and later translated by Szekely. The young Szekely gained access to the archived Essene documents through a series of life changing events. Out of print copies of his book, "The Discovery of The Essene Gospel of Peace: The Essenes and the Vatican" published in 1975, by Szekely can sometimes be found on-line. In it he states that the original manuscripts were found written in original Hebrew and Aramaic text and lay in the secret archives of the Vatican.

The young European Edmond Szekely attended a prestigious catholic school & priory. His headmaster was so impressed by Edmond's thesis on Saint Francis that he made a bold recommendation for a special internship at the Vatican. The prefect of the archives of the Vatican accepted Edmond as a visiting "monk." The prefect elder did not know that this young man was not actually of a religious order. Despite this he recognized in Szekely a thirst for the real inspirations of St. Francis. Over time, the powerful Essene manuscript was given the light of day.

The opportunity to translate the manuscript was the beginning of Szekely's life mission; to search and unlock the secrets of the ages. Fluent in classic Greek and Latin and with the best Aramaic and Hebrew dictionaries in hand, Szekely's painstaking translations began. The prefect elder eventually implied reportedly to him that a copy of the ancient document may have been discovered by Saint Francis himself. Francis was known to have shown great interest in old "holy" fragments of the early church.

He went on to travel the world, earn multiple advanced degrees and translate many lost languages. His work on the first book of The Essene Gospel of Peace was originally printed in French in 1928 and in English in 1937. Identical fragments of Essene writings were found later in the Dead Sea Scrolls near the Dead Sea. It took till the late 1970s before books two and three were published in English. The Essene Gospel of Peace: Book Four, The Teachings of the Elect was published posthumously in 1981 according to Dr. Szekely's wishes representing yet another fragment of the complete manuscript.

There are fourteen Angel Communions from the ancient manuscript. To commune is to join with or connect in your mind and your heart. There are seven communions in the morning and seven more in the evening. With my notes, I could really immerse myself in the energies. I shortened them from the books original long narrative, so I could get to the heart of each communion quickly.

The following are my Essene notes. I wrote them as though I were explaining them to the reader. They later formed the body of notes for a workshop I would teach on the Essene Communions in 2011 and 2012. Here are the condensed communions I put together from no other book except The Essene Gospel of Peace: Book Two, translated by Szekely.

"To lift your eyes to heaven, when all men's eyes are on the ground, is not easy. To worship at the feet of the angels, when all men worship only fame and riches, is not easy. But the most difficult of all, is to think the thoughts of the angels, to speak the words of the angels, and do as angels do. And one man spoke: "But Master, we are but men, we are not angels. How then can we hope to walk in their ways? Tell us what we must do." (Szekely 1981, p. 31)

"As the son inherits the land of his father, so have we inherited a Holy Land from our Fathers. This land is not a field to be ploughed, but a place within us, where we may build our Holy Temple. And even as a temple must be raised, stone by stone, so will I give to you those stones for the building of the Holy Temple. And all the men gathered around Jesus, and their faces shone with desire to hear the words which would come from his lips. And he lifted his face to the rising sun, and the radiance of its rays filled his eyes as he spoke." (Szekely 1981, p. 32)

"The Holy Temple can be built only with the ancient Communions, those which are spoken, those which are thought, and those which are lived. For if they are spoken only with the mouth, they are as a dead hive which the bees have forsaken, that gives no more honey. The Communions are a bridge between man and the angels. And like a bridge, can be built only with patience. Just as the roots of the tree sink into the earth and are nourished, and the branches of the tree raise their arms to heaven, so is man like the trunk of the tree, with his roots deep in the breast of his Earthly Mother, and his soul ascending to the bright stars of his Heavenly Father." (Szekely 1981, pp. 32 and 34)

ANGEL OF THE SUN - *"She who cometh each morning as a bride from her chamber to shed her golden light on the world. O thou immortal, shining, swift-steeded Angel of the Sun! There is no warmth without thee. No fire without thee. No life without thee. The green leaves of the trees do worship thee...Angel of the Sun, Holy messenger of the Earthly Mother, enter the holy temple within me and give me the Fire of Life!"* (Szekely 1981 p. 34)

ANGEL OF WATER - *"She who makes the rain to fall on the arid plain. Who fills the dry well to overflowing? Yea, we do worship thee, Water of Life...All the waters the Creator hath made are holy...Angel of Water, Holy messenger of the Earthly Mother, enter the blood that flows through me, wash my body in the rain that falls from heaven, and give me the Water of Life!"* (Szekely 1981 p. 36)

ANGEL OF AIR - *"Who spreads the perfume of sweet-smelling fields, of spring grass after rain, of the opening buds of the Rose of Sharon. We worship the Holy Breath which is placed higher than all the other things created. For, lo, the eternal and sovereign luminous space, where rule the unnumbered stars, is the air we breathe in and the air we breathe out... Angel of the Air, Holy messenger of the Earthly Mother, enter deep within me, as the swallow plummets from the sky, that I may know the secrets of the wind and the music of the stars."* (Szekely 1981, p. 37)

ANGEL OF EARTH - *"She who brings forth corn and grapes from the fullness of the earth. She who brings children from the loins of husband and wife... This wide earth do I praise, expanded far with paths, the productive, the full bearing, thy Mother, holy plant! He who sows corn, grass and fruit, soweth the Law. The Lord sent the Angel of Earth, Holy messenger of the Earthly Mother, to make the plants to grow, and to make fertile the womb of woman, that the earth may never be without the laughter of children. Let us worship the Lord in her."* (Szekely 1981, p. 39)

ANGEL OF LIFE - *"She who gives strength and vigor to man... Go, then, toward the high-growing trees, and before one of them which are mighty, say these words: 'Hail be onto thee, O good, living tree, made by the Creator.' Then shall the River of Life flow between you and your Brother Tree, and health of the body, swiftness of foot, quick hearing of the ears, strength of the arms, and eyesight of the eagle be yours. Such is the Communion with the Angel of Life, Holy messenger of the Earthly Mother."* (Szekely 1981, p. 41)

ANGEL OF JOY - *"The Lord is not worshipped with sadness, or with cries of despair. Leave off your moans and lamentations and sing unto the Lord a new song...Let the field be joyful, let the floods clap their hands...The mountains and the hills shall break forth before you into singing. Angel of Joy, Holy messenger of the Earthly Mother, I will sing unto the Lord as long as I live."* (Szekely 1981, p. 42)

As you can see there is a timeless validity to these practices. Just reading them through can bring relief to a mind craving connection with life. I have found that if you go to your heart and then find the inner light, the outer beauty of the natural world can make itself known to you and bring you joy. No matter where you are living on the planet you can delight in nature's miracle. Mostly, just let joy fill your heart to overflowing. I know I did, from the time I first began to practice these communions in 2008.

EARTH MOTHER - *"She who sends forth her Angels to guide the roots of man and send them deep into the blessed soil. We invoke the Earthly Mother! The Holy Preserver! The Maintainer! It is she who will restore the world! We worship the good, the strong, the beneficent Earthly Mother and all her angels, bounteous, valiant, and full of strength; welfare-bestowing, kind, and health-giving. The Earth Mother and I are one. I have my roots in her, and she takes delight in me, according to the Holy Law."* (Szekely 1981, p. 44)

I suggest the reader commune with the give and take, energetically, of the angel of the earth. Notice how the energetic connection activates the glandular flow. See how regeneration of the overall body's health takes place through a giving and receiving. Lie on the earth, if appropriate, and feel its regenerative powers. Commune and seek to absorb the life force of the earth, especially from the trees and forests. Become one with her majesty the earth.

I have discovered that the whole planet is in dynamic interaction with the human organism. Feel this life force heal the body and restore its ability to be in harmony with the earth. Being the sacred Tree of Life for a moment is a gift! If you commune with the energy and unity of man's physical organism with the earth, you will experience something restorative. I found myself feeling deep gratitude toward the earth for the nourishment that comes through and from plant life.

Overall give as much attention in prayer, to the Earthly Mother, as to the traditional Heavenly Father. Practice each communion until it fills your heart and soul with warmth and unity. Here is further advice on how to commune with the angels from The Essene Gospel of Peace-Book Two. The following are what are known as the evening communions.

"And then one man spoke: Master, we are filled with eagerness to begin our Communions with the Angels of the Earthly Mother, who planted the Great Garden of the Earth. But what of the Angels of the Heavenly Father, who rule the night? How are we to talk to them, who are so far above us, who are invisible to our eyes? For we can see the rays of the sun, we can feel the cool water of the stream where we bathe, and the grapes are warm to our touch, as they grow purple on the vines. But the Angels of the Heavenly Father cannot be seen, or heard, or touched. How then can we talk to them, and enter their Infinite Garden? Master, tell us what we must do?" (Szekely 1981, p. 45)

"My children, know you not that the Earth and all that dwells therein is but a reflection of the Kingdom of the Heavenly Father? And as you are suckled and comforted by your mother when a child, but go to join your father in the fields when you grow up, so do the Angels of the Earthly Mother guide your steps toward him who is your Father, and all his Holy Angels, that you may know your true home and become true Sons of God....Only through the Communions with the Angels of the Heavenly Father, will we learn to see the unseen, to hear that which cannot be heard, and to speak the unspoken word." (Szekely 1981, p. 45 and 47)

THE ANGEL OF POWER - *"Through thy power will my feet tread the Path of the Law; Through thy power will my hands perform thy works. May the golden river of power always flow from thee to me, and may my body always turn unto thee, as the flower turns unto the sun. For there is no power save that from the Heavenly Father; All else is but a dream of dust... There is no man that hath power over the spirit."* (Szekely 1981, p. 47)

THE ANGEL OF LOVE – *"Whose healing waters flow in a never-ending stream from the Sea of Eternity. Beloved, let us love one another: For love is of the Heavenly Father... Those who walk with the Angel of Love, they love the Heavenly Father, and they love their brethren, and they keep the Holy Law. Love is stronger than death."(Szekely 1981, p. 48)*

THE ANGEL OF WISDOM - *"Who maketh man free from fear, wide of heart, and easy of conscience: Holy Wisdom, the understanding that unfolds, continuously, as a holy scroll, yet does not come through learning. All wisdom cometh from the Heavenly Father, and is with him forever. Wisdom hath been created before all things."* (Szekely 1981, p. 50)

THE ANGEL OF ETERNAL LIFE - *"Who brings the message of eternity to man...do not wait for death to reveal the great mystery. If you know not your Heavenly Father while your feet tread the dusty soil, there shall be naught but shadows for thee, in the life that is to come. Here and now is the mystery revealed. Here and now is the curtain lifted. Be not afraid, O man!"* (Szekely 1981, p. 52)

THE ANGEL OF WORK - *"Who sings in the humming of the bee, pausing not in its making of golden honey...In the song of the maiden as she lays her hand to the spindle? If you think that these are not as fair in the eyes of the Lord as the loftiest of prayer echoed from the highest mountain, then you do indeed err. For the honest work of humble hands is a daily prayer of thanksgiving, and the music of the plough is a joyful song unto the Lord."* (Szekely 1981, p. 53)

THE ANGEL OF PEACE - *"The sixth Communion is with The Angel of Peace, whose kiss bestoweth calm, and whose face is as the surface of untroubled water, wherein the moon is reflected. I will invoke Peace, whose breath is friendly, whose hand smoothes the troubled brow. In the reign of Peace, there is neither hunger nor thirst neither cold wind nor hot wind, neither old age nor death. But to him that hath not peace in his soul, there is no place to build within the Holy Temple; For how can the carpenter build in the midst of a whirlwind?...Peace dwells in the heart of silence; Be still, and know that I am God."* (Szekely 1981, p. 55)

I pondered many of these words over the course of months studying the communions that first year. Often I was washed over with a soft *"hush...from spirit"* followed by an invitation to again sit, meditate and be at peace. Some days after doing the communions I would sense a palpable strengthening of my connection with all of life around me and within me. My very cells seemed to hum with a joy I had not felt in a long time.

THE HEAVENLY FATHER - *"Thou hast made the earth by thy power, hath established the world by thy wisdom, and hath stretched out the heavens by thy love. Do thou reveal unto me, O Heavenly Father, thy nature, which is the power of the Angels of thy Holy Kingdom. Immortality and the Heavenly Order hast thou given, O Creator and the best of all things, Thy Holy Law! I will praise thy works with songs of thanksgiving, continually, in all the generations of time, with the coming of day I embrace my Mother, with the coming of night, I join my Father and with the outgoing of evening and morning, I will breathe Their Law and I will not interrupt these Communions until the end of time."*
(Szekely 1981, p.57)

"And over heaven and earth there was a great silence and the peace of the Heavenly Father and the Earthly Mother shone over the heads of Jesus and the multitude." (Szekely 1981, p. 60)

I liked to think that anyone could learn from The Essene Gospel of Peace: Book Two. Wouldn't it be amazing if we could all begin to *"think the thoughts of angels, speak the words of angels, and do as angels do"*, because then we could, *"learn to see the unseen, to hear that which cannot be heard and to speak the unspoken word?"* (Szekely 1981, p. 31)

I went through a period of daily silent meditation for a minimum of two hours at a time in my home for about a month. I finally realized I needed to give myself the proper environment for a deeper connection. I decided to go somewhere for undisturbed retreat. Sometimes we all need a clean break from our personal lives to enliven a serious practice.

In addition to my deep fascination with the ancient teachings of the Essenes, I had unfinished curiosity about Swami Rama. Ever since I read his biography years before I wanted to learn more about his life. I looked up his residential institute in Pennsylvania. It was still in operation and they were holding a special candlelight ceremony in a month. I decided I should go there and combine my studies. I received a warm hug from my husband just before leaving for the airport in Jackson Hole. Bob probably knew I needed some spiritual renewal and quiet time.

In the late fall of 2008 I boarded a flight east. I had reserved a seven day stay with plans for mostly meditation time at Rama's Himalayan Institute. It was time to go closer to this Indian sage's former home and learn more about his teachings. Once I arrived, I discovered my room was in a very old building and section of the campus. It was built many years before as a Catholic home for nuns. I thought about the nuns that had lived in the old buildings decades before when it was like an Abby. The echoing hallways and old plumbing was quite an experience in itself. The older buildings were linked by enclosed hallways with the more modern structures built in the 1970's. I decided that the austere antiquated atmosphere was a useful place to be for my studies and inner work. While there, I visited the bookstore near the lobby and bought several of the books written by the Swami and by his protégé Pandit Rajmani Tigunait.

I found my way to the main meditation hall where a candle was staying lit for nine days in honor of the Swamiji's birth and life. I learned that about fifty or so people were in attendance at the time I visited. Each day I practiced the fourteen communions from The Essene Gospel of Peace: Book Two, but mostly I kept to myself.

During a walk in the woods nearly a mile from the main buildings of the Himalayan Institute, I experienced something really bizarre! I had paused on the trail and heard spirit say to me, "Do what you came here to do." I stopped for a moment and then connected with the earth. Suddenly there was a powerful anchoring of energy in and through me with everything all at once.

In the vacuum of space/time I was instantly dissolved and then catapulted faster than light upward and then sent down from the sky anchoring a point somewhere in the earth under the main building of the institute. Another way of saying it was that I was a stationary point and everything rushed up to me then went vertical and then shot into the earth. Either way I was *whooshed* back onto the forest path in a twinkling.

I was very shocked at the powerful time/space anomaly that had just taken place for a moment! Next the cool fall air caressed my skin and the body breathed. It was hard to describe, but something had just anchored energetically into the earth as viewed from the sky. I walked a little faster after that to get back to my room and regroup. I was somewhat thrown by it all, but nothing like it occurred the rest of the week.

I attended one class on nutrition by the resident MD physician. The woman was very knowledgeable and interesting. There were yoga asana classes offered every day but I was not doing that anymore. I was there to sit and do the inner work. I noticed after a few days that my daily silent meditations varied in quality, but I did not know why.

I continued to use the communions for energetic prompts. I even tried different rooms in each of the main buildings to assess what location had the best vibe. The places where I could access the sunlight streaming through a window had a good feel, but nothing was as useful as reading from my Essene notes and then dropping into their message energetically. I was excited at the prospects for physical healing and enhanced meditation skills with all that I was learning from the many books I had on the Essene way of life. It felt important to have time to myself.

As the week came to a close I was excited to learn that there would be a special open tour of Swami Rama's original living quarters. About twenty people signed up for the tour. As we walked down a formerly locked hallway and climbed some stairs I noticed the first distinct trace energy of this teacher. I became impressed as I entered his living space. I felt a subtle energy that I usually identify as from a presence in higher consciousness. The room or apartment was left just the way it had been when he lived there.

Swami Rama had been dead since 1992 and had not lived in the United States for a few years prior to that. He spent most of his last years in India. A painting of him hung on the wall of his former apartment at the Institute that was very serious looking.

Someone giving the tour said that Swami Rama did not like his portrait once it was done and banished it to the woods in a moment of disgust. Instantly it disappeared. Hours later it was retrieved when someone found it resting far from his room and out in the woods but unharmed leaning next to a tree. It was put back in his living quarters after his death for visitors to see.

By 2009 I was beginning to realize that in hindsight I had been restoring my inner spiritual template by revisiting old teachings. I now saw I was becoming ready for new things. Through a series of prompts from my guides I discovered the modality of *Integrated Energy Therapy* (IET) in early 2009.

Integrated Energy Therapy has roots in a healing modality called Reiki. The founder, Stephan Thayer, was trained as a Reiki master. His modality also includes energetic attunements similar to Reiki. Thayer was deeply inspired by the presence of Angels and they guided his development of Integrated Energy Therapy. He shares their insights in a book he wrote with Linda Sue Nathanson called INTERVIEW WITH AN ANGEL.

I headed south to Sedona, Arizona and became certified from Basic all the way to the Level of Master Instructor in a week long intensive training in Integrated Energy Therapy. I could feel the angels had steered me to this experience to regain skills and learn new insights. It was fun. I enjoyed playing in the energy with the angels and discovered the IET methodology came easily to me.

The practice of Integrated Energy Therapy focuses on eight integration points on the body. I am told that these points on the body match up with the energy meridians. We were taught to use a very light touch on the area of the body for a moment and to allow energy to release. There is also an energetic imprint of higher energies. This description is an explanation for the Basic level only. It has many layers or skill sets up to the level of an advanced practitioner. Each level was even more fun.

Just to review, in my years of experience with angels, I have come to view them as that which improves communication with truth. By this I mean the truth about yourself, your source, your world and so much more. They speak to us through the heart and support our willingness to act on things with courage and faith. Think about the rays of light and all its spectrum of colors both seen and unseen. Angels are just beyond the veil of creation and yet their home is not here. I delight in their warmth and insight.

Angels encourage the flow of communion with what is right now available. Infinite possibilities are with us and will occur through our heart and mind's playful engagement, if we realize we are always connected to those possibilities. Calling in the presence of angels is like asking to be surrounded by their light. They provide a clearer connection with light. They work through our inner light as they bring us into proper alignment with our creator. I wrote this description soon after my Sedona training and had it on my website to help explain and clarify what angels are to me. I believe they are something far more universal and consciousness based than the IET methods teach.

At the training to become a master instructor of Integrated Energy Therapy, I was aware of an unusual group energy that took place during the attunement training. When we were practicing the different attunements on others taking the training, I began to notice subtle energy patterns lining up. I sensed it was not part of the instruction and seemed to come from above.

One of the women I was attuning at that point looked up at me after I finished. She said, "I saw you as a galaxy of stars." She looked wide eyed. As I moved to the next woman in the inner circle of attunement receivers, I felt a subtle but connecting energy weaving in and out of everyone present. The colors of clothing, the name tags on the people, all became part of a fabric of something beautiful and transformative.

During the next attunement I saw the heavens open up above us. I felt a massive energetic pattern unlock. Multiple layers fell away as joy filled my heart and mind. I could sense a gateway for greater communication with our source was being allowed to open, not just for me, but for every living thing. The room became very bright for a moment. The earth seemed to sigh a little in relief.

When we finished for the day, many of the twenty-four or so participants were buzzing with comments about how "high" they felt. The teacher was visibly giddy or drunk on energy. She admitted she was feeling it and then explained that it had been a long week for her. She said she had arrived early to attend the native ceremony going on in the nearby town and had also gotten too much sun on her fair skin. She looked sunburned. Everyone became curious about the native gathering she spoke of. She gave quick comments and details about the rare event.

The next day was day nine of the ten day ceremony called *The Return of The Ancestors*. Two weeks earlier I had received an email alerting me to the event near Sedona. I had planned my departure from Sedona to allow for a day of participation in hearing these indigenous leaders from all over the world. Perhaps there was a connection between the unique energy alignment and activation at our Integrated Energy Therapy event and this Mayan prophesized gathering of indigenous people. To my delight and intrigue I was now really looking forward to attending this important event the next day at least for an afternoon. I would then have to head home.

By morning I realized that I also wanted to spend some time hiking around the red rock canyons. The red cliffs near the Church of the Rock were especially powerful that morning. I also drove up to the Chapel Rock church parking. I thought I could do some meditating inside the church. I walked up the wide pedestrian spiral walkway to the entrance.

Once inside I felt the need to sit for a moment. I closed my eyes until I felt deeply rested, as though I was being wrapped in the spirit of Christ. Comforted, I enjoyed the early morning air with another short hike. I then got back into my car and drove down the highway to the nearby town of Cottonwood, Arizona. I watched for signs directing me to the big event! It was a very hot day. The mountains around Sedona had a unique feel. I understood why the area was a popular place to visit and explore.

13

A RETURN TO THE
WAY OF THE ANCESTORS

It was April 2009 as I headed to the site of *The Return of the Ancestors*. The central location for the event was in Cottonwood, Arizona. It was a gathering of Indigenous Elders from all over the world to share wisdom, visions and insights into the coming Earth changes. The Mayan calendar predicted this event would take place and where it would happen.

I attended day nine of the event and heard hours of translated messages along with over 100 people in a circle around a ceremonial fire. Cameras were aimed at a central microphone, with a crew recording the unique international gathering. One after another the representatives from many tribes and indigenous people from all over the earth came up to speak. Each spoke with an intensity of purpose. The men spoke and then the women spoke.

I stood for a few hours watching from the back. I managed to discretely snap some photographs not sure if this was allowed or not. No one said anything to me. I felt a subtle energy as I stood watching and listening. There was a serious tone to the flow of messages coming from each translator or speaker.

At one point a wise indigenous elder came to the front and spoke of his concern that many ancient teachings could be lost if there are big changes for the earth. He encouraged everyone to remember the old ways and pass on information about them if it is respected and valued. He believed that women were the leaders of this new time that is dawning.

He asked the men to protect the women so that they could find strength and courage to speak out and have their thoughts known. He believed the earth spoke to the women of our planet in many ways and that people would need their guidance in the years to come. He emphasized that the conflict and separation of many groups of people across the planet was a big problem. He said we humans would need each other in the times to come. I was very inspired by this wise elderly man from South America.

For many years I have known I had past lives where I was schooled in native teachings, probably several lifetimes. Many different tribes have keys of wisdom that call to me. I have had years of personal experience with native teachings, but I am not a Native American in any genetic sense.

I returned home and wrote an article called "The Medicine Wheel: A Return to Harmony" from my personal notes and experiences, so that at least I had done my part. I have shared copies with friends and clients over the years since. It is a way of life sorely lacking in our modern world. I would later rename the article "A Return to the Ways of the Ancients." I believe that the message of the medicine wheel teachings can bring us into a better alignment with the natural world around us.

Like the ancient Essene communions, they bring us into harmony with the cosmos. I had benefited by immersing myself for a time in their ways. The teachings of the four directions were a bridge to my ancient past. Inner and outer awareness along with a perception of above and below, have always had a place for me in the rhythm of life.

Most people in the modern world view life as proceeding in a straight line, as if each individual is separate from everything and heading down some highway of life. Many people live their lives stuck on that road somewhere, oblivious to all the wonders of nature they could tap into if they opened their eyes. Time is perceived as linear and there is a preoccupation with the past or future, while the present is mostly missed altogether. In reality, our lives move in cycles. We can return to a more natural state of being by contemplating nature's seasons and rhythms. By following the path of the sun and being aware of our connection to all things, we begin to restore balance into our body, mind, spirit and heart.

At first glance nature may seem unforgiving or inconvenient to our daily lives. The sun rises whether we are ready for it or not and winter can come with challenging energies and circumstances. Each season has its gifts and its trials. The inner workings of the earth will set the tone for each day, each moment and invite us to listen in to her changing patterns.

If we fight these tides of daily change and unpredictability, we find an increase in our physical, emotional and mental stressors. Yet nature is really reflected in our bodies, our thoughts, our feelings and our very souls, if we begin to pay more attention to the messages. When our awareness becomes quieter, we can pay more attention to the things going on around us. The hum of a bee nearby and the feeling and smell of the breeze is going on all the time. It will bring a flow back into this moment. To embrace the circle or cycle of life is to slow down and observe the inner self and the outer forms of creation. Nature has a way of saying "Be here NOW."

We begin to notice what is all around us when we stand and breathe in the air of this moment. Become aware of the direction you are facing and your sense of standing on the earth. We are constantly traveling in some direction even in our minds, until we stop and take in where we are and what we are really doing.

If you were to see a Native American medicine wheel, you would see that it contains the four directions of north, east, south, and west. There is a center hub of some kind and the entire area is marked with a circle of stones. As we stand on the earth near it in a conscious way, we are also able to look above at the sky and below at our feet resting on the earth. There is a sense of what lies deep below our feet within the earth and what is far above, beyond what we can see.

If we were to enter this medicine wheel, we might walk to the center and become familiar with each of the four directions as we faced each, moving in a clockwise direction beginning with the east. After one complete pivot from the center of the circle, we might feel it has a sense of completeness and continuity. A circle can be a sacred space that we see in many places in creation. In the Native American teachings of the west, many insights are offered when contemplating each of the four directions in a sacred circle or medicine wheel. When these insights are applied to daily life the struggles fall away and the harmonic returns to our being. It can even open doorways into the center of creation's song, the NOW. This moment is the only moment there is, in truth.

For personal study, some individuals have created their own small medicine wheels and marked the directions accordingly. The symbols, elements and energies of each direction can be placed on the markers. These visual aids can help engrain the metaphor or energetic influences of each direction. Put your attention on all four sides of your body, in its relation to these four directions: east/west and south/north. Give thanks to each energetic field as it extends out in each direction. (See the diagram)

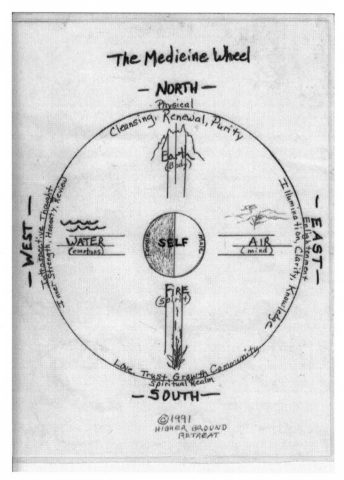

(My 1991 Class Hand-Out)

Contemplate the most basic teachings of each direction by seeing east as the rising of the sun or the beginning of a new day. Think of receiving awakening and insightful energy flowing into you from the east. The south is the full activity of the day and sends you the playful energies of sunlight or high energy. The west is where the sun sets and we begin to wind down our energies, reflect on our days past and prepare for sleep. The west sends soothing sunsets of calming energy. The north is where we enter our period of rest and commune with higher wisdom. Allow cellular rest to occur and rejuvenation for all aspects of your body, mind and spirit.

Now look more deeply into every aspect of each of the four cardinal directions. The south carries the element of fire and represents spirit. It could be said to reflect the energies of the noonday sun when life is awake, active and engaged in work or play. The south is also a place of community and interactions with all people, places and things. We realize we are part of the greater community of humanity. We see how each person is always part of a greater whole. The Great Spirit is like the sun shining down on all things.

The great Mother Earth is also seen as the bringer of nourishment and sustenance. Mother Earth should be experienced beneath bare feet, so that nothing blocks the exchange of vital energies. It can heal you and reaffirm you. It tells you to remember that your right to exist is equal to every living things right to exist.

Mother Earth will never reject you or demean you in any way. Let her expansive energy and beauty heal you. Say to yourself, "Beginning today, I will come to an understanding of my special relationship to Mother Earth and the greater society, as a whole, by releasing my sense of separateness and aloneness. I am not alone!"

The south also teaches us to understand humility and belonging. We each share a piece of the universal energy within all living things. We can use this common bond, this universal connectedness to provide support for others on the path of wholeness. Say to yourself, "Beginning today, I will seek a greater understanding of my sacred connection to the entire universe." The south reminds us to nurture our own spirit by remembering to also honor our inner self or child self. Innocence and trust are gifts from the south.

If you feel you are in a place of disconnection with your sense of the greater whole and your part in it, it will show up as patterns of vulnerability, loneliness, and a loss of your sense of direction in life. The south will ask us to acknowledge our fears, desires and feelings of distress and offer them up to the Great Spirit and then turn and reach out to a member of society and ask for help. Say to yourself, "Beginning today, I will reconnect with the Creator's light in myself and another in order to reestablish the universal bond we share with our brothers and sisters in life."

As the sun in the sky moves toward the west, it sets below the horizon and night falls upon us. Our attention turns from an outward focus to an inward reflective focus. The west is the realm of introspective thought. It's a time of transformation and completion as day turns into night. It teaches us to release the thoughts and energies of the business of the day, relationships and the activity of community. The west might ask us to look at our problems as well as our accomplishments of the day or from the past. We are encouraged to make a commitment to some form of positive growth or change in the old patterns.

The west can also represent the unsettled energies of the darkness of night. We must face our emotional energies and the element of water. Uncharted waters of the psyche may come to the surface of our awareness. The west tests our integration of the gifts of faith and trust that the south offered. We address our fears in the west. We may uncover ways in which we have managed to control others or our environment in order to maintain emotional stability.

The nighttime teaches us to let go of the day and all our worries of tomorrow. We thank our ancestors and departed loved ones for their contributions to our life. We forgive all that was perhaps not perfect about those relations. The west is less active physically as we wind down and prepare for rest. Say to yourself, "Beginning today I will be responsible for my emotions, my reactions and my responses to life."

The north is represented by the deep night and complete physical rest. The night sky also reveals the cosmos and galaxies of stars. Native cultures often referred to this direction as teaching us about the great mystery of life or the unknown, unseen levels of existence. We thank the Great Spirit for all the unknown aspects and sources of support in our life.

The north can bring deep contemplation and silence. As we surrender into deep sleep, we turn our hearts and minds over to the care of the angels and wisdom keepers of the north. The north also represents the physical earth that, in winter, is dense, solid, frozen and asleep. Our physical body receives rest and rejuvenation in the north. Many seeds are dormant now and activity is at a standstill. The hibernation cycle of a bear can also be a reflection of the energies of the north.

Say to yourself, "Beginning today, I will take good physical care of myself." Our bodies naturally attempt to heal or cleanse away the unneeded elements of the earlier cycles. Many layers of stress and toxic energy in the cells seek complete relaxation to realign the energy centers with vital flows of the life force. Say to yourself, "Beginning today, I will come to an understanding that change is a process." Like winter, the seeds of change need warmth, safety, encouragement, but mostly time to rest in order to find the strength to reach the eventual surface and warmth of the dawn's sunlight. Hopefully the element of purity will find its way back into the energies of the body during our time in the north. Great strength comes from the north when its wisdom is embraced. Remember to slow down. This is a time of rest and renewal.

The east brings the dawn of a new day, as the sun stretches out over the landscape. The life force of nature comes awake, and our minds shift from a deep sleep. The east is the element of the air. The wind can reflect the thoughts of the mind blowing serenely or with force. The air can bring clarity, knowledge and enlightenment. It's a new day for new thoughts and new resolve. We expand our views and rediscover our zest for living.

In the east we are invited to awaken to creation and all its beauty. All things are touched by the light of the sunrise. The desire to live can be strong in the east. We find ourselves capable of moving quickly through the dark soil of our former existence, towards the source of light. Something beyond our self is calling our name and triggering a release from the shackles of the earlier cycle when we were the sleeping seed.

The east reminds us to look to the light of the horizon and realize that the sky and the wind can bring gentle rain or tornadoes and hurricanes. The wind can be powerfully cleansing as well. When we watch the sky, we see there is a balance established between opposing forces over time and over the face of the earth. Within these forces of nature, new beginnings come and take shape, some of which are unexpected.

Say to yourself, "Beginning today, I will embrace the energies of the wind and sky and ask them to guide me toward my greater destiny and happiness." The east is a time of action and initiation. It's a time to release former narrow points of view and seek out people and activities that will enhance personal growth and development. The east can help us reclaim our life dream or sense of purpose.

We have come full circle, as we see the return of the sun and move toward the greater community of life in the south. The time you spend with each direction brings you closer to embodying the center of the circle and experiencing balance and harmony in your life.

Moving beyond the cardinal directions, the fifth direction will take your awareness straight down the vertical axis into the core of the earth. This will increase your sense of stability and root you to a seat or stance of empowerment and strength. The sixth direction takes your awareness straight up the vertical axis into the sky through the top of your head. The Native American Hopi called this "kopavi" or "the door at top of the head." Here you can access the gateway to higher dimensions, worlds and states of consciousness.

Finally, the seventh sacred direction brings your attention back down and inward to your core, also known as the "temple of the heart" in many traditions. Know that this temple is a hearth of light that burns as a spark from the source of all light. When your heart, mind and spirit are informed by the seven directions, your awareness resonates with the totality of your energy field's potential. You become more and more expanded.

The qualities of each direction can be recognized also as phases our lives must pass through. Acceptance of these rhythms of nature can bring wisdom back into each moment. Let yourself be born fresh and new each day. The heart, mind, body and spirit will soar to the heavens. Above and below are integrated, as you reach up and then down toward your feet with your hands.

Making a move toward the outer edge of the circle, you become aware of the energies outside of the circle and feel gratitude for the sacredness of your circle. Moving and dancing towards the center brings a sense of drawing in each layer of awareness, as you face out, then in, while moving around the circle. Your process within the dance will eventually feel complete and you will find yourself in the center of your circle, resting in the stillness.

Working with the medicine wheel can be a journey into a greater understanding of all life. We thank our ancestors and wisdom keepers for bringing these teachings down through the ages and keeping them alive in practice and ceremony. They can restore our connection to the earth and our Creator. We must begin again to walk gently on the earth and let our hearts soar to the heavens.

Contemplating the energy of the four cardinal directions exists in other traditions. In my studies of important saints I began to notice the practice of turning to the four directions actually exists in old diaries of Saint Francis. He would stand at the entrance of a new town he was entering and first turn to the four directions, asking for protection.

I enjoyed playing with the pattern of the medicine wheel until late 2008. Around this time I was guided to deconstruct my property's large medicine wheel. I felt like I was setting free the energies of the wheel. I did the same with my sweat lodge and put some of the willow and blankets in a bonfire. It felt peaceful. I was then ready for what became my new healing vocation in 2009.

Just as a side note, later on during the winter of 2015, I decided to join a group of women for a one day drumming workshop led by a skilled drumming instructor named Christine Stevens. It was fun to take out my twenty year old Egyptian drum and play it along with others drum types at the workshop. In addition to some basics, we learned the *sounds* of the four directions. I had never heard of sound being paired with those teachings. I loved learning that the four directions also include the dimension of sound! The sound of the east was said to be the sound of a rattle or voice/singing. The sound of the south is the drum beat or what calls the community together. To the west is the sound of the bones of our ancestors clinking together or sticks tapping and the north is the sound of silence. Ah, how I loved the feel of each.

A few years prior I brought home a CD of native songs of the Iroquois. Singing the songs of the Iroquois was and is deeply real for me. My soul has a memory of or roots across time and space with those old ways. I have also loved singing along to East Indian mantras both vocally and emotionally. I particularly enjoy a CD by Benjy and Heather Wertheimer called "Sri Shantala." I must have done this as well somewhere in time because it felt familiar. I had come a long way since my childhood resistance to practicing a skill through repetition. The light of the divine needs the spontaneous to inspire or lead the way, while repetition like drumming serves to reinforce the connection.

Authors Note: With regard to native or indigenous teachings, I recommend using thoughtful discernment when participating in native ceremonies. I have a special interest in the ethical practice of any sweat lodge ceremony. Make certain it is constructed with organic, natural materials to avoid chemical fumes. Plastic structural piping is a dangerous substitute for willow branches. Also, a sweat lodge experience should be led by an ethical experienced teacher who will allow you to exit the lodge at any time. Clothing types should be cotton fabric and loose fitting.

14

MIRACLES AND THE MATRIX

Understand that zero point, is not about nothingness. It's a designation of infinity. Perfect stasis is perfect equilibrium: The Holy NOW, from which everything takes shape.

There is but one Spirit, the continuous and unbroken matrix of all existence. Through internalized communion, the whole becomes aware of its variable possibilities. This is your personal point of truth.

Glenda Green, LOVE WITHOUT END-Jesus Speaks

Every step on my journey has thankfully provided a clue or insight into my next step. I taught and certified my first student in Integrated Energy Therapy (IET) by the fall of 2009 and worked with clients out of my home. I enjoyed the IET energy work but wanted to keep my heart open to other new possibilities. It was subtle energy work and genuinely effective at assisting people with a spectrum of issues. I enjoyed just allowing the flow of energy and noticing that the angels like to inspire us to be conduits during the sessions.

That fall my husband and I along with another couple attended the Jackson Hole Wellness Festival. We had won two nights at the Teton Club located at the Teton Village ski resort. One of the larger conference talks was particularly good. The speaker was Byron Katie. I learned that her spiritual awakening was rare and powerfully transformative. We were both very impressed with her energy and concise method for questioning the mind's tendency to stay in a pattern of unnecessary suffering. I highly recommend Byron Katie's book, A THOUSAND NAMES FOR JOY.

By 2010 I was told about a website called matrixenergetics.com with some amazing testimonials. After looking at it and feeling adrenalin shoot through me, it was obvious my guidance was directing me to train in Matrix Energetics and be fast tracked into a certification with it. I booked my flight, hotel and seminar all at once. I also ordered the book MATRIX ENERGETICS by Richard Bartlett, ND, CD. Soon after it was ordered it arrived and I started to read it. I was also getting ready to leave for a nine day silent retreat. This was the same Buddhist community retreat I had gone to seven years before. I decided to bring my new book along even though I understood that books were not encouraged for a silent retreat.

By day three of the Buddhist retreat I was aware that something was not agreeing with my digestion. My abdomen was becoming increasingly bloated and tender. The retreat was being held at a remote ranch in the mountains, so I could not easily get to any medical aid. My guidance was not giving me any clues, but I kept my sense of humor and called my stomach my Buddha belly. Deep down however, I was growing concerned that something was really wrong.

I finished reading the book Matrix Energetics just before bed and shut off the light. Suddenly a very clear male presence hovered above me. I could not see him with my eyes, but I distinctly felt a strong but friendly personality who was aware that I had an issue. I somehow knew it was the founder and teacher of Matrix Energetics, Dr. Richard Bartlett! He did not speak with words but instead did a sort of mime to communicate. All I could see/sense were his hands gesturing.

A minute later my hands were filled with his intention to investigate more closely, as my own hands palpitated my abdomen, like a physician would. A moment later, I felt him smile with clarity. My hands became my own again. Then in the air above me, his hands revealed a tiny black and white pill that now was being offered for a remedy. I nodded OK and then it disappeared into the air. He disappeared as well.

I lay there mesmerized by the intensity of this teacher's extraordinary abilities and unassuming nature! Now I was *really* looking forward to his seminar. I was so grateful I had brought the matrix book too! The next morning my swollen belly was flat and I had no further issues with the food. This was very exciting, but I could not speak about it, because after all, it was a silent retreat.

The retreat was being held in a hunting lodge in a beautiful setting in the mountains of Wyoming near a wide river. The Tibetan flags and scarves were draped over the antlers of elk and deer mounts on the walls. The teacher's instructions each morning after breakfast were somewhat disappointing. The message seemed to be to put your attention on your body and watch your mind. I understood the practice but noticed that my body stiffened up when I focused on it. I returned to my long held practice of putting my attention on an energetic connection. Everything lightened up.

I could tell by the end of the week that I was happily energized by my silent walking and sitting meditations, but many others were not. One woman even cried at the final evening share time about how much pain she had been in during the sits, but she was getting through it and learning about her mind.

A few weeks later, I was in Seattle for the nearly week long Matrix Energetics practitioner certification training and level one and two seminars. It was all being taught by the founder Richard Bartlett who is a chiropractor and naturopathic physician. Also on stage teaching with Richard was his daughter Justice Bartlett and Melissa Joy Jonsson. I went on to attend another seminar in San Diego at the Hotel Del Coronado, three months later. This completed the required attendance of two Level I and Level II seminars, renamed later as Fundamentals and the sixty hours of documented session work. This was all within a few months, giving me another practitioner certification.

As for my own developing healing work, from the start I loved the free flowing dynamic of Matrix Energetics sessions. I worked on people multiple times at each seminar and it never ceased to excite me. My own body experience, when I was worked on at seminars by participants was sometimes so cool! I would become suddenly fluid like and go down joyously to the carpeted floor laughing. When I was working on someone, it was incredible to feel his or her body become water under my fingers and pour onto the floor below me. The quantum effect or wave patterns that science describes these days really come to life at every matrix seminar.

I began doing Matrix Energetics right from the moment I boarded the airplane heading home from the first seminar. Back at home my friends would smile and swoon during sessions. I did them for free at first. I came to learn that many profound effects of complete change could take place when I engaged with the "field" of possibilities.

One day I decided to employ Matrix Energetics on our dog Cashew after she was urinating uncontrollably all over the house for nearly a week. The veterinarian said she was likely in kidney failure. After looking into my dog, I could *see* into her organs. Her kidneys became a bright glow of pink. After another moment or two something moved, shifted and then pushed me backward. I knew something had happened but went on with my day. Our dog stopped peeing all over the house! I was thrilled with the change.

I was then guided to take her off all medications for her hip dysplasia. The vet admitted that these meds were what had affected her organs. For a while her arthritis seemed worse, but then I was nudged from within to apply my healing skills to her mobility. I honestly felt this took more faith.

To my surprise after a few sessions on Cashew's hips over the course of a few weeks, there were big changes. My dog could now get up the stairs again. She looked happy and generally in less pain and with no more medications. When the condition returned it was my opportunity to practice and not give up. It always worked and in general our dog looked much better within a year.

One evening that summer while I was at a friend's home, her dog came up to greet me. I was waiting for the other dinner guest to arrive. The dog was looking very old and probably ill. It had thin, matted hair and had difficulty walking. My heart poured out to this creature. I had a sudden urge to reach down to "see" and touch it and do a little Matrix stuff. Before I knew it, the encounter with my hands sent out a vivid spin of violet light from the dog. I laughed at the "kick" of it and went back to visiting with the friend, talking about the meal.

Minutes later she asked, "What did you do to my dog?" She went on to explain that her dog was in advanced liver failure and was dying. She pointed down at her dog in astonishment, because it was drinking and eating! She added that it had advanced hip dysplasia, as well, so could barely get outside to do its business. We watched as her dog was starting to run around the room, limping still, but looking very happy. By the end of the dinner, the dog was coming up to me looking so full of life. I heard my heart whisper to the dog, "Now don't overdo it." It trotted away and headed down the stairs to the kids play room to my friend's amazement. She mentioned that the dog was seventeen years old.

Two weeks later I stopped by to say "hello." Her dog barely looked like the same animal. My friend had to insist it was the same dog. Its hair had come back in and the dog wanted to go in and out a lot. It had put on weight too. Unfortunately my friend was annoyed because she had to keep getting up from the couch to let the dog out.

She had a knee problem that was being treated by her doctor and had to limp around in pain. I noted the paradox and sensed my friend's impatience. She had not asked for me to help with her knee. I realized I had to notice my friend's knee as an uninvited personal pattern in front of me. Despite this I was able to sense it was tied to several issues involving her unhappy marriage.

She would eventually get a divorce and become much happier. Seven weeks later that dog died in its sleep without incident. I thought "how awesome!" The dog was given a new lease on life and enjoyed a few extra months before exiting peacefully.

That fall was the annual Wellness Festival in Jackson Hole, Wyoming. As a practitioner I had hoped to have a booth at it. I learned that it was too late for me to participate. They had only a small area for the practitioners to set up and they had already selected the people. The good news was that the Teton Wellness Festival had a very intriguing individual coming from Croatia. He was the featured all day event in the large conference hall. I glanced at the promo image of this man smiling and immediately became excited about the weekend event. He reportedly had begun visiting the United States in 2008.

Before bed, I decided to look this Croatian healer man up on the internet. I quickly discovered dozens of video links and stories about him. Many clips had him standing in front of crowds of people from all over Europe who were converging on one of his "gazing" sessions. They called him "Little Brother" in Croatian, or Braco. It was pronounced, "Bratzo."

I played one of the video links of him standing on a balcony in Europe before hundreds of people. Tears ran down my cheeks, but I did not know why. I watched another one and something came out of my mouth like "Wow that is a big Angel!" I sensed that his gaze could act as literally a portal to the higher brighter reality. My heart longed for the freedom of that reality, but I also knew I had more work to do.

I went to bed thinking how cool it was to be attending the event in Jackson Hole tomorrow and seeing this unique man. I drifted off to sleep. I was awakened around 3:30 a.m. to a very distinct sense of his presence filling my bedroom. Again, I did not *see* him, but I felt him and could hear his accented voice speaking urgently to me.

He said to be sure and come to the event but that he could not be there physically. He seemed to indicate that men in black suits were preventing it. He went on to say that he was going to try something new and that it was an experiment, so please come! As soon as I nodded in eager agreement, he was suitably reassured and disappeared.

The next day I arrived at the Wellness Festival in anticipation. I joined many others in a room of very upset event planners, all buzzing about some problem. Something had prevented Braco from being there. One woman was in tears as she finally spoke on the microphone. She explained that his travel visa had been pulled by our state department and he could not board his plane in Croatia to be here now. Many good people began calling from Jackson Hole to offices of the federal government to find out how this could be remedied.

Reportedly someone knew Hillary Clinton—then secretary of state—well enough to get this cleared up. The audience learned that Braco now had an artist visa, and would be on time for the rest of his booked events around the country. But for us, however, he was still in Croatia and would like to do a *Skype* group presentation for today's event.

In front of the room was a large screen that allowed a few hundred people to see a projected image of his face. I felt good as I listened to all of this. It explained my interesting encounter last night with Braco. The presentation began with a video of people's testimonials of experiencing "Braco's gaze," and then we all stood up. Braco came onto the screen live all the way from Croatia and gazed at our audience via his personal computer for seven minutes. After a period of silence the audience was invited to share on a microphone their experiences. People made statements like "I felt so much emotion" or "my body could feel a gentle energy buzzing." I noticed a strong wave effect that dissolved me a few times. It was powerful and intensely unique.

I participated in three more forty five minute sessions, one after the other and really enjoyed the variety of experiences energetically. We all viewed his face up close on a large screen. I loved that he was just *being* a portal for the *light* to shine through to the world. Our local Wellness Festival became, inadvertently, the launching of what would become "Live Streaming with Braco" for years to come.

I learned that Braco does not speak anywhere or teach anything, so it quickly became apparent that he was meant to serve people in a universal capacity. He has a remarkable story of how he came to be doing this work since 1995. You can find a book and articles on him if you would like to learn more. Some have guessed that he has been viewed by hundreds of thousands people in person and by millions when you count the "Live Streaming" online connections. Healings of all kinds are well documented everywhere. For me, he was a welcome change in the landscape of our world. I saw him as a "brother" serving as a beacon of hope for so many thirsty people. He never liked being called a healer, however. He supported all the healers of the world in his own way.

I wanted an office, but had to wait for the right one to come available. In 2010 I established and registered the business name ENERGY HEALS as a DBA in Idaho. I also created the Facebook page and alternative registered business name of Energy Healers of Teton Valley. By early 2011 I had opened an office in Driggs, Idaho and designed and created my own website. I taught myself how to use the software for my website. I went on to create several upgraded sites.

I created the first "Teton Community Healing Arts Festival" in our town at the Driggs City Center building before it was its remodel was completed. I noticed it was a great large open space at first. It sat this way for a couple of years while funding was raised to complete the build out for what is today the Geotourism Center and climbing gym. If you recall I had done several events like this years before in Boise in the 1980's. I hoped the festival could bring many practitioners in our area together under one roof. I wanted to give new practitioners a place to meet the public and share their innovative work.

The first event for our Healing Arts Festival included a Friday evening keynote speaker from northern Idaho. She was an energy practitioner and new friend of mine named Genie Monte-Pellizari. She is the founder of "Source Connection Therapy" and the author of the book of the same name. She gave an interesting talk to our modest gathering. Our venue the Senior Center had double booked the room and confused community members who thought a fundraiser for Sand Hill Cranes was supposed to be there that evening. The mistake cost the festival some attendance.

Saturday was devoted to an all day festival of hands-on practitioners and there were workshops on Sunday. I had a booth and did sessions and taught a workshop. On Sunday my two hour workshop was an introduction to The Essene 14 Communions. With the help of friends, a Healing Arts Festival was held in 2012 and 2013 in our town. I brought in main stream businesses like physical therapists and massage therapists as well. I was the event planner and director of each. Despite many forms of advertising and word of mouth, the events were never large but those who participated and attended each year said they really appreciated that we held these festivals.

Beginning in 2011 I also began attending and participating in the Sun Valley Wellness Festival. I set up my booth in a large banquet area they called "Hands on Hall." I have been a visiting practitioner each year since then. All of this work and exposure to people with various challenges and issues has been the best experience for me. I have noticed that there are common themes to all the different techniques and practices out there. Through Integrated Energy Therapy and Matrix Energetics, I have been delighted to be part of the world of transformation, as a healing practitioner.

So far Matrix Energetics is the most interesting and expansive field of study. In 2011 I completed my first level four, later renamed Self Mastery, Matrix Energetics seminar and training. My second self mastery three day seminar was in 2013 and I loved both! The manual alone was worth the price of admission. It had so many ideas and tangible healing approaches that could be applied. I could use it for years and not have experienced all of it.

I have attended Matrix Energetics seminars every year and they offer a variety of options especially for the advanced practitioner. I have made friends from all over the world by attending many conferences and offering sessions. People are what make this work so compelling. The work I do involves all aspects of life that are open to transformation. My session work has grown more and more spontaneous and consciousness based. Each session is unlike any other.

Every moment we are surrounded by energy patterns of all kinds pulsing and rippling outward. Most do not see or feel the dynamic interplay of energetic expression that is at work in our everyday lives. As a healing practitioner, I sense this "field" of energy all the time and have learned that I am interfacing with living fields or patterns that are in a constant state of communication with everything else. Our bodies are communicating all the time with these patterns in our environment along with everything else. What I have loved is the discovery that the universe wants our "union" or our joy to be complete.

The universe hears our cells, our minds and our very being, communicating all the time. It wants us to remember how to hear it as well. The universe accommodates our picture of reality each moment and does not judge our preoccupation with day to day life. I have learned over many years that it would like us to come home and engage co-creatively.

When a spiritual awakening begins, we discover that the universe knows us, like an old lost friend and wants to play but first it needs to bring things to our attention. It wants us to all notice what we are doing, saying and being each moment with our thoughts, emotions and energy in general. So begin to notice yourself on an energetic level. Often it is very much more negative than you might believe. Turn each thought around and embrace the possibility that there is a solution to each challenge in your life and the lives of others. There are infinite possibilities all around us!

In recent years, some would say our world has become like a sad and tragic movie script. Its plot is full of heart wrenching losses, mass murders, and personal disasters like floods, fires and foreclosures. Regional wide scale natural disasters seem to be on the increase. Too many can say they know someone personally in a health crisis and death is coming to those who seemed so healthy last time we checked. It can be very unsettling even to the most solid character.

When we watch the news, we can be sucked into the dramas of political upheaval and dysfunction or the many health scares being broadcast. Environmental disasters have grown so common that we feel almost numb, if not alarmed. Even if you don't seek out the news on TV, radio, or the Internet, almost anyone can feel the ebb and flow of energetic tension in the air. The vibe some days is unmistakable.

Great swells of emotional and mental energy are rippling through large masses of our planet's population. Some moments seem to be pushing for a type of stampede effect. Political upheavals have changed the shape of a number of governments in the Middle East and are still unfolding.

Other swells of energy seem to inspire a powerful inward focus and a quelling of all movement. In these instances, it is as though a sudden command of the heart happens. It is saying, "Hush, and be still!" I have felt this and have known it is very important that I stop engaging in anything distracting and be silent for awhile. I tune into the patterns unfolding and engage as directed. I experienced this at the time of the Boston Marathon bombings. It was a very deep, "Oh no!" feeling, like a silent alarm followed by an unprecedented call to respond at every level.

After about an hour or so of floating in a strange but expanded state, I was intuitively nudged to turn on the television to see what it might reveal. We can all remember the riveting scenes that unfolded via news of the bombing footage that day. I did not sleep that night and felt swept up in visions of hospitals filled with life saving efforts.

In these accelerated times, many have felt the need to disconnect from the busy world and spend more time in nature or in an activity that calms the heart. Powerful focused energy is passing through many people's energy field for days at a time. For many, sleepless nights have become common. Those of us who have listened to the deeper calling have a sense of being part of the turning of the tides away from destruction in event after event. Despite how bad things look on a given day, we have a strange deeper sense that it most assuredly could have been worse. There were fewer deaths than expected, the asteroid did not hit the earth, the floodwaters retreated just in time, the large solar flares did not take out our entire electrical grid, etc.

So what is happening? I believe human consciousness is discovering an opening of sorts into patterns of possibility previously unavailable. We are being invited into a field of dreams so magnificent that we are momentarily spellbound by the very *feel* of it. Life can unfold with surprising lightness and include rebounds from seeming calamity. Uncanny synchronicities can occur in daily interactions with friends and strangers alike.

Even mystical unprecedented miracles are being witnessed in real life situations more and more. For those who have been in extreme difficulty and experienced a sudden unprecedented change, they feel a stunned effect as everything becomes good. The relief is followed by the thought, "Wow, how did I make it out of that mess?" There is a very real shift in perception of one's world all of a sudden. It's like realizing you *are* loved and help *did* come.

Each day more individuals are recognizing their instinctive connection with all life and with a greater field of awareness. For some, the distinction between the chaos and the coherence is energetically palpable. Energy waves continue to move in and out of each day. Many are sensing subtle doorways of possibility coming into their awareness. The heart urges us to take the leap of faith and go forward. Before we know it, one opportunity leads to another, we are suddenly in a colorful world of gentle people offering assistance and the skies appear clear again.

People for the most part are acting from their hearts and help is finding its way to the areas affected. For those choosing to surrender to their heart's deeper knowing or to the general goodness of our world, despite their predicaments, they are awakening to a new feeling. There is a brighter sunlight shining into the landscape of their lives. A deep exhale releases the tense past and they are choosing to embrace what *is* beautiful in and around them, rather than dwell on what seems lost.

Some people have become aware even of the humor of the moment and have provided a much needed comic relief for many. The adventure of life is full of exciting twists and turns unfolding each day. No one can call this era of history boring.

Over the past few years, many of my clients and family members have shared with me all sorts of intense challenges they have found themselves in. I have offered many types of energy sessions, meditation instruction and general counseling to address each call for help. I have witnessed many miracles in my healing work and in my life for years.

In 2012 I felt a need to begin offering a monthly study group to begin teaching consciousness tools to address the wild energy waves moving through so many individuals' lives. I titled the class "Playing in The Fields of Consciousness." I had two classes going each month for a couple of years. We are all in accelerated energy, for better or worse. I was offering consciousness awakening tools to discover these infinite fields of possibility that are all around us.

For those who understand the language of Matrix Energetics might think I was attempting to teach their tools, including a process called a "two point" in my monthly classes. I was not, because as a certified practitioner we have an understanding that only the Matrix Energetics seminars are allowed to do this. In my classes I worked with universal principles of miracle mindedness and awareness expansion. The word "field" was already very ingrained in my consciousness from my exposure to Master Teacher and my years of awakening beginning in 1991.

I teach my clients that it begins with a willingness to play in those same living fields of possibility. I was very pleased to see that this concept of "play" was taught and even emphasized at all of the Matrix Energetics seminar trainings over the years. I like the word "play" because it immediately removes the tension, strain and heavy attachment to outcomes, thereby opening the doorway to the brighter outcome being sought. The attachment to outcomes is a linear, left brain habit. Too many have lost touch with the innocent open minded, heart centered state of play that we used to do as children.

Imagine what is available to you if you truly decide to take the leap of faith and let infinite possibilities be so. As adults, we need to drop down out of our heads and into our hearts. It is a profound shift out of fear and toward moment to moment awareness. You have heard many people talking about being in the NOW. I believe children do it naturally. We can do well to return to some of that innocent perception.

Children are very sensitive to what is authentic and what is not. The heart knows where true authenticity resides. There is a power within each one of us to choose once again, or to start fresh with the heart and eyes of a child, when approaching difficulty. I have had my most profound outcomes when I did just this.

I believe everyone with a willing heart and an open mind can learn to access healing possibilities and life changing transformations. These skills are not just reserved for the really smart, special or holy people either. If anything, I think we are all invited to the table of infinite possibility. What is required is a new awareness of the field of the heart. The field of the heart is the timeless, original foundation of our *being*. The physical heart is the first organ to form after conception and so you can say everything else follows it. I believe that through our inner light we can find a true connection and communion with Source-God-Oneness.

Through the heart field, we discover where all fields of consciousness converge, communicate and connect. I believe consciousness is communing with everything all the time. I view our bodies as dynamic pulsing fields of light and information interfacing with other patterns every moment. The mind is really just a lens, and a powerful one. But it should be led by the heart. If our minds are in charge, we can lose out on all kinds of wisdom in the moment. Our hearts have a quieter, but deeper method of communication. It takes a slight adjustment to remember how to hear the wisdom of the heart and to learn how to become an active extension of it.

To access a pattern of energy is to *be* for a moment innocently communing with what is possible. Patterns will show up and merge with your conscious field of awareness until a shift happens. Everything is in a wondrous interplay of potential patterns. When energy patterns move to a place that is complete, you will feel that too, like the last note in a musical composition. Expansion and contraction are the steps to the energetic dance the universe is showing us.

I invite you to sit still for a moment and consciously drop down out of your head and fall into your heart field, like a pebble being dropped into a soft watery pool of potential. Feel the quiet ripple relax your shoulders and straighten your spine. Do it again and this time really let yourself fall deeper into that heart/hearth or inner temple. Now decide that you can look into any pattern, situation, or condition.

Remember, everything is a pattern of light and information pulsing each moment in a particular way. What do you feel drawn to? Keep everything simple and brief. If it is your body that gets your attention, what area in your body are you drawn toward? Go toward the first thing that occurs to you. Be aware of colors, textures and feelings of any kind. Experiment with zooming into and out of areas of the body. Relax and just be aware of whatever occurs to you.

This is not a linear process, so remember to laugh and be surprised rather than cling to the old habit of trying to figure out where something is going and why. As you move toward any point, notice if any part of you feels burdened or heavy and needs to be lifted or released. Notice if some part of you wants to be set free. When you look inside your body, go anywhere that attracts your attention. *Be* with it for a moment and listen to what the heart is trying to show you or tell you.

Drop into the heart again and again, playing with energy, patterns, images and thoughts. As you become more aware of your heart's prompting and the energy begins to ripple, the patterns of possibility will become more distinct. You will be amused at the unexpected insights and real physical sensations as change becomes apparent.

So remember, listen with your heart, feel with your mind and move with your body to find the groove or opening into a place of momentary coherence. Let go and flow with it. These are some of the methods I use to assist others in accessing their infinite field of potential. If you recall, I learned as a teenager from a channeled book called THE NATURE OF PERSONAL REALITY by Jane Roberts, that the universe rearranges itself to accommodate our picture of reality. Around that time I also learned that everything is energy and is therefore in motion, not static. It was now many years later and I had begun to learn the new sciences behind the nature of our personal reality.

In 2010 at my second Matrix Energetics seminar, a physicist named Claude Swanson was given an opportunity to speak about his book LIFE FORCE: The Scientific Basis. His book covers thirty years of extensive research into healing energy and phenomena. Dr. Swanson holds a degree from MIT and a doctorate from Princeton. Through his interviews with the founder of Matrix Energetics, Richard Bartlett CD, ND, he became very familiar with Matrix Energetics breakthrough healing demonstrations or miraculous transformations by witnesses to many of them.

Dr. Swanson gave a short talk on energy to all of us seminar attendees. I came home with an autographed copy of his very large book. It is chock full of research into the energy of "life force." Typically, I am not known to be drawn to research papers, but I had to have Swanson's book. My father, a medical doctor, asked to borrow it right after he saw it. Later my father said he wanted his own copy and has since purchased one. Recently my dad commented specifically on Swanson's book. He said that any page he opens to becomes a fascinating read. I have enjoyed reading parts of the book, but the science is sometimes quite advanced.

In 2012 I was approached by Dr. Swanson at a matrix seminar in Denver. He approached me near the restaurant area and asked to speak with me that morning before the day's seminar began. I was surprised at the request, but invited him to join me at my table. He said he interviews healers often for scientific research purposes. I felt open to sharing some of my life experiences with healing. I spoke of the dog I worked on that came back to full health after being diagnosed with kidney and liver failure. I also shared a little about my spiritual awakening experience with a reality beyond this one. The interview was cut short by the need to get back to the seminar. The morning presentation was gearing up in a nearby conference hall.

Since then I have learned many things about the dynamics of energy as it pertains to transformation, especially from watching interviews with Dr. Swanson. For layman science geeks like me, Dr. Swanson explains things well. Swanson explains that in the 1950's an astrophysicist was studying what stars do. This scientist linked bio-photons with torsion fields because stars exhibit a flow of energy in the shape of a moving torus or torsion field. I remembered that funnel-like energy phenomena had shown up in my intuitive awareness before. I was delighted to begin to really learn about them from the scientific standpoint.

Dr. Swanson teaches in one online interview that an electron is always orbiting or cycling. "When electrons become synchronized they suddenly *see* each other" he says. In energy work we call it coming into coherence with a pattern we are working with. Swanson would say that when you shift your frequency or phase conjugation, you become aware of different electrons that are simultaneously now aware of you!

A parallel reality exists this way. These bio-photons at first could be on a different plain of awareness like sheets of paper. Each sheet of paper can be completely unaware of the one right next to it. When there is an opening into infinite possibilities, the planes of reality can become suddenly aware of each other and change can happen.

According to Swanson, there are torsion patterns in everything and this is how healing can happen at a distance. He states that bio-photons are produced by DNA messaging. These light pulses are holographic in nature, so any point of reference can link with any other aspect of the hologram, according to Swanson. He goes on to say that when torsion waves, that come from your attention, go somewhere out into infinite space, there is a sudden coherence that makes awareness come together.

This reminds me of the saying, "Where attention goes energy flows." An energetic dialogue can now happen. Swanson also states that torsion fields can travel forward and backward in time without losing energy! In Matrix Energetics this is called "time travel" and it allows for even more fluidity to physical reality as well as the possibility for change.

The new physics has so many important keys to understanding our underlying reality and to the nature of healing. It was exciting to realize that a respected physicist has established viable research into the arena of metaphysics, life force or energy and consciousness. Read Swanson's book and impress your friends!

To recap, today more people than ever are aware that we live in a very complicated or layered reality. Another way of interpreting our collective reality is that we are swimming in and through patterns in nature and in all matter, even in thought itself. So to begin to access the inherent intelligence that is all around us, we begin by getting out of our cognitive, "I already know" self. We need to look away from our learned stored database and instead ask the "unified field" an open ended question.

Pause and feel a current or directional impulse. I like to follow whatever gets my attention and seems interesting. Calmly let go of whether any of the answers matter at first. It becomes fun as your attention takes you into a whole lot of energy or sensations that are palpable.

As I have already said, Matrix Energetics is one of the leading consciousness technologies for transforming our personal reality with the unified field in a mutually beneficial way. If it is done accurately, it is as if you have dropped a pebble into a pond deep within you, yet all around you. The open ended question IS the pebble that you toss out into the field. Remember that in reality your heart is all around you as well. It will respond or interact with the universal intelligence. Our physiology needs to relax and shift into a secondary mode of paying attention. Be in the world, not of it for a moment. Possibilities pop up in every moment and become opportunities to engage with reality in a whole new way. Every point of reference is useful. It is always a real time assessment or measurement and can change instantly. You are interacting with a dynamic flow of possibilities.

Relax and be ready to see, feel or experience guidance. Have an innocent trust knowing that your unconscious self is always listening and is linked with the Source of all creation. Be more open minded to the unknown wholeness of the potential reality. Remember that fears manifest when we allow our lazy mind to run the show. The softer measurement of any event is what God offers us.

When in a session I will often experience a sudden awareness that my client is suddenly becoming much younger under my hands. I can see often a younger version of them. I might share the age that is showing up in my awareness and then I will learn that a traumatic event occurred at the age I mentioned. Each clue leads deeper into a pattern until the whole system reboots sometimes at multiple levels.

The client will often describe many sensations during all this and may recall memories later to me that match all the different phases of the session. I have seen chronic illness begin to change significantly, injuries lift and fade in intensity and overall moods improve. More positive changes may reveal themselves days after a session. It is always exciting to see.

I believe God wants us to play with the living fields of intelligent life that are all around us. Through this grace you are given the freedom to know and return to a state of wholeness. Only in hindsight can you fully see the miracles, but they do begin to shine like jewels behind you on the trail of life.

The most surprising healing for my own body continues to unfold with amazing shifts away from pain and illness. A dramatic example was when I received a cracked rib after falling face down on an icy road with arms out from holding my dog's leash. For several days I just lived with the situation. The pain kept increasing until the thought of someone coming to me for help with a broken rib had me wondering, how would I help that person? Before I knew it, I was seeing someone in front of me theoretically with complaints of a broken rib. Next thing I knew my own twisted rib was experienced moving into place! My pain was cut in half! Feeling my ribs for a moment in gratitude, I realized I had actually healed myself! I also knew I would know what to do if it were someone else. I imagined working on them and it mysteriously helped me!

I attended a new training this past year called "Master Harmonic Resonance Technology" presented by Richard Bartlett, D.C., N.D. As I already stated, he is the founder of Matrix Energetics. His new modality has exciting skill sets that relate to the body hologram. I immediately used the insights on my clients in my office upon my return from the training. Another new approach was to ask a client to turn over. I now can work also on the back side of the body while applying interesting powerful energy modules that bring together many dynamic possibilities!

On a different front, I recently explored tuning fork technology or sound vibration healing this year. I received a session from a certified tuning fork practitioner and friend from Spokane Washington. I met her during a visit to her city to teach and offer sessions. She was one of the many sessions I did, traveling around the area to remote locations. I was amazed to learn, as we visited, that she had met me years before in Teton Valley Idaho in 1991. She spoke of how much she missed the Teton Mountains and its energy. Nothing had ever felt the same since she moved to Spokane with her husband.

After her session with me we stayed in touch and before too long she came for a visit to see her old Teton stomping grounds. While in my town she gave me one of her tuning fork sessions. I noticed during the session that I could see bright colors with some of the tones. A rainbow lit up in my mind's eye when multiple sounds were struck, especially at its completion.

Overall I love the importance of sound and vibration in healing. During sessions and sometimes when meditating alone my voice spontaneously likes to do vocal tones including the typical "Om" sound. It reverbs through my whole system and can be useful on clients. Remember vibration is energy in motion. Sound is a distinct form of vibration.

Whether it is advanced quantum consciousness techniques, a tuning fork session or sounds and vocal tones applied with energy, I do believe there is a place for these tools in the field of healing. There are many consciousness based approaches to healing available at this time on the planet. Find what works for you.

15

ENERGY BLESSINGS

Back in the year 2011, the word "blessing" became a new area of interest for me. Previously, it was not often in my vocabulary. People sometimes implied that they thought I was blessed in certain ways. I never knew quite how to respond to them. I understood being grateful, deeply grateful to God, to Yeshua and to all the many messengers of God, for all they have done for me. I believed that any divine intervention is a "blessing." I also knew of the concept of being "blessed" by someone, but I otherwise did not think much about it. If a blessing is real, I tend to believe it would have to be an extension of God's love, affecting someone in a special way.

In 2011 I heard about a movement whose members are part of a group of people now in many parts of the world that has its origins with the "Oneness University" in India. These people are being led by two Indian Masters, one called the "Sri Bhagavan" and the other "Sri Amma." They established a large campus in India open to people seeking a path to enlightenment, from all over the world.

Many of the teachings center around the giving and receiving of a particular practice called a "deeksha blessing." I assumed this hands-on practice was attuning people energetically in some way. After learning of the movement showing up in my town and knowing some of the people drawn to "Oneness University," I looked it up on the Internet, to learn a bit more.

A year later, a few local people in their organization chose to have a booth at one of the local healing arts festivals. After they set up their booth and were checked in they offered the free deeksha to the public at our festival. The blessing giver's hands are placed on the top of a person's head for a few minutes. I would later learn of a "gazing" aspect to the deeksha offering that is less common.

In 2011 while working in a booth at the Sun Valley Wellness Festival I had a very unusual, unexpected experience with the *deeksha* blessing. A friend who was working at the booth next to mine introduced me to a man who was a member of the local Oneness Community. After brief introductions, he told me a little about the Oneness Community. He then asked about the work I was doing in my booth. I spoke about some of the Matrix Energetics experiences I have had with people and animals. I also spoke of my general enthusiasm for healing work. He became excited about the level of transformation I described to him. He seemed impressed to hear of all my experiences with miraculous outcomes and energy phenomena.

The crowd of people passing through the room had diminished, so he asked to sit down in my booth. I was not busy at the time. He looked at me with an expression of bold inquiry and asked if he could do the Oneness Blessing on me right now? I thought about it for a moment and felt my heart saying sure, why not?

I was already sitting in my chair, so he moved over and stood behind me and laid his hands on my head for a few minutes. I felt only his sincere presence, but somewhere in it, I realized that this was an opportunity to experience his Indian teacher, Sri Bhagavan. After a minute I realized I was not picking up on any presence. However I did begin to feel that something unique was being offered, but it needed my agreement as well. I sensed that this man was led to me by God. I did not want to overlook any of what was actually being offered.

With my awareness deepening, I entered into a kind of trust with what was happening. I began to sense a need for a female connection to assist this process. Through my connection with the man standing behind me, I tracked energetically to his teacher, Sri Bhagavan without actually feeling any personal connection with him. I suddenly sensed a connection was lining up and bigger forces were at work. With an awareness of certainty I could feel something unlocking deep within me. Something I had placed in a sort of secured quarantine within me could now be sent to Sri Bhagavan safely. I understood instantly I had fulfilled my part with the situation.

Awareness then spread through me that a burden had been lifted from me. I had passed a payload of heavy stuff on to one who seemed capable of receiving something needing this level of care. I knew it was from the thirteen months of walking between worlds back in the year 2000 and 2001. That assignment now felt complete. My new friend seemed done as he sat back down in the chair in front of me, most likely unaware of what had actually taken place.

To my surprise I then said, "Now I will bless you." I stood up and moved over to him, gently laying my hands on his head. I was aware of the spontaneous nature of my offer to do this and followed through obediently. I had never done something like that to anyone that I recall.

A few minutes passed, I sat down, sensing it was complete. We both smiled and could not talk for quite a while. As a familiar energetic deepening took place within me, I grew in need of him staying until it was complete. I needed a feeling of sacred space for a while since we were in a busy room full of people passing by now.

After a good ten minutes of silence, we tried a few times to speak and then laughed, because it was too difficult to form words. We were both feeling the energy still at work. When he finally spoke, he carefully said that he had not seen anyone receive the blessing quite like this. He said that when he first began to move into position to give me the Oneness Blessing, he saw many saintly souls, all coming forward wanting to bless me through him. As they began to line up all around him he paused, unclear about how to proceed. He decided to join with his teacher in India, as he had been taught to do by his Oneness Trainer.

I thanked him and tears began to flow down my cheeks. I admitted that I had not sensed any souls lining up to "bless me" but I did sense a female energy, perhaps Sri Amma, in the experience at one point. I also remembered asking for "Mother Mira" (Mother divine Guru from India) to assist if possible. My tears were a combination of momentary fear followed by relief that he had followed his heart and not been distracted by eager spirits. I felt certain that it was all over now and things felt complete. I told him that I appreciated him allowing me to fully integrate the experience without his getting up to leave.

He smiled and said, "I was not able to get up and would not do that to someone." Eventually we hugged, both still a little teary eyed before he left my booth. I was busy giving sessions to the public the rest of the day. Only later did I think about the unusual nature of it all.

∞

Later in 2011, I learned about a very different blessing experience being led by Glenda Green, the author of the remarkable book *LOVE WITHOUT END: Jesus Speaks*. I heard about it from the author's website. I thought about it and decided it was timely to learn what this author was presenting as a blessing experience from Jeshua's guidance.

On my way to my first Blessing seminar taught by Glenda Green, I felt Jeshua with me on the airplane, invisibly smiling, as I flew south to Arizona. His joy was surprising but reassuring. At the seminar, it was thrilling to meet others like me who also felt a personal connection with him, outside of organized religion. As the seminar unfolded, I sensed he was very pleased with my attention to his subtle direction and participation.

The blessing itself was a delight to discover on day two of the training. It actually included the four cardinal directions that I knew so well from native teachings. It also included the energy of specific stages of Jeshua's life and mission. When all the pieces came together, it was quite intriguing. It had a universality to it that really worked for me. I also noticed that the process of participating in giving the blessing did not involve touching anyone or even standing near anyone that was being blessed. I enjoyed the flowing openness of it all.

The Spiritis Blessing experience had many unique aspects to it. It was aimed inward first and then outward, as if our hearts had to become so full, at one point, that we instinctively share the energy and the light in every direction. But, more importantly, it involved connecting with HIM first and then with all the heavenly hosts and elemental levels of creation. By the end of the weekend I had become a certified member of the newly formed International Spiritis Blessing Team, led by Green in July of 2011. When I attended the training for a second time, I remember sensing the possibility that a more innate, almost organic phenomenon was possible if I continued to immerse myself in Jeshua's instruction.

Back home I discovered how amazing it felt to participate in different settings such as my home and outdoors. I enjoyed engaging in the eight or nine minute exercise by myself. The energies of love really invite you in as it does the work. Just to be clear, this blessing activity was not part of my energy session work with people in my office. Also no money is ever charged for offering the blessing.

At the next year's seminar early in the first day I sat listening and swaying to the music that signals break time is over, Jeshua prompted me to look at my energy. My aura was a moving dynamic flowing out of my heart up above my head and out, and then down and back into my body below. I felt Jeshua wanting me to understand that this was what I looked like, on other occasions to him. He was showing me a clue about what is happening when I am "in- energy" sometimes. I had seen this phenomenon before.

In my session work I see all kinds of small spiraling spinning energy with my visual sensitivity. That year I had seen drawings of this type of aura in a diagram on new aspects to look at surrounding quantum physics where energy moves in the shape of a Torus. I spoke of it in the last chapter.

When I got home from the second Spiritis Blessing seminar, I was nudged by spirit to do the blessing outside on my deck. The smoke from many forest fires had become unbearable in our area. My own lungs were beginning to hack and cough from the smoky atmosphere. As I began to complete the exercise, the air began to clear to my surprise! Within about thirty minutes it was clear in every direction for many miles, yet there was no wind! It had been very smoky for weeks up until then.

On another occasion I applied the blessing outside in response to the severe drought in our area. I had been feeling the parched conditions of the surrounding flora more each day. During the blessing protocol I started to smell and feel rain in and around me. Clouds began to show up soon after. To my delight it rained hard the next day, after many weeks of no rain.

I loved that this Spiritis Blessing addressed my interest in being involved with larger patterns, not just for a person to receive an energy blessing. Over the years I offered only a few Group Blessing times for a handful of people to sit and receive with pleasant results. My real interest was in the energy dynamic itself.

For many years I was aware of a need to address a whole town, a group of people and even the weather. Meditating and joining with a larger pattern was what I had already been doing for years. A practice of accessing aspects of the elemental field, along with above and below and then linking with the powerful gifts of Jeshua's life and unique path, did anchor something intriguing for me at a core level.

I came across a diagram on social media one day that struck me as a perfect description of the three geometric aspects of the Spiritis blessing when I experience it. I loved how the diagram matched, like layers of a puzzle that come together at the end. The first aspect was called "Field Patterning," and looked in the physics diagram, like many spirals coming together at the center. When in a native ceremony an individual will often stand and turn in or pivot in a clockwise direction. The earth's atmosphere and elements move in spirals as well.

The second image was called "Vector Geometries" and appeared to be many intersecting angles of lines, like the "seven sacred directions" already covered, plus every diagonal direction as well. When energetically facing each cardinal direction, there is an exchange of information that brings stability to oneself within the harmonic of nature.

The third image was called "Flow Dynamics" and perfectly depicted an active torsion field with energy flowing out the top and then curving out and then back in at the bottom. I became excited thinking about helping with the pollution on our planet, and overall health of the Earth. Perhaps this physical moving energy expression could assist in clearing and cleansing the larger fields of nature. I wondered if we could collectively trigger a type of clean up or transformation for the planet's atmosphere if more people could really activate a torsion effect from the heart.

I knew we would need people participating in it and doing it at many key locations on the planet. Trusting that Jeshua had things in hand, I just enjoyed the feeling of connecting with the elements of all three expressions in form for myself. I also realized my experiences with this may not match the other blessing giver participants. Perhaps each person brings a unique quality to the practice of this Spiritis Blessing.

At each Spiritis Blessing seminar after that, I continued to meet new friends from all over the world. In 2014 when I was on the airplane flying home from my third Spiritis blessing seminar with the author Glenda Green, Jeshua prompted me to begin writing down my own thoughts on the "blessing," as if I was teaching the seminar myself. I jotted down several pages, before I reached home. My notes would prove handy later that summer. Within a few weeks Glenda announced in an email the dates of her first Master Blessing Teachers online training. She would be offering it to seasoned attendees of her Spiritis Blessing Seminar beginning that June.

In the summer of 2014 I became one of about a dozen individuals worldwide, certified by Glenda Green, in her Master Blessing Teachers Seminar (on-line training). First I created my own teacher's manual from my notes and the class hand outs. This gave me a complete teaching manual. I then taught two small weekend workshops before the end of that year for some of my own interested clients.

For me the Spiritis Blessing technique fulfilled a unique cohesive pattern of expression for some situations in life. I have a sense that I have learned from it and integrated what I needed from it. I enjoy the feel of moving in an energetic way and accessing the patterns in nature when I feel inclined to do something dynamic. The Spiritis Blessing has useful tools in it for people at all levels of experience. I recommend learning to do it if the spirit moves a person. It is offered annually in Texas by its founder, Glenda Green.

∞

In late 2015 I picked up a book in hopes of learning more about the official deeksha blessings offered by the Oneness University initiated Trainers and the hands on blessings by baseline deeksha givers. If you recall I spoke about it in an earlier when I encountered this group in 2011. I was interested in this growing community of people and their concept of being "awake." Having had extensive experience with energy and awakening since the 1990's it was time to learn what they had to offer. My earlier chapters cover the topic. The book I found is about the Oneness blessing by a person with the last name of Rosenfeld. By reading it I learned only a basic overview of the Oneness University in India. I had hoped there would be more information on the history of that movement. I would learn more from new contacts years later.

In the book there were several very brief stories from people in their community describing their process of becoming awake. The term "awake" was being applied to many people without much of a description as to why. Rosenfeld's book eventually outlines the criteria for being awake, but it left me puzzled. I couldn't help but feel that they overuse the term or water it down. Her description of a spiritual awakening states that it is nothing more than a neurobiological shift. She writes the following. "For some the shift will be so subtle as to be barely noticeable, gradually integrating over time." Labeling anyone as part of an awakened elite group is truly unfortunate when they may have not actually awakened. I advise those given titles to dismiss them quickly. Stay open to the innocent true self and you will become an instrument of light that arrives on the scene in service to the ONE.

According to this book, their program assigns the term "awake" to people based on some observed verbal and mental practice of being in acceptance of what is. While that state of mind is healthier to live by, it does not really encompass attainment of enlightenment. Yet I do appreciate their commitment toward inner peace and a deep acceptance of life in general. Further, the daily devotion to connecting with, what they call the divine is a noble practice.

One of my concerns, however, is that their organization tallies the number of awakened people on the planet using their criteria. I believe that some of the most important embodied spiritual players on the planet are not visible, unless they want to be. Many more souls with tremendous value have chosen a path that may never find its way to their model or methods.

Counting up the number of awakened people is odd. Remember that awakening is all about a powerful process that lifts the veil in a profound way from the illusion of separateness. Counting up separate parts (people) is strange and certainly unimportant to a truly "awakened one." I should also add that there are many aspects about the Oneness University methods of energy transference or deeksha that are thankfully helping people. I do appreciate the giving of a form of assistance so freely with the deeksha. Any practice to initiate the readiness of a student towards an early stage of preliminary spiritual awakening is helpful but is as good as the givers readiness.

However, I believe being truly awake spiritually is remarkable and powerfully obvious. And even then there are many mysteries within it. All in all, it is important to emphasize that there is much more to being awake than is presented in Rosenfeld's book. Having said this, Oneness University was still an intrigue to me and like all types of blessings they each have something to offer when they are given with integrity.

In regards to becoming more awake, I knew there was so much more to the topic of being initiated energetically or made awake to ones authentic self. It helps to look deeply at ones name as well. It seems simple, but it can be useful to really go deep into the code-like nature of our names over time.

.

16

WHAT IS IN A NAME?

You may have noticed that as an author, I have an unusual name. When I write my full legal name, I put "SoLaMeé" in parenthesis so that it is included. It is the name I prefer to be called. I wrote in an earlier chapter about how it came about and the gifts that came back in 1991. It has been a burden at times to have a name that is not typical. Some days it would draw me inward just thinking about my name. I have never really liked the written appearance of it but it feels right when it is spoken. I questioned how it appeared to the world and would soul search the meaning behind it in my life as a whole. The universe eventually heard me and seemed to whisper, "Be patient and let the energy work its way through it." For the record my given name is Patricia. Growing up it was replaced with "Patty" to my family and friends. I have already shared it faded in my late twenties.

I learned long ago about the significance of a name. In college I majored in Sociology. I became fascinated with historic practices and patterns of groups of people across the earth. I had been a psychology major initially but noticed that social pressures, customs and expectations have significant impacts on a person. My studies of the North American Indian first exposed me to common practices of the naming and renaming. Other indigenous cultures as well have been known to rename a tribal member after a significant event took place. They did this in all likelihood because a big event changes a person. After bravely killing the charging bear, for instance, the tribe might honor that individual with a renaming ceremony. From that point on he would be called "Charging Bear."

In contrast to honorary renaming, I pondered my childhood memories of bullies and the shaming of someone by flinging a hurtful name

THE SPIRAL TO NOW, Patricia (SoLaMeé) Heneage

at them. I knew school yard taunts of "freckle face" and "fat lips" even from my brothers. Paying attention to the power of a name came early for me. I was called many names intended to wound me.

I chose over time to change my sense of self from the inside out. I listened and noticed how nature treated me and found my value there. Animals have always tended to like my energy. When the world is cruel and people reject some aspect of you, I recommend spending time in nature to attune your mind and heart to a more reliable mirror.

When I was in my teens my mother revealed to me that she had a different name originally growing up. I became very curious about how that happened. My mother explained that when she was born she was named "Judy." As she grew older it never felt like it matched her, she said. She put up with it like most people do when they dislike their given name. Her mother died unexpectedly when she was thirteen. The trauma of this loss impacted her deeply. After she turned eighteen she legally changed her name to "Lynne." This was bold but she implied that it gave her a new lease on life. She saw it almost as a way to finally find her own sense of self.

Why does a name matter so much? Should it? The spoken word has vibration and the power to bring about a change in a person's self esteem. Self talk as well can impact the forming of the individual. "I am....ugly, fat, stupid etc." as opposed to positive identifiers such as "I am pretty, smart, strong etc." Words make a difference. A name can really affect many aspects of a person. The health and happiness of people overall is often partly linked to the name they are given or the name they choose to be called.

Some names carry historic triggers. Different languages can influence the feel or experience of the spoken word and the name that is given to a person. Baby books often are thumbed through by new parents on the search for the "right" name. Looking up the meaning of a name can be very interesting and informative.

I was acutely aware over the years that society does not tend to look kindly on change. When it is your name and the prevailing social opinions are not in your favor it can ripple profoundly. Yet some people delight in the fresh energy of being given a new name. While others are almost shocked that something so sacred like your given name would be altered or disliked. I have encountered both of these types of people many times over the years.

In a previous chapter I explained how I encountered a common spiritual practice of receiving a new name. Eastern religious sects for thousands of years included the practice of receiving a new name from a teacher. I was exposed to a process where the name comes through an intuitive personal experience.

To recap, back in 1988 I went through an experience that opened up my awareness to an angelic energy. When it was complete I had received a flood of memories that felt celestial or from higher consciousness. I, along with the others at the workshop had received an angel name. I sounded it out slowly at first, when it came through. I heard "Aja lea Ta Ja." I also received a mudra that seemed to express my name silently with hand movements. It felt emotional and vulnerable at first but I liked the feel of it. I had many friends with new "spiritual" names from that workshop. I enjoyed asking each one to say their name for me so I could experience their names as well as share mine.

In an earlier chapter I explained how the above experience eventually led me to taking the new name "Tajalean" for a few years. Having accepted and embraced a new name that was not of my choosing took a leap of faith. It helped that I was surrounded by many friends and associates that also had new names. Most of us did not worry about making our names legal. They were just who we were socially and spiritually and they seemed to warm our nature.

Many years later I discovered a book on the Sanskrit language called The Language of the Gods by Judith M. Tyberg. I examined my angel name again out of curiosity and learned of a similar set of letters. "Anja li" means "to anoint, to dissolve." It certainly felt like I went through both of these within a few years of receiving my angel name.

I stated in an earlier chapter that by 1991 a new name came in that at the time was loosely translated to mean "river of the sun." I thought the name was linked with water more like a stream-of-the-sun. It came in slowly and I sounded it out, So-la-meé. At first I did not like it and wondered what to do. I knew to state it out load and feel it to sense the energetic connection behind it. I noticed it did not want to be spelled "mae" instead the energy was insisting on the letter "e" twice as in Solameé but with a French "e" at the end.

When I stood up and said it out loud I began to like it. The sound felt good but the letters, not so much. I decided to accept it. Within a few years I decided to put it on my personal bank checks but in parenthesis. People consistently remarked over the years that the name sounded good and fit me. Over time I learned that my name was similar to the biblical name of *Salome*. Some scholars referred to her as one of the "hand maidens" of Jesus. That name was common back then in the Middle East according to some.

Not long after becoming Solameé I visited the Wisconsin spiritual community. My new name was quickly accepted without any need for explanation. The Master Teacher there renamed many people, but in some cases the names were unexpected. I recall names like "Amazing" and "Glorious" even "Lala" was another person's name! Several residents were given a different name but not an uncommon one.

Master Teacher would just look at someone and say, "I will call you Jake as in Jacob's ladder." The man's real name was David. Most of the loyal students embraced the new name from that point on. It was a powerful really good way to quickly shed an identity that holds you into a pattern. It can get rather funny when referring to someone over the phone with the name, "Amazing." Amazing was a nice man who called me back once after I had left him a message. Imagine hearing, "Hi, this is Amazing." I paused and then realized who I was talking to.

In more recent years my inner guidance began to prompt me to loosen up the way my name is written and notice each syllable, as I did when it was first received. For a time it was like seeing each syllable as musical notes as in "So la meé." Having been a singer who loved music my whole life, this did not seem strange. I loved the movie and sound track of "The Sound of Music" and the lyrics "Do, Ray, Me, Fa, So, La, Tee" is all about musical notes. I played with it by singing the notes of "So" "La" and "Me". This may all seem silly but the push to begin to write it this way along with the extra French "e" was persistent so I obeyed.

Later this pulled apart emphasis on syllables began to haunt me in a strange way. I felt like a past life was coming to the surface and it was not an easy memory. Often a name is specially designed to trigger energetic things to open up. Deeper soul memories can be revealed and eventually integrate.

It all came together one day a couple of years later. I was working my way through an online comprehensive course on the roots of unified physics. The program covered the history of great thinkers in science and mathematics. In that module I came across an image of a woman with a name that immediately got my attention. She was Hypatia of Alexandria and known to be a mathematician, astronomer and teacher of the Neoplatonic School of philosophy. She lived from AD 370 – 415 in Alexandria Egypt. Her teachings were mostly lost but some accounts through her student's written works taught that everything in the natural world emanates from the One. She taught that human beings lack the mental capacity to fully comprehend ultimate reality.

Hypatia was well known and a highly educated woman. Her teachings valued science over superstition. She reportedly made the growing Christian community threatened. It was a time of civil unrest and riots were emerging around the region resulting in great change. Hypatia was a symbol of learning and science, which were largely identified by the early church with paganism. I discovered in my research that she was "torn to death" by an angry mob armed with sea shells! This sent a chill down my spine.

I then read on about how Hypatia loved the Library of Alexandria and all its treasured knowledge. It was created in the third century BC. It was the brain and heart of the ancient world but was burned to the ground not long after her death. I felt a sense of loss so deep for a moment my eyes became watery. The records estimate that 70,000 scrolls of lost advanced knowledge in mathematics, physics, biology, astronomy, literature, geography and medicine went up in flames around this time. It determined the unfortunate dark ages that followed.

Could it be that this is why I have a deep fear of mobs, especially riots? Becoming famous has never been on my bucket list either. It all began to make sense. Is it really a past life of mine? Who knows, but her sketched face on that document looked very familiar to me and left me feeling deep loss, almost grief, for a few days.

Eventually the pulled apart way of writing my name came to an end. On a practical level it needed to come together so my name would not be split up from one line to the next when written. The capitalization of the syllables in my name mattered however. I also could not just go back to how it used to be written.

After doing some soul searching I realized that if I do this, my name may draw attention to me and it might not all be good. A friend settled the matter for me. She said she liked my way of writing it with the bold capitalization of the syllables. It has been the hardest name to embrace and "wear" in my life, but I knew it was necessary. My name then became the current written form of *SoLaMeé.*

Since then I have wondered if more people are changing their names these days. I meet people all the time that have new names many of which they created themselves. I enjoy anything that gives people permission to express themselves authentically. These days we long for an age when mankind sees his neighbor as himself. Oh, what a world this could be.

17

LOVE IS THE JOURNEY

A few years before I began writing my life story I was made aware of an important old book called HE WALKED THE AMERICAS by L. Taylor Hansen. I decided to order it. After the book arrived, I learned from the introduction that this author had three master's degrees in archeology, anthropology and geology. She was the daughter of the co-originator of the Taylor-Wegener theory of continental drift. She was an authority on the natives of North and South America and studied among them for thirty years.

Hansen's book pulls together many legends, orally passed down from many different tribes. Taylor Hansen's book has numerous descriptions as told by the indigenous people, of a white man and prophet who arrived by boat first off the shores of Peru 2000 years ago! The legends indicate that he came from across the Pacific. This legendary man reportedly traveled to nearly every tribe throughout the Americas. Hansen came upon these stories of this bearded prophet from many indigenous tribes in the Americas during her thirty years of research and explorations.

He Walked the Americas conveys story after story about a white man 2000 years ago that was well known throughout the region of the Americas. He was called by some "the god of wind and water" because he walked to shore across the water from his vessel! He reportedly never gave a name for himself but instead asked the people he met to call him whatever they would like. This furthered the mystery surrounding his travels to the Americas.

According to Hansen's book and research there were many stories handed down through the different native oral traditions that speak of a man that appeared very different from them. His eyes were the color of the sea.

He reportedly could see into the future and heal all that ails. He dressed in a simple tunic with a belt. He had skin colored by the sun, long curly brown hair and a beard. He said he came from a land of many bearded men. He reportedly would be gifted with anything he needed. He often was gifted new sandals and clothing embroidered with golden thread around the hemline by the various tribes.

One might wonder at this juncture if there is proof that these stories were true. The author describes artifacts such as pottery and art with angel images and etched crosses on painted hands. Carbon dating was matched to the time of Jesus. The native stories all speak of his ability to heal the sick where ever he went and teach peace in a way no one ever had.

The *Bloody Sacrificers*, as they were called in the Central American regions, attempted to kill the mysterious prophet at different occasions, but to no avail. Many of their bloody ways died out during the long era of peace established by this prophet, only to return much later.

As I finished each story or chapter, I grew utterly lost in thought, almost overwhelmed with it all. I was struck with the possibility that Yeshua had done so much more during his life than anyone imagined. I thought about how the Bible's Jesus (Yeshua) is described as living only to the age of thirty-three and that his mission ended with his death and resurrection. I now knew in my heart that long ago, he had done even more than we have been told. He was miraculous in every way and could have done anything he was asked to do by the Creator. The commonly accepted written records of Jesus through scripture appear to have resisted viable evidence of his many travels well beyond the Middle East even from a young age.

What if his resurrection allowed him to be a fully physical presence again far beyond the early sightings? The bible does indicate he was seen multiple times after his crucifixion. I learned in Hansen's book that according to these indigenous tribes, this mysterious prophet left the region of his birth in the Middle East and traveled east, eventually heading out over the Pacific Ocean and on to the Americas. It was all too amazing to believe!

In the book, He Walked The Americas it states that over the centuries, natives did not want any of their people to tell the stories of their beloved prophet to outsiders, for fear it would not be believed and could harm their sacred memory of him. Some tribes even passed down ancient vows to never reveal the legends to any white man. One man was threatened and then blinded for revealing his knowledge of the prophet to researcher L. Taylor Hansen. The native man did it anyway because he believed it was time that the world knew the truth. She reported in her book the unfortunate loss of his sight but not his ability to speak and share the old stories.

As I read this book, I felt my soul being revived and renewed. This began to change my mind and open my heart to the possibility that truth *is* stranger than fiction. Since then, I have reread several sections of the book and found it has an energy that brings everything about the story of Jesus into a new light. Perhaps many people throughout the ages have been afraid to imagine the truth of all this. At the end of the book there is an indication of artifacts of importance being stolen or destroyed, leaving his journey lost to the ages. Jeshua's teachings appear to be spread across time and space. There are signs all over the globe, awaiting our heart's recognition.

This reminds me of a very moving quote from THE KEYS OF JESHUA by Glenda Green. Here Jeshua revealed insights to Glenda Green about his reason for taking a human form 2000 years ago.

"Each human being is a temple to the Creator's presence. When I came to Earth these temples, or mansions, were broken, fallen, or challenged with inadequate or wrong understanding. It was my love, my choice, and my duty to enter the temple of human form and to restore it from the inside out, that you would have a place to live, in which your spirit could flourish and fulfill its destiny. I came to prepare a place for you, and that place is within your very own being. Now it is up to each soul to choose whether or when to accept that restoration."

I can appreciate those who have too many painful memories associated with places of Christian faith or worship and seek God instead in the forest or on a mountaintop. They believe they were harmed from traditional conservative church leaders and their doctrine. They discovered that they do not need a minister to feel the love of their creator. Freedom to seek a relationship with God in a form that fits for each person is the most important path for mankind. I found jewels of wisdom in many unexpected places during my journey. I think that others can do the same.

No one on earth or in spirit has ever affected me as much as the presence of Jeshua. He has walked with me at several junctures in my life. I feel he has fulfilled his promise to find me, even when I could not find myself. I never needed anyone to tell me he was the beloved, my teacher and Master, but the intensity is still veiled for my protection.

I believe Jeshua respects and cares for all, even those who struggle to understand him and need to keep their distance from him for some reason. Jeshua/Jesus does not judge us, he simply informs us of better choices that are available to consider. Love is what he is. Love is what he teaches us to remember. His real mission has always been to assist us in our remembrance of God's love for us. Jeshua holds an eternal place for each of us in God's family. I believe he works in harmony with every faith, yet often behind the scenes. He wants us all to rejoin the ecstatic unity of life, light and love. No one can block your relationship with him—no one.

Through much contemplation over the years I now believe the energetic fall that I experienced around the year 2000, was God's plan to forge a pathway out of the deeper domains of hopelessness in our world. It was as if I was being sent into the depths of this world to retrieve those ready to make a change. I did not know what I was heading into, but trusted that God's love would carry me through it.

There are many unknowns to such an assignment. I discovered as a witness that true inner power is the ability to make a new choice when offered one. I have been assured that many souls made a new choice that gave them a doorway forward. I also had to decide to trust that I would make it out of those depths and regain access to my beloved life of light and joy. We can probably agree that faith will most assuredly strengthen the bridge between heaven and earth. Many of the important experiences in my life have included looking for the light or signature of God in a teaching or book, even within a group of people.

Eternal truth is found in the very foundation of this world, but it needs a witness to bring it forth and see it flower. I like to feel this guiding light of God coming to the forefront. Religious teachings have a place, but can also become a step away from what is known as the "living word." "My kingdom is not of this earth" is a famous line from the New Testament in the Bible. What is he reminding us of? He is reminding us of our true home in heaven with our creator. He did not speak of death as the way. He spoke of life as the way. He showed us a path that brings life back into every moment and connectivity with all of nature. He overcame death because he had not lost any connection with the eternal truth of his Source. Fundamentally he showed us how to choose faith and life over fear and death.

I cannot emphasize enough the importance of all the ways to join, or energetically connect with patterns, energy, and states of consciousness of the living fields or quantum states. Remember that the ancient Essene practices seemed simple at first, but they can transform a meditative experience. Communing is a powerful skill set. In the Essene practices they would merge with words or thoughts. Euphoric feelings arise directly out of pure awareness and can carry a powerful field effect. Euphoric feelings are unconditional and therefore limitless.

The source of all energy and order can reveal itself when we are being in the awareness of connectivity, without having any sense of ownership over it. You dissolve into it and it recreates you. Have you ever merged with the sound of water or the gentle feel of a mountain meadow? If you truly accessed it, there was no identity for a moment. You disappear into the sound, the feel, the smell and the vibration.

In recent years I have experienced Jeshua showing up to my surprise, at spiritual community events and revealing hidden players and teachers to me that were at work behind the scenes. Jesus and the other masters and angels offer assistance everywhere. To see them at work is a delightful awareness. Love is the true oneness spreading quietly between groups and organizations as the collective desire to move beyond fear and separation continues to expand.

Speaking of Masters, according to many sources, Mary Magdalene was known as Miriam in her time. I am certain that she was not in any way linked with a sinful life portrayed in the modern bible. That was one of the errors some sources seemed to repeat despite evidence to the contrary. Our current Pope Francis has officially declared that Mary Magdalene was NOT a prostitute. When Miriam met Yeshua/Jesus she was an honorable woman but a distressed and grieving widow with a daughter named Sarah age 9. To be a mother 2000 years ago in Palestine that had no living husband or male relative was to be pitied or worse. Jeshua would have understood this and protected her in some way. I do not believe they shared physical intimacy but I can imagine they shared a love beyond what the other disciples could understand.

Since then I have contemplated my spiritual name and have come to accept that I probably knew Mary Magdalene in that life. I also feel she was a mentor to me back then. I even think she taught me how to stay out of the lime light. I feel her spirit emerging from the vastness of space, quantum space. I feel her silently pointing the way out of the chaos toward the light of truth and freedom. She is so utterly without ego that it is very hard to detect her presence. I have wept some moments at her grave in past embodiments for the level of her sacrifice.

After a lot of contemplation I have come to believe that she was an advanced soul. Some books about her suggest she may have been more intelligent than most of the male disciples. Jealousy of her is documented in scripture. She was the one he reportedly entrusted with advanced teachings. She needed to be discreet in that age. Many knew she was a rare soul that could be killed if she revealed too much to those hungry for a sign of the master's presence months after his death. Some records suggest she left the Middle East with a small group of devoted souls to a new land where they would be safe.

I feel that perhaps over the ages since Miriam's lifetime as the beloved disciple, her spirit continued its devotion to truth and liberation for all. Like her when we devote our selves to Jeshua's ultimate message of awakening, it can be a difficult calling. I remember vividly the dynamic levels in consciousness I had to navigate at that time in my life. I understood it involved being an instrument in a powerful but innocent filtering of souls. I believe the activity of my being in this multidimensional discerning dynamic was the hardest thing I have ever been asked to do spiritually. I know that the light within assisted in my successful navigation through it.

18

THE POLITICS OF CHANGE

Many times before in my life I had been challenged spiritually, emotionally and mentally or psychically. Around 2015 I began to discover that I was slowly feeling more stress in my life. I was aware intuitively that some of my more ominous predictions for our world were starting to heat up, not unlike the planet itself. Since my book had published many countries had begun to address global warming. It had become a real understood threat by most of the world while our united states was in dire need of a wakeup call.

There were magnified political upheavals going on everywhere. Even more extreme weather events had taken place in our own country and intense cosmic solar flare activity and anomalies of all kinds were on the rise across the planet and solar system.

During some of my reflective moments or meditations, I realized I had to begin to really look at myself. I had to almost relearn how to cope with stress. I wondered some days why I was becoming so doubtful that everything will work out. There was a growing tension deep down inside me whittling away at my faith. I kept a good face on most of the time for friends and clients, but admitted at times that things were beginning to really test my energy. I could feel waves of anxiety all over the world on some days that made my hair stand on end.

For intuitively sensitive individuals like me it was a lot to absorb. I wondered at times if I was sensing a species wide concern about extinction level events coming. I received email newsletters from other teachers like myself reporting on the increased solar activity and subsequent emotional and psychic strain out there. They too felt the intensity of our world and knew humanity was starting to grow exponentially more chaotic.

My life after the initial launch of this book back in 2015 was a mix of stressful scenarios. I had to work very hard to correct errors in the early editions. The same errors would show back up after I had sent it to the self publisher company. I think I corrected some errors three times over in that year of new editions and printed copies.

Early on I hired one of the editors with the company for a substantial amount of money, but the service was limited. The woman did just one pass through the early manuscript. She also missed errors of mine. I asked some friends to read the early copy and report errors. Often they became so caught up in the intensity of my story that they could not remember where the errors were.

Unseen forces pushed me to work through it all and get my story written down anyway, as well as establish my copyright with the Library of Congress. I spent a lot of money with copyright registrations. Rewrites along with fresh expanded sections were becoming the routine. Overall the stops and starts with my book resulted in a few early editions that did not have the proof-reading they needed.

I did what I could to try and wrap it all up with the 2017 Special Edition, but deep down I felt unsatisfied with it all. I sold books to dozens of people locally as well as mailed copies off to family and friends and received warm responses that became some of my early endorsements and encouragement. I was invited to give author talks at our local libraries during those years, which was nice but attendance was low. I enjoyed giving the talks, yet knew something was still preventing me from a feeling of completion and peace with my life story.

On top of this, by early 2016 my life was inadvertently thrown into the world of local politics. My husband was solicited by locals to run for office in our county. We began to attend local monthly Democratic Party meetings more often and his campaign began to take shape. I noticed that I was increasingly surrounded by people that did not have much in common with me or my spiritual pursuits.

Now I was the wife of a candidate for county commissioner. This identity was perplexing at first to me. On the one hand I knew my husband better than anyone else, but on the other hand I learned that wives or spouses were often excluded from all strategy and planning. My husband noticed this and tried to include me. I went door to door with him at times and did other volunteering. He felt the stress like any candidate in a competitive election but kept with his teams approach for better or worse. He admitted some frustration with it all.

Election night 2016 was historic nationally when Hillary Clinton lost to Donald Trump by a slim number of Electoral College votes. She reportedly won the popular vote by 3 million votes! Trump's campaign all year had revealed many dirty tricks and unethical standards for a presidential nominee. We could only gasp in horror when he was announced as the winner. The world seemed to be tilting off course into chaos.

My husband lost his election locally as well. It was a quiet, sad, concerning time for many people. My sense was that humanity was about to be tested like never before because of Donald Trump's rise to power. Some would even say, because of him and the extreme version of the Republican Political party controlling both houses of government; we were now fighting for the soul of our country and the very earth's survival.

2017 brought me a wave of new clients and students. I was busy and generally calm despite the television and Facebook news cycles. I marched locally the day of the Women's March along with four million people across the world that cold January day. We all needed to protest the election results along with this new president's complete disregard for women's rights. It felt refreshing to see so many people becoming compelled to take action and speaking out about issues. Even though we lived in a red state politically, we saw many people out marching, as well as all across America.

I felt called to speak out at times through different outlets. I had to play my part as an American citizen. It seemed important to stay alert. I also realized my higher spiritual instincts about world events were beneath the surface of my awareness. Despite the seeming threat of this new president and his growing corrupt band of players, I knew that there was an intrinsic divine framework to all of what we call our existence. Everything is actually held lovingly in place by a larger energetic field than any human ego can fathom.

I pondered these deeper truths at times when the world events continued to grow chaotic. I needed to remember that what is happening to our world has a plan built into it. There is a way forward in all this! We are undergoing a massive wake up. We need to not lose out on our potential as human beings. We have to grab hold of our power to make new choices and act on our instincts en masse as voters and people of vision. We can no longer sit on the sidelines of life and assume it will all take care of itself.

That August 2017 was the North American total solar eclipse. It passed directly through our entire mountain valley and across the whole of the United States. My husband and I had been looking forward to this cosmic event for many years. We invited family and a few friends to witness it with us. I became caught up in the hosting of 17 people and overseeing food and housing at more than one location, but otherwise was excited about it. When the time finally came, I experienced a rush of emotion during the one minute and thirty-four second total blackout. We could hear cries of elation across the valley floor at times, while others were overcome with tears. (See the eclipse map below)

Everyone in our group cheered from their lawn chairs after it ended and clapped like happy fans of the big show. I was overcome with a need to rest and just be with the foreboding impressions about it all. I also could not help shake the feeling that something very vast and intelligent had peaked in on our tiny little planet for a brief timeless moment.

I later pondered the deeper aspects of what the eclipse all felt like and wrote a few short words about it. I found an amazing photo of the eclipse that was shared freely on Facebook. I could not find the author for it. I decided to use is with my words and frame it for my office. I wrote the following: "What is an eclipse? Passive, infinite potential or Yin energy steps in front of loud, intense, assertive Yang energy long enough to hush the noise and allow the greater cosmic ocean all around us to be experienced."

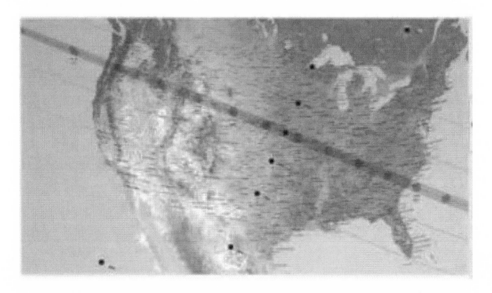

∞

In early 2018 my husband decided to run again for the office of county commissioner. This time we both wanted to do things differently. We teamed up and shared with each other all the things that we wanted to do. Our Democratic Party went through important changes as well. I had so many ideas and thoughts about strategy I began to brain storm often with

Bob and his team when I had any time free.

I was invited by the Democratic Party to become a precinct captain in my region of the valley. It was a small elected position in the party that had no opponent. I was on the primary ballot that May along with my husband who had a minor primary challenger. He won his primary and off we went full steam. During the primary he hired a bright young campaign manager that listened to his ideas and implemented strategy.

I found a woman neighbor interested in joining up with me as a deputy precinct captain for the Democratic Party. Together we went door to door for months and it restored some of my faith in humanity. So many people were friendly as we stepped up to their front door. Many were self proclaimed lifelong Republicans but did not turn us away. They often welcomed our information on candidates. Some admitted they were scared for our country and were open minded to Democratic candidates and ideas.

I organized two events for our party and watched a swell of new faces joining the cause. I helped with roadside sign waving during rush hours on both the primary and fall elections. By fall that meant very cold winter conditions on Teton Pass half way up the mountain. It felt good to be part of something in the local community again, but my own energy healing work had reduced considerably. I wondered if it was a political push back. I sensed a stress building deep within me again, but mostly just kept doing my part for my husband and our party.

In my spiritual teaching and energy healing work, I offered sessions and assistance each week when work came in. I knew how to help others in a variety of ways and received many thanks from the clients that I helped. It was always a nice break from politics and group dynamics. In sessions or classes I taught, I often reminded my clients that every moment we are in a flow of light and information whether we know it or not. Curiosity is essential to beginning the process of awakening to the inner witness. We must begin to peel away the defense mechanisms that block connectivity or the ability to be in contact with our higher mind.

I felt rejuvenated by the energy work on my clients and ready to head back to the demands of my husband's campaign. The ongoing barrage of news on the national political scene was also often in the center of my awareness. My personal meditation practice had fallen away in all the political activity. I began to notice that I was becoming way too defensive about some things. I understood this inner struggle was a trap to get into. The belief in the need to defend oneself, even with a deep spiritual foundation, can keep coming back until deeper programming is cleared. When the mind defends itself we are inevitably weakened, when we believe we are vulnerable in some way the inner light dims. Knowing this and staying on top of this are two different things.

Late that summer of 2018 I came across a book by Michael Singer called THE UNTETHERED SOUL. Michael Singer's book came to my attention when a student of mine mentioned it. She said the author's information sounded a lot like my meditation lessons and advice. She was amazed I had not read it before. The book apparently came out in 2013 and was a best seller. I was warmly validated by her praise. She went on to say that I seemed a lot like this author in my journey except that his awakening took place many years ago in the 1970's–80's. I jotted the title down, making a mental note not to let this information get by me. Not long after this I bought Singer's book online along with one called THE SURRENDER EXPERIMENT. It was all about his life story.

It is funny looking back on all of this. I was not always taking my own advice to stay out of the conflict of life. Here was a great teacher teaching many of my own insights in a fresh new way and who had forged his own path. I missed my inner still point. I missed having the time to unblock my energy and feel that coherence as it magnifies. When I was in my groove I was like a sensory instrument, able to detect the finer, subtler vibratory fields. I trusted that I would get it all back when I had the time to apply myself.

I not only studied his books for several months, I began a class at my office centered on the book's insights along with some other sources. I created a six week curriculum for four devoted students of mine. Together we all became really honest about the stress of life and the ways we can get back in touch with the seat of the soul.

To get me back in touch with my internal witness I became aware that I might need a real break but before my husband's campaign and our party activities reached an end. Being more of a witness to everything slowed down my energy in a good way but the pace of things made it hard.

In September I signed up for a two day event out of town that had a curious title. It was called "The Beautiful State" and was being offered by the Oneness University. If you recall, I have already mentioned this Oneness University and its main teachers in a previous chapter on blessings. Getting out of town for a break sounded great! I was ready to really focus on my personal spiritual energies.

The weekend workshop material was presented by two American Oneness Trainers named Lea and Elizabeth. It included plenty of visual video talks by the main teacher from India, Preethaji and at times her husband Krishnaji. His father is Sri Bhagavan and mother is Sri Amma. They were the master teachers for Oneness University for many years. I learned that Preethaji and her husband Krishnaji had been passed the responsibility of leading instruction from now on for what had been called Oneness University. It was now renamed O & O Academy under this younger couple's leadership.

The Beautiful State weekend course was very new and written by Preethaji. I appreciated its affordable price and accessibility. The training was interesting and useful. I received energy transmissions during the process from the two trainers. Each time it was offered, I made use of the energy blessing or "deeksha." It cleared my field and renewed my spirit. Before experiencing the deeksha energy blessing there was attention put on information around the topic of one's harmony or disharmony with oneself.

The preparing for the energy transmission or deeksha from the trainers began with what is known as holistic intentions. They taught that intentions can be the seeds you plant/sow in your field of awareness. A holistic intention always emerges from a beautiful connected state. I was told that when we move with right action or effort we are in a beautiful state. The beautiful state also always takes into consideration the well being of the whole.

We can choose to move back into the flow of life, light and infinite potential. To do this we must energetically reconnect. We allow life to flood back into our awareness. We can become aware of new ideas, information and places that are available. I understood that the divine is dependent on the observer or witness. The deeksha or *diksha* is a divine initiation. When done well, deeksha can initiate a neurobiological shift in the brain.

We are in an interconnected state with all things when harmony with others includes a sense of connection. Some might say that the deepest suffering within the human existence is loneliness or disconnection with others. There are only two states of consciousness for all of humanity at any given time. We are either in a connected, peaceful, grateful, loving, accepting state or we are in a fearful, suffering, disconnected state.

That made it simple! I was familiar with the older teaching of everything is either based in love or fear. I was looking at the material being presented here and realized many people needed it and it addressed important new insights. This was all not new to me but refreshing to review with the others in attendance. We were reminded that the experience of love is nourishment to the human brain and the human soul. We all could understand that love unites and restores connectivity. I appreciated that the universe had led me to this event.

Another area of intrigue for me was the energy of fight/flight. In my training in healing I knew well how it leads to disease and general distress. The fight/flight collective response follows an atmosphere of division, separation, politics, and gossip. There was plenty of that energy flowing back home in the heat of the election cycle. Power struggles were aplenty.

Preethaji's video lessons taught that in groups there can be a form of conscious leadership that can transform the work atmosphere into a collective whole that includes each person as an integral aspect of the whole, not unlike a family that has members that are essentially part of this whole. No one is excluded. We can move past the push/pull of a conflicted state or fear for survival, because everyone is "fed" and important. Every form in life itself is viewed as having a function that is valued. A beautiful state within the workplace can create a passion driven playing field of synchronicities. This was all great information to focus on and have energy work around.

During the "The Beautiful State" weekend training I received several important insights into my current unrest. I knew it was time to make a leap. During one of the breaks in the weekend, I felt drawn to look at a large full color book on display. It was mostly photos of the temple in India where these trainers had visited and received much of their training over the years. It had an effect on my energy just looking at the amazing geometric structure.

Later during one of the many meditation times I received a direct message from some old Indian sage I did not know. He said "Come, come!" I tried the idea on of traveling to India and noticed there was no resistance in me. Instead I sensed a friendly energy flowing in from across the planet. India had called me. I was also pleased and intrigued at how different the Oneness University felt overall.

When we came back from the break I shared with the group how for most of my life I had no interest in going to India. I arrived at this workshop thinking I was still that person, but then those images of that temple in India known as Ekam flooded in and spoke to me. I said I knew I probably needed to go. Everyone clapped in approval.

One of the trainers named Lea also worked as a travel guide it turned out. I said I would call her when I got home and firm up the commitment to join her group. She hugged me and said that for a small fee she would help me with a travel visa and airline tickets etc. This was another huge sign that I was being helped to take this leap into the unknown.

I learned from my new friend and trainer that The Oneness University had changed its name to O&O Academy. Many things had apparently changed in the organization the previous year so everything was new. It was sponsoring the first ever "Ekam Enlightenment Festival" in

December at the intriguing temple inland from the city of Chennai, India. I drove home feeling much better and ready to take on a new challenge.

When I got home I went online and booked my accommodations and reserved my ticket for the week long "Ekam Enlightenment Festival." I would be traveling with seven other people also making use of Lea as the travel guide and Oneness Trainer. We would be going across the planet farther than I had ever been. I was in some stress just thinking about all the things this would entail, but it also felt very exciting to witness to the stress and yet work through it.

My husband's campaign was less heavy on my mind as I finished out the campaign season with gusto. I would be on a big travel adventure in a few months. When November 2018 rolled around my husband won his election. I was very pleased. I knew he would do a great job. I noticed there was a sweep of democrats that took office in our own Teton County, Idaho and across the country. Perhaps not a massive blue wave took place across this country, but with all the gerrymandering by Republicans, it was a relief Democrats made a good return to some seats of leadership.

Over the next three months with the help of Lea, I worked on getting an Indian visa. I was gratefully shown how to begin the process online and even received help with filling out forms as well as getting my airline tickets lined out. When I had the completed form, I mailed it off to San Francisco with my passport and waited. I received a confirmation via email that it had been received and was being processed.

The difficulty came the following week when my passport and travel visa did not arrive on the appointed day. This was my passport! I would need it to travel out of the country. Having to replace it could take months! I called the national delivery company and discovered their records had it as delivered two days prior. I assured the man on the phone that it was not delivered to my address. He said he would track down the driver.

I then heard by phone that the driver insisted he put it near an aluminum planter near the front door. We do not have such a planter, I said! I was left filing a missing item report and put a $600.00 loss on the item. I called the federal agency that had mailed it and reported that it never arrived.

It was all as though time began to slow down. I meditated quietly on what might have happened and sensed the item was possibly nearby or stolen. I called all my neighbors and left messages asking if they had any package left at their door addressed to me. After that I jumped in my car and drove up to each house in our large subdivision. All the properties in our subdivision were on 4.5 acre lots. I found nothing.

After returning home I sat back down on my couch in silence. Not long after that my husband came home. I carefully told him my whole story. I shared my concern that this could be a big drag if I had to replace my passport and Visa. I said I may not be able to go on my trip. He listened and then walked outside and began to hike up to a nearby neighbor's home that I had already visited. He too thought the package might be somewhere in our subdivision.

Something made him look off in the distance to the house across the way. The sunlight reflected off something dull and silver near the door. He then hiked to that doorway and noticed an aluminum planter. He then just began lifting up items. Underneath the doormat completely hidden from view was my thin package with my passport inside! The driver for the delivery had placed it there.

My husband happily ran home and burst through the front door grinning from ear to ear and shouting, "I found it!" What a relief it was. Thank God for Bob's resolve to look again for the missing package with my passport! After opening the package I sat staring at it with its India travel Visa embedded. This was a test for sure and also something that can happen to anyone. Over the next month or so most everything slowly fell into place.

19

INDIA CALLED

Your awakening begins with the singular endeavor to make the journey toward the light and love of our source. As with any journey, you do not know where or when the journey truly begins, until you know there is a place to get to that is not where you are. I can still remember the first time those words flowed through me back in 1993.

At this time in 2018 I realized that I was not really where I wanted to be in my life. I loved my session work. It was a gratifying vocation yet I felt a little bored. My father had coincidentally gifted me money. With this money I could make bold choices. I knew where I was being directed. India had called me to her door. I knew it was time to jump into the adventure again and watch the miracle of enlightenment. This time I was a mature woman and seasoned veteran in the field of transformational healing and energy upgrades.

Just before the departure date for the trip my new colleague and friend Lea had plans to come to Jackson Hole, WY. She decided to do The Beautiful State weekend course near my area with a local Oneness Trainer named Edie. Despite the fact that I had already attended one of those weekends, I signed up as soon as I knew. I figured it could only benefit my preparation for the big trip to India. A friend of mine decided to sign up also. The two of us headed over the mountain pass that December day in my car. We found our way to the large room upstairs at a physical therapy business in downtown Jackson Hole. We settled into some seats after greeting other participants.

As the event was beginning to unfold, I noticed something near the door of the room not of this world. It was the spirit of a large man in an ornate guard like attire from Egypt. He was tall, dark skinned and standing near the door looking at me. He appeared to be an Egyptian guard of high rank wearing the headdress of a jackal also known as Anubis. I thought to myself, is that the god of the dead? I thought wow, now that is quite a sight. He wore an arm bracelet of gold wrapped around his upper bicep. Suddenly my arm had one of those bracelets on it! I shuddered for a moment, but also knew it was OK to just trust it. He then disappeared. I didn't feel I could share this with anyone at the time.

The weekend training went well but was familiar. I had attended the first time in September. The energy transmissions or deeksha were good and my meditations revealed many interesting things. I offered deeksha at the end to those who wanted it along with the others that were trained now.

As everyone was gathering their personal items to leave I knew I needed to speak with Lea the trainer and travel guide about the packing list for India. Somehow it was missing from my emails leaving me with many questions. I remembered that weeks earlier she had referred to it in some of the group messages, but I could not find it.

Once I had her attention I noticed she seemed irritated that I had not downloaded the "WhatsApp" software for free messaging overseas. She said she had placed the packing list already on our group site with that App. She said she will be using it to communicate with everyone during the trip and it was important to have it already loaded. She took my phone and helped me find it and set it up. Standing there watching her made me realize I had just swerved away from a proverbial cliff if I had not spoken with her. I now could communicate with the group overseas on a free message app. She said she will send the packing list again and then turned on her heel to prepare to head out.

I headed home remembering that God is with me and even now it has all worked out in time. The packing list came in my phone by the time I got home and it was a long list. I would be on the plane in two days. A part of me realized I will have to really take care of myself and not just assume others will be looking out for me. Lea had an independent nature that required her people to travel wisely with or without her. I resolved that tomorrow I will shop for whatever I need for the trip.

I was excited as I packed for the trip my last day. I was curious about what might be similar to what I experienced back in 1991-92 during those high energy talks and sessions in Wisconsin with Master Teacher. I also was open to what India could offer me in terms of awakening in general that I did not yet know of. It was time to simply make the trip across the planet where so many other seekers have gone since time began.

I would be attending the seven day Ekam Enlightenment Festival event in December 2018 along with 2000 people from over 60 countries. We would be given seven days of instruction and periods of high energy upgrades at the very unique and large temple like structure called Ekam inland from Chennai India.

My journey to India was an adventure all by itself. I drove myself to the Boise Idaho airport singing to a CD of the Moola Mantra by Deva Premal. Once there I met the seven people all traveling with Lea. Our travel guide was the last to arrive, cutting it close. She had booked all of us from that airport with a connection in Seattle all the way to India.

When we boarded in Seattle it was the largest airplane I have ever been on. I was traveling on Emirates Airlines and it was a first class operation. Because it was going to be a 17 hour flight I had chosen to upgrade to business class months earlier when the tickets were booked.

Not long after I boarded I became fascinated with my accommodations. I had a large seat that stretched out into a bed and delightful food and beverage items. The flight attendant was very helpful at showing me how everything worked. I finally settled on a movie and relaxed. It was not until after I had watched half of the movie that I realized our airplane had not left the hanger! They announced over the loud speaker that there had been electrical/computer errors discovered during the preflight inspection. It had to be corrected, but we could now depart. I was calm and intrigued by it all. It had been almost two hours at the hanger!

I was very comfortable most of the way there. The flight route took us over the North Pole, with a plane change and connection in Dubai. However, after landing in Dubai, we barely made our connection due to the delay in Seattle. Nearly 150 people on our flight needed to make the connection to an India flight long held up by our flight. The airport had to usher us quickly as a mob through the massive terminal to our distant gate. Still I felt calm yet alert through it all.

We landed at 3 am India time. It was a wet hot atmosphere as we departed the airport looking for our prearranged taxis. By 5 AM we checked into our rooms at a very beautiful hotel and rested a little until breakfast. I got to know my new friend Geneal a bit as we chilled most of the day in our shared room. She had also attended the September Beautiful State workshop and we had become acquainted then. It was nice to see her and visit.

The following day I joined a few others from our group to visit the city for shopping in a shared taxi. I spoke with our taxi driver at one point while waiting for a few of the shoppers in our group. He spoke very good English and was happy to tell me more about the sites nearby.

I asked him about a very old cathedral we had passed by. He explained that this was the original site of the church founded in India by St. Thomas. He enjoyed telling me the story of St. Thomas' reluctant mission to

India as a disciple and how he later produced many famous miracles. I loved that I was India and yet I was learning about Jesus' disciple Thomas. God was filling my cup each day with little extras.

After our brief stay in the big coastal city of Chennai for the jet lag, we loaded into pre-reserved cab rides for the three hour final leg into the countryside to our respective campuses. The roads were busy and chaotic. The driver noticed I was new to India and laughed a bit. It was becoming dark so I settled into the ride and tried not to get motion sick from the jarring driving style. We arrived late in the evening to Campus 3.

After registering at the front office, I eventually was able to settle into my assigned room. First I met my new roommate and we had an instant sense of soul connection and friendship. Her name was Noreen and she was an American who lived in Italy with her Italian husband. They had and raised two sons there. She had been to this campus and the Oneness University several times before and knew much of the history. She was also my travel guide's, sister! We were given a room on the second floor with a balcony. Noreen explained some of the rules of the bathrooms and some campus etiquette. We laughed and talked a lot before I fell asleep easily.

When I woke early for morning meditation, I joined many others as we gathered at a corner of the campus called The Sacred Space. A soft chanting music filtered through the air. I looked for a spot to sit with many others and noticed the rock garden area first. It seemed like a harsh place to sit. For some reason I thought about someone hitting the hard surface if they fell over. Instead I moved over to the soft, wet grassy area and settled on a yoga mat. The chanting sounds over the speakers were the words, "Humsa so hum Akam" which meant "I am you. You are me. All that exits is the One." Eventually I would know this chant well and hear it in my sleep.

The first morning that week my roommate Noreen discovered she had a terribly hard mattress. She was in a lot of pain in her neck that morning. After examining it I suggested she remove the "mattress" from the room. I had noticed that my mattress was very good, even comfortable.

Noreen did not want to complain to the monks. She was nearly in tears from the thought of having to sleep on that painful mattress a second night. I agreed to speak on her behalf to the head office and request a new mattress. I headed out and took care of this for her. Later I did energy healing work on her in our room and it cleared some of the distress. She thanked me as we walked to the buses. The new mattress was there by the end of day to her great relief.

That first day after breakfast we were transported by buses to a nearby campus for a special opening fire ceremony called a Puja Hamas presented by the senior monks. It was designed to remove all obstacles to enlightenment. It was longer than I would have liked.

After nearly three hours I began to fade in energy physically. As we headed back to our campus and on to lunch, I realized I was too wiped out to take part in the afternoon trip to Ekam. By body felt very strangely weak. It did not feel like it was just lingering jet lag. My organs seemed to be in some sort of stress.

That afternoon I returned to my room and fell asleep for several hours and missed dinner. When my roommate arrived late she asked if I was taking electrolytes every day. I said no, I did not know I needed to. She became alarmed and ran off to get me a small packet of powder to stir in water and drink.

I learned that the water in India was typically distilled water. This meant it had zero minerals and it is not enough for good health. After a few days you feel like nothing is hydrating you. I found in my luggage some Air Borne brand vitamins and minerals for airline travel that I had bought when I shopped with the packing list. I thought they were for avoiding airline transmitted colds and flu. I now realized I would need to take some in water each day until my return home.

The following morning I felt intuitively guided away from the sacred space meditation area. I knew I needed to find a place of my own to sit and soak in the silence before breakfast. I wanted the softness of a chair or couch. I felt weak. I spied a quiet spot with a sitting area on the open air second floor of one of the main buildings. After I settled comfortably on a cushion, I could hear the sweet sounds of birds and early morning bustle of nature. It was a meditation of peaceful cellular rest.

I joined everyone for breakfast. I settled down at a table with familiar faces and learned to my alarm that something had happened at the group meditation site that morning. I of course had missed it when I discreetly chose not to join the others for meditation at The Sacred Space. One of the women from Jackson Hole named Edie sat down at the table. She reported to us what she knew. She said that a man collapsed in the rock garden area during meditation and was taken away in an ambulance. This was the cause for all the noise during the morning meditation.

We learned by the end of breakfast that he had died. I froze for a moment lost in thought. Death wow! Was it too far a stretch to imagine myself dying as well had I not rested yesterday and got started on those electrolytes? I had this odd feeling that I had come close to something seriously fatal. My internal guidance had also kept me away from the stressful incident that morning.

Like so many things in India, I would learn that the people there take everything in stride. The monks seemed to avoid the topic of this man's death at first. We learned a couple of days later that the deceased man was Japanese and that he had come with about a dozen others from Japan.

The monk shared that on the day he died a woman staying at one of the other campus and participating in the festival, gave birth to a healthy boy. The monk implied that this was important news as well. Indeed it was important news. It was all an unexpected aspect to the general atmosphere of this festival.

Keep in mind that any interest in moving toward enlightened states of consciousness requires a desire to clear away the old patterns or imprints before bright insights begin to flow across your consciousness. Just attending such an event and being there is generally not enough to experience such things. All patterns of protecting the inner self must be addressed.

I was facing my own death in a way. I could not deny it. I was seeing primal layers of self protection taking care of me. There are deep seated fears of harm coming to our bodies, our minds and our hearts in everyone. The fear of death is a very primal thing. Some people change when in a large group and become disconnected from their own best interests.

Other times people are too preoccupied with self needs and miss the group energy that is being offered. I was looking at it all with great humility. It was interesting to look back on my decision to stay on campus and sleep that first afternoon, not to mention meditating alone that morning. With each decision I made, I noticed I was a "witness" to my thoughts and my nervous systems subtle reactions.

The following day I had to be reminded to come back to the early morning group meditation at the Sacred Space area of the campus. I walked through the quiet morning air as others came from different points of the campus to the designated meditation area. Once there, I noticed it was uncomfortable at first to sit but settled in. Thoughts lingered inside me of the man who died while meditating earlier in the week.

The previous summer's "Untethered Soul" book study and weekly class prepared me well for this trip to India. Sitting at breakfast my mind wandered to thoughts of a ripple across a pond when the breeze blows or a twig gets tossed onto its surface. Your skin is the surface of that pond. I was very aware of my energy and my nervous system.

I tracked my own posture as it changed or adjusted to a seeming stimulus. To be the witness as a practice is the way to transform the consciousness of the self. I knew I needed to be non-judgmental and yet inclusive as I watched all that was beginning to happen around me. My mind for the most part was able to be quiet and not indulge in analysis when something seemed strange or unexpected.

One of the discussions presented early in the week by one of monk instructors was about all the ways we may become blocked from reaching higher states in consciousness. The monk's name was Kiranji. We all sat in one of the large meditation halls on Campus 3 one morning after breakfast. He explained that often an individual doubts that they are always protected by the divine.

Many thoughts ran around in me as I sat listening. I did feel safe, I also felt aware of a need to be alert or at least awake to my inner guide. Eventually I remembered this topic was a similar topic at times with my students over the years who struggle with their faith in the divine. They sometimes admitted that they doubted that enlightenment was even possible. I used to respond by telling my students that it helps to first establish an underlying faith in God when accessing higher states of consciousness. This was all a good general topic to cover early.

The monk Kiranji listed off three common blocks to discovering one's connection with the divine. Ingratitude - People focus on what did not happen instead of what did happen that was actually fortunate. Blaming the self, life in general, or blaming others even God is the second block. The third or last block involves destructive perceptions about the divine itself, such as "God tests us." He suggested noticing beliefs that undermine a feeling of connection with God and being protected by God overall. The monk went on to add that it is the untruths that are the inner enemy, but with consistent self inquiry we can discover what IS true.

I would like to emphasize there are several practical considerations that are helpful to maintaining a healthy connection with the endeavor to reach enlightened states. I was happy that they provided some insights into optimum effectiveness at the festival. They said that attendees should try to limit their intake of food and stay hydrated.

The monk suggested that participants limit talking by practicing "mona" or silence as often as possible. Kiranji said it helps to be conscious also of time externally while being free of its clutches internally. Finally he suggested letting your presence be like honey – sweet, as you interact with others in the group. I believe these were all very helpful and useful for all levels of experience at any event that involves a lot of intensity and energy.

Day two I was excited to experience my first trip to Ekam. We would soon be seeing the mystical structure I first saw in a photo back in

September while at the weekend Beautiful State training. We were transported on buses each day for about thirty minutes in order to arrive at the steps of Ekam. Our foot wear had to be removed and everyone entering the structure had to be searched or walk through a metal detector. We walked quietly up three flights of stairs and around the entire balcony and outer area of the upper structure before bowing and entering the great hall.

Here is a photo I took of the massive structure of Ekam from a book I bought while there. The entire structure was made mostly of white marble with many intricate inlays of stone. Once we entered, I could barely make out the far center of the room where there was a roped off white marble pedestal with a large golden globe or sphere on it. I was content finding a floor cushion with my new friend Noreen more toward the back.

There were thousands of seekers from all over the world needing to get settled into floor cushions and chairs before our instructions for the week began. This took well over an hour. Our host Krishnaji is a relatively young man that appeared to be in his early forties. He was a charming communicator. His spiritual development began at a young age because of his father's insight to create a school of enlightenment for young children. The story goes that a large bright sphere of light was with his father Sri Bhagavan from a young age before disappearing from his awareness after he turned twenty one.

Many years later the bright golden orb came to his son one day when he was ten years old. The young Krishnaji asked his father about it. His father suggested he try to convey it to one of his class mates. Without thinking the young boy put his hands on his class mates head and the student became aware of a bright immanence. Krishnaji's father and mother Sri Amma led this school for children for many years. As the boy grew into a man he went on to become a world teacher along with his wife Preethaji. Together they created many successful teaching endeavors and companies worldwide.

I sat with the masses of eager seekers in the great hall at Ekam. Krishnaji was received with applause at first. His face was projected onto a large screen so we could see him clearly. He began by saying that with regard to enlightenment, he believed there were many states possible. It may even be infinite, he said. For the purpose of instruction during this festival, he was going to focus on just five. The first state he said was identified as The Witness State, or known in the ancient language as "Sthitha Prajna." How funny! I had been immersed in this practice now for months almost as though I was being prepared for something. Krishnaji's wife is Preethaji and spiritually is impressive. She spoke next. She presented her thoughts and messages each day to the large hall with great precision. She had a compelling presence and voice.

Preethaji and her husband taught that once enlightenment is attained fully, you are in a state of unwavering wisdom. You are unperturbed by the movement of thought or the movement of life. You are an observer, a witness to the flow of life-neither averse to any experience nor craving to hold on to the experience. Equanimity is a word that comes to mind.

Krishnaji taught that the second state of enlightenment is called "Bliss", while "Ananda" is the ancient word for bliss. "Aa," means from all sides, while the word "Nanda" means Joy. In this spiritual state of consciousness, joy pours into you from all sides. Every experience of life feels alive, blissful; seeing, listening, talking, walking, solitude or relating. Your consciousness is like a sponge that soaks up bliss from the universe.

I loved the simplicity of so much of the messages being presented. Sometimes the Hindu methods are steeped in mystery and complexity. The mystical experience can often elude the seeker far longer than many would believe. I personally have experienced Bliss before and know it by the surge of intense energy that floods my nervous system and emotional field from all directions. It is hard not to voice a response of delight. My body sometimes feels a ripple of heat followed by a jolt up my spine. I need to be free to move a little to fully engage with it.

Each lesson of the day at Ekam was interspersed with long periods of music and meditation time. At first the crowded room was something I had to adjust to. I moved around and tried different locations during the week. That first day I knew I needed to make use of this energy any way I could and not just sit with familiar faces. First I moved to the far back near some empty chairs.

After a while I could sense the energy and felt comfortable as vivid images flooded my awareness during a meditation. I was seeing myself in ancient Mexico for some reason. The colors were intense as I flew over pyramids and saw a prominent leader's massive golden headdress. The Mayan calendar came into view. The images flashed by quickly. I thought, OK this is not what I expected.

As the music started again and the lights dimmed I let go completely to the energy of this building and the time/space of the moment. Surges of energy came and went. Then suddenly to my right there was a distinct opening in the atmosphere. Brilliant silver energy poured in and pierced by heart. My body leaped and arched from the intensity. I almost stood up. Something guided me to stay seated in my chair.

The next thing I knew a brilliant golden light was now shooting into me from that same opening in the air to my right. This time I could make out a powerful geometric pattern was forming in me. The energy was activating something and waves of energy were expanding outward from a deep center within. My hand reached down to the side of my chair spontaneously and then my left hand did as well. This time the left hand could feel warm currents of energy below my chair. The room disappeared and I felt like a navigator on a cosmic sail boat tracking my voyage with the stars all around me. I felt thrilled and confident in my ability to track with my hand a path to a new world! My chair was somehow my vessel! It faded as the lights came back on and it was time to soon head back to our buses.

Back at the campus the following morning during breakfast I was asked how I was doing by one of the veteran oneness trainers. I shared my experience of the silver and golden energy that had pierced me admitting it almost felt like a powerful female and male energy blessing me personally. Was it Sri Bhagavan and Sri Amma, the former founders of this place activating my field? The woman loved that I had shared my experience with her. She said it was a great story to share with others and hoped I would share more with her later.

The lessons unfolded each day after we settled into a seat in the great hall of Ekam. Jeshua/Jesus appeared a couple of times watching me from across the room. He seemed to be nodding approval. He appeared another time during a deeper meditation standing in a large passageway shaped like a keyhole opening that was lit with soft golden light. I sensed I was coming closer to an important threshold in my life.

During the next instruction period we learned that the third state of enlightenment, according to Preetaji and her husband Krishnaji, is called the state of "Thou Art That" or known in the ancient language as "Tat Tvan Asi." You are in a completely non dual state of consciousness. You go beyond body identification. You go beyond all limiting mind projections or past identifications. You find yourself in a state without any limiting mind projected definitions. You are in a state of being ONE.

In the past when I have experienced this state my body disappears completely and I explode into an infinite sense of expansiveness. Joy comes too with this intense nearly indescribable liberation of form. My earliest experiences in this energy happened through the teachings embedded within the book, A Course In Miracles.

I was taught years ago to open up to the realization that "I am not a body, I am free, and I am still as God created me!" Laughter, even tears can spontaneously flow for no apparent reason as the reality of the truth dawns across your mind and heart. The physical body often starts to vibrate from within at a high rate of speed. You feel like a live wire.

I noticed many people around the great hall appearing to be in this type of energy. It was loud at times. Laughter and shouts of joy were a common sound as well as crying. Some of the people in the room appeared to be almost throwing up energy at times. They would hunch over and cough a lot. That was not something I had ever seen happen from a lot of high spiritual energy. Perhaps some sort of purging was taking place with those people. I should add that a number of festival attendees were obviously sick with colds, adding to the sounds in the large room.

Later in the week we learned that the fourth state of enlightenment is called "The Great Compassion," known in the ancient language as "Maha Karuna." Krishnaji taught that one must gaze deeply into the nature of all suffering and recognize that the pain of all beings is actually being felt by your heart but you have buried it. I understood this one well and knew I was beginning to reawaken to this larger pattern of energy called the pain of the world. They taught that you awaken to the connectivity of oneness with all human experience. A preliminary state often produces a great love for your fellow man.

During this festival day we arrived in the evening and spent the whole night in the massive structure awake and in and out of energy and instruction. I remember seeing and feeling bright soft yellow light everywhere that night and the awareness of a Kwan Yin type energy. I also remember time traveling to other places on our planet in vivid detail. I felt surges of love for our earth and its rich biosphere.

My mind saw images of places all over the planet. One place had a large crowd gathered outdoors somewhere in Mexico around a teacher of wisdom and healing. It was a woman with brown skin late middle age. I could see her white dress up close with colorful embroidery but not her face. Moments later I was back in the awareness of the temple hearing the emotional sounds of people in energy all around me. Many were also asleep by now and stretched out all over the massive floor.

I thought back to many years ago when I visited that spiritual community in Wisconsin, how powerful it was to feel the pain of this world for even a few moments. I remember I held it back at first, as the sheer volume and magnitude of this energy began to build up around me. It terrified me until a fellow student and teacher at the Wisconsin community reminded me that it was all just energy. She said simply "just give it to God" or let it go up to God. I realized it was not meant to be held onto or controlled.

Back then when I was feeling the pain of the world, the dark but vibrant energy surged in from all directions and then shot up through me and out of the top of my head, to my great relief. I remember I wept for the world for a moment with gusto and it all then released even more. The energy was free and reconnected to its source. I did not have to solve it, fix it, or change it. I just needed to allow it to pass through me and go to its source. Since that time many years ago I have looked upon all people as another myself. As with the concept of a hologram, there is a little bit of me in everyone and everything. I understood that nothing was ever really separate at all. These memories felt potent and meaningful to recall.

It had been an all night vigil at Ekam offering the experience of the The Great Compassion. With the sun coming up in the sky, we all piled onto the many empty buses at the front gates of Ekam. We headed back to our campuses for breakfast. It had been a long night for some. I felt clear and awake but ready for nourishment.

Later that day we were invited to go into the foothills of the countryside and hike a short distance. We sat and meditated all over the rocky forest area. It was the second hike of the week. It felt better overall because this time there were hundreds less people walking on the trail. This allowed for everyone to take in the meditation out in nature without so many festival seekers. I enjoyed softly singing up on a hill with many others the chant, "Humsa So Hum Akam" repeatedly as it echoed across the rocky foothills.

The next afternoon we went again to Ekam and the great hall. Outside Ekam many of us took photos of each other in front of the huge temple structure. My new friend and roommate Noreen snapped this photo of me. I felt truly blessed deep within my heart to have made this journey to India. It was a journey into my hearts inner temple.

It was time to experience the fifth state of enlightenment taught at the Ekam Enlightenment Festival. It was called "The State of Cosmic Consciousness" known in the ancient language as "Aham Brahmasmin." This tends to be an explosive enlightened state of consciousness. It is one in which the individual self has realized its inseparability from the cosmic self or ever expanding universal self. You are all forms and formless. You are all existence and beyond it. You are the macro and the micro universe. In early stages of it some may travel through intense experiences of being at one with such states as water, fire, air, earth. Preetaji taught us that you also realize you are the One.

In my experience this state is more uncommon and includes a complete turning inside out energetically. It is so profound that you are fully lifted up into what is known as the Greater Reality. You cannot make this happen. It is with the assistance of Reality. It recognizes you first.

As you realize you want reality much more than anything else in existence, you manifest a powerful longing. Nothing but your true home is where you want to be! There is a great yearning and you move beyond all aspects of the universe. Particle mass of all kinds is recognized suddenly as the illusion or dream of physical existence. This is the real awakening at its most transformative state. When you return to the awareness of being back in the world of dense bodies and things, your cells are not the same.

When this took place for me years ago, I remember not being able to walk or speak at first. It was all very strange and difficult to have to function in these very dense bodies. I knew as before it was all a dream. I also knew I would never be the same again. The physical world seemed dense and dim for a while.

Back in those days the daily energy experiences assisted me in finding the opening into the greater reality again and again until I became familiar with the launch up into the brighter states of consciousness. I also became comfortable with the natural falling back down into the denser realities of physicality. I wrote about all this in great detail in an earlier chapter.

I understood I was here at Ekam to complete more of my own experiences of oneness and all that came with it. I also knew I was officially awake to the truth of what I was as before. I was of my source, which was LOVE. I was also NOT of this world, but I could stay and assist in the great undoing of separation in my own way. I could feel the energy in Ekam offered the same platform of great potential for awakening humanity as Wisconsin did for me so many years ago.

I know that our daily existence includes a flow of impressions and experiences that may not always appear "awake" or "enlightened." I knew to not judge self or others. The practice of being in the witness state is a foundational tool that can assist you in bringing yourself back to a perceptional lens of seeing where you really are.

In the course of daily life, harmony and disharmony may still fluctuate at some times more than others. What shows up in your lens is meant for inquiry and examination momentarily. Remember you are a part of a flow of existence. It has many dimensions to it. I believe meditation should include a full spectrum of experiences from deep rest on up to highly energetic and expansive states when desired and possible. I always say it is the quality of the meditation not the quantity or length of time spent that brings the most satisfying outcomes.

On the last full night of instruction and energy I again found my awareness swept away to other beautiful remote places on earth. I saw vivid images of myself in a canoe for example on the Amazon River paddling with another person. I felt strong and capable even fearless. That is not something I can even imagine wanting to do in real life! Hours later the meditation wound down.

It was then time to celebrate the last night of the festival with everyone moving into a more playful mood. A rock band with musicians from South American country's played with gusto. I danced joyfully with the festival attendees from across the planet to the talented band as they played into the night at the main hall at Ekam. I moved around the room freely.

I moved to the center of the large hall and studied the alter area with its marble floor imbedded with beautiful ornate geometric patterns made of healing stones like lapis. The standing marble pedestal at the center point was topped with a 12 inch diameter golden sphere. I felt a need to look at it all one last time. I seemed to be asking this alter and the immense structure to speak to me of its true purpose. I would be leaving the next day for home and wondered still how it all fit.

My past experiences with high energy did not involve any form of large temple, only people of high caliber and expanded consciousness. Many things had changed in my life since the early 1990's. I was open to larger places of meditation and study, but wondered if I would ever come back to India and this golden city. I wondered about all the costs and investments that it took for this temple place that took over ten years to make required. This huge unique structure called Ekam was expensive to build in many ways. I also thought about what it cost me personally to travel here for this international festival.

I sensed there was an adjustment in the energy in that moment. Something seemed to hear my call when suddenly in my mind's eye the pedestal grew very tall and large and rushed up to me as an after image of light. A large eagle appeared in the air as well! It seemed to be representing true freedom. My own country of America came to mind as the eagle is our national emblem. I remembered my own concerns back home with our country's integrity as a nation under the current corrupt administration. The energy of the pedestal held up freedom. It also wanted this energy to go to America. It needed me to do my part. I felt my inner core calibrated with it all. I was content and grateful that I was part of this energy.

To be clear, the very concept of a pedestal seemed less relevant than the concept of a pillar holding up something. The sphere was more a representation of wholeness that is ever present and available when invited and received with a humble reverence perhaps. I wanted to continue to be receptive to it no matter where I found myself.

I made use of my every moment while there, but left feeling like it all now had to be carefully processed over the next few weeks. Did I have some new experiences of deeper cellular activation? "Yes!" Did I see and feel many familiar energy vibrations not new to me at all? "Yes!" In summary, it was a very long way to travel for this type of thing. Having said this, I knew I needed to go to India at that time.

On the plane ride back I had time to ponder many things about this trip. Much of what was being taught all week was not new to me. I sometimes lacked the awe and intrigue others seemed to exhibit. I was fortunate to have had years of high energy upgrades and encounters with advanced teachers and very bright expansive minds.

At the end of each day we would be bused back to our campus often a bit worn out from the ordeal of having to be with so many people in a multi day event. I was not unhappy but realized that this type of multi day energy experience needs rest and renewal built into the schedule at times. The nervous system is receiving an upgrade and not unlike a computer, you will need to shut down and reboot your system. Either way, high energy can take a toll on anyone.

In other matters, when the basement restrooms at Ekam were crowded, the newer restrooms were a long walk from the main temple. I did a lot of walking. Meals from my stand point were served too late in the evening to digest well. These were some of the random thoughts that tumbled through me as I traveled home on my long flight.

In January 2019 I attended The Beautiful State weekend training in Sun Valley Idaho with Oneness Trainers Lea and Elizabeth. I could not pass up an opportunity to see the friends again that also went to India, as well as make use of the energy being offered. Some important insights came together for me during the weekend. Some of it did not pertain to what was being taught. I have learned that my spirit has its own agenda with energy sometimes and it helps to go with it. I chose not to share too much with the group.

I noticed during one of the meditation times that my aura or energy field popped out encompassing my whole existence. The tree of life appeared hundreds of feet tall in my mind's eye. It anchored within my womb somehow. Before I knew it, all the important family members or loved ones in my life had a place inside me. I experienced a huge rush of energy as the pieces all came together and seemed to be activating a spinning sphere-like field.

I went home feeling a deep understanding about the need to allow the important people in your life into the equation of transformation. They are all a part of you, and you a part of them. I had held some loved ones at a distance, thinking before that this was necessary. No longer would I do this. I wanted and needed to let them in and to notice who and what they really are to me. I sensed that becoming a more whole being required new dimensions in forgiveness and love.

∞

That spring my husband and I were interested in taking a vacation to somewhere fun. Over the winter I had the opportunity to plan the trip in April to Mexico. We both were ready to see and experience the ancient cities and stone structures of the Yucatan. I made all the arrangements.

We stayed in the town of Tulum at a resort for ten days. It was a two hour drive from Cancun. We visited the Tulum ruins first. The hotel had bicycles available to use for getting around town and to ride to the parking area for the Tulum state park. The heat was notable so we left early in the morning each day to explore the area.

We rented a car for the rest of the stay so we could drive to interesting ancient sites. We went to the lost city of Coba during one of our day outings. It was designated a state park some time after its discovery in the 1990's. It was lush, quiet and less worn out by tourists being less known. Coba had miles of trails through the jungle and many stone engraved stele's that recorded the history of the people from that region. One described female leaders and a peaceful society.

My husband and I were thrilled to hike around Coba all morning. Near the center of the park I scrambled half way up the very tall pyramid of Coba until I felt some vertigo. The jungle canopy was far below. It is the tallest pyramid in the Yucatán.

After sweating happily through the jungle pathways we would dip into fresh water plunges whenever possible. We swam in several deep clean cenote water holes that week at several sites that were open to the public. One near Chitchen Itza had a very powerful feeling of life force energy. The beautiful vines grew hundreds of feet down into the volcanic water whole. A long stone stairway leads down into the ground to reach the open area. Several carved platforms allowed brave ones to jump or dive from various heights into the very deep water. As I floated and swam to the opposite side of the pool, old tension really lifted permanently from my cells and body. I sensed I was receiving a healing of some kind just being in the Yucatan or old Mexico.

We went to the famous ancient city of Chitchen Itza. It did not disappoint but had a lot of venders selling their wares. There were many signs in the stone structures of a warlike society throughout Chitchen Itza. We saw carvings of Panthers eating the head of a man and numerous depictions of bloody human sacrifice.

I could really sense the lost knowledge as we walked all through the many ancient sites. Some of this lost knowledge included the concept of women in leadership. The lost city of Coba has been a site of recent archaeology efforts. The topic of women leaders became revealed when the steles stones with engraved messages were decoded. That area had many signs of a former peaceful society that became lost or abandoned. We enjoyed walking along the long pathways in the jungle with very few tourists. Coba had a very different feel compared to Chitchen Itza and all its crowds.

We could all learn much today about these ancient massive monolithic structures in stone. Each time we returned to our resort I enjoyed just soaking in the sounds of the ocean and the feel of the warm breeze by the pool. Over all I loved being there and felt peacefulness in Mexico as a whole. I would love to visit again and see more of that area of the world.

∞

Overall my healing work picked up in 2019. I had many intense sessions with my clients both new and old. I was able to work in a shorter span of time and access the deeper patterns more quickly. I was also solicited by a national radio program to be interviewed on air and recorded. I ended up getting good ratings and was asked to do two more premier shows. It felt good to be interviewed and speak on the topic of Quantum Consciousness and the Energetics of Healing. I later received several calls of congratulations and praise from friends and family that either heard me live or heard it through the links to the recorded interview. I decided to post a link to the three recordings on my website for customers.

By June of 2019, I decided to work again at the Sun Valley Wellness Festival for four days in a booth. It had been four years since I had been in it as a practitioner. The energy work was so successful people came back for more and brought their friends. Overall I am grateful for the interesting new clients that have given me their trust. I have seen so many amazing things improve and fall away from a pattern of disease.

As an example of energy healing recently, I had a friend and client with a bad bug bite on her elbow. It had created a large area of redness and swelling. She had been to the doctor but they could not do much but give her a prescription for a steroid. They had drawn with an ink pen around the edges to mark the size of the area affected. She was told to come back in if the swelling became any larger. She was in my office a few days later and mentioned plans to go to Hawaii soon. Her arm looked pretty inflamed. The idea of her traveling to a humid climate concerned me. I knew she needed healing right then. I felt guided to my essential oils on a nearby shelf. One in particular from the aromatherapy set stood out. I asked if she would allow me to apply some to the area. She agreed. After a few drops fell to the area I touched her other arm and closed my eyes. I saw a bug up close with long antennae. I said out loud I do not think this is a spider bite. After a few more minutes there was an agreement from the bug.

I explained to my client that the she needed to be aware of words and energy that she puts out into the field. I asked what she remembered from the day this bug bite took place. She recalled telling someone that she was proud of herself for sending love to spiders and bugs. I asked if she wanted them crawling on her. She said "No!" I suggested that she rethink her tone toward bugs. I gave her permission to respect them but to ask that they stay back from her person. We meditated for a while in silence. Once we finished the meditation, to her surprise her arm felt completely different. It even looked much better. I received a text the next day from her that confirmed it had all cleared up. Her arm was normal again! She did not have to take the medication the hospital had given her after all.

Each session is a unique exploration in consciousness for me. Life rolls on and each day is a new beginning. I pray our journey as human beings unfolds with more unity of purpose and less division and corruption harming people's faith in our government and our world. All governments are made up of real people and some are better than others at their job. See the light in them if you can. Either way it will show you the best path forward. The world is still at a time of great change and intensity. The sorting of the wheat from the chaff of life does honour everyone's internal nature. We are all being asked again and again to make choices that reflect our understanding of infinite love and peace. What we put our energy behind becomes us.

20

YOUR JOURNEY AWAITS

For those who are curious, my own experience long ago taught me that there are three cosmic forces that aid each of us in our journey of awakening. Awakening needs all three to fully emerge and they may proceed in a different order than the one I am going to outline. Your eternal self carries a signal within your very soul to ignite the flames that liberate. One of the cosmic forces embodies the fires of truth or spiritual teachings to quicken the pace. This is divine revelation. From my experience to speak from revelation is to be spontaneously conveying a deeper truth that is capable of affecting everyone within ear shot.

For instance when I heard my master teacher speak years ago, whether in person or through a recording device, I noticed immediate visceral affects on my mind, heart and spirit. The whole room would shift suddenly and a new reality would become palpable. He had no notes and could not always repeat what he had just said. It was in real time, a happening to witness to. The power of words spoken from a higher state of consciousness will alter the listener if they are ready to hear, feel and taste the truth in that moment.

During another stage of an awakening many people will be flooded by cosmic forces that feel like an ocean of God's love rippling overwhelmingly through them. Joy and emotion are impossible to contain. This stage allows for a process of change in their conflicted emotional and mental layered self. Many layers will need to be shed or undone to cleanse the field and ready the aspirant for higher level activations.

The third cosmic force is known as the Kundalini. Once triggered, it will travel safely throughout the body, as long as all the energies of judgment and fear have fallen away from the very cells. When we remember to give everything to God, the conflicted patterns energetically flow effortlessly on through one's physical, mental and emotional fields. Nothing is held onto, thus allowing eventually a certain level of readiness for the greater awakening into Reality.

At this stage many people can falter because of a lack of faith in the supreme intelligence of God. "Awakening into NOW" chapter six describes in detail the literal collapsing of space/time and sudden magnetic pull up and into a blinding Reality of limitless joy and light!

I believe that too many people want an end to a process of change so they can hang it like a certificate on the wall, in essence and be done. The temptations of the ego will continue, however. They include the thirst for recognition and a sense of superiority. The second temptations of the ego are a need to be in control of others and situations and the need to feel safe at all times. We are safe in the light of God. All that comes into our sense of reality will challenge this, but we are safe just the same. In reality our personal development is never fully done until we are no longer of this earth.

You may be asking, what is the spiral to NOW? Let's revisit some basics. The earth is orbiting in a grouping of planets that are within a larger spiral of the galaxy, and so on. In many ways we are being affected by the energy of this moving dynamic, but each in different ways. The molecules in everything spin and are never static. Spiritual awakening dissolves the rigid structure within an identified self just enough to allow for a remembrance of this spinning dynamic. This momentary access into the NOW doorway is very exciting to the nervous system.

I suggest a full immersion into this portal of light. Dissolve into this energy envelope and it will take you into a new world of light and sound. The body is a physical manifestation or emanation of energy. Some individuals may resist the lighter energetic potential of their body and soul but it is eventually the only undiscovered territory. All human beings have an infinite potential to grow and mature. Any activity that can heal or attune the energetic of the body-antennae is useful and potentially life changing.

There are many ways to shift resonance or upgrade the circuitry of the human body. One way to shift into a more harmonious state is to simply move closer and closer to your desired resonance or condition of influence. It requires a clear focus but without personal energy pushing on anything. The honed centered state combined with a willingness to join into the energy of NOW will bring you into coherence with brighter body hologram potentials.

Stand up and learn to stabilize your sense of self in and with the structure of space/time. Look past your immediate environment and into each of the four cardinal directions. Feel your awareness connect and stretch in each direction for a moment, far into infinity. Notice the energy that comes back to you from that direction as well. Turn and face a new direction and notice how it feels.

Continue until you have done a complete pivot. Now just notice your sense of standing upright. Feel it all in your body as you straighten your spin. Look up to the heavens but with your inside eyes. Look up through the top of your head and notice a feeling of connection with what is above you.

(Pause) Look down into the earth and notice a feeling of connection with what is below you. Now turn your attention only to what is inside you. You are not a body, but you are a living dynamic with an emanating core of light. You are in it just as it is within you. It is a spinning field of joy and promise. It quite simply can be a journey through the eye of the needle and a journey of profound change.

I believe the main goal in the practice is for you to become total or all inclusive energetically. In every fragmented state you will be *having* thoughts *hearing* words and *thinking* about something. When you can *become* the thought, *become* the sound or *become* the underlying nature of the words themselves, you will know you are being enveloped by the unified field. It is the shifting of gears out of separateness and into energy consciousness. You will become pleasantly magnetic, more resonant and singular in your vibration over time.

Looking back now, I can see that my life has encompassed so many unexpected experiences and teachings of awakening. Writing about my years of awakening has been a surprising step in my overall integration of the journey into the spiral to NOW. I have begun to return to a pattern of joy and light that increasingly emanates wholeness. Self healing or self mastery continues to grow more vivid as I repair my body after injury or limitation and step through new doorways. I also appreciate the profound levels of transformation in my private session work that continues to amaze even me.

I have begun to crave the inner fire and the deeper silence. It is becoming clear to me that it is time to again make the commitment to the full endeavor. My heart remembers that it is all about a lot of energy that gets set in motion and transforms the body back into a vehicle of spinning light. I have begun to have new experiences of spherical consciousness that are powerfully intense. All that encompasses my world is experienced sometimes as in a sphere like state of consciousness. Each vivid connection of great love and service to my family I now see was essential to my growth as well as theirs.

I feel that I am moving into some sort of sacred connectivity with a keystone like opening into a brighter light of potential. My practice each day continues to be about finding the love and the truth of the moment. Letting the energy of it all in and spinning it all back out again. I feel I am rising like a tide with each return to this moment of great awakening to the NOW.

I would like to invite you to jump into the flowing river of life and feel the excitement of a spiritual adventure unfolding before you. Join me in this full endeavor of personal and global awakening. God will help you with this journey. You are important and everyone is essential to the work that is unfolding. Sit and consider what is at stake. Humanity has a chance to pass through many difficult current global events as billions of people sort through the collective fears yet make better choices for tomorrow.

I see humanity beginning to choose an original peace, an original love, and a returning to our roots within the Kingdom of God. With a little help from everyone, we are moving toward a healing that pops mankind over the rim and into the pristine beauty of the promised era of true coherence. We must have the willingness to transcend surface appearances and the courage to reach directly into the heart for answers to today's challenges.

Every moment is a choice. Make every moment count. Then be ready to receive the spiritual fire when it comes. Welcome its intensity and feed it everything that separates you from the truth of who you are. Do not stop until all manner of dross has been burned away. Only then you will witness a spiritual fire worthy of being identified as waking up.

My sense of commitment to this process has never changed. As I sit in quiet, I know that a day will come when it is possible for us all to catch the wave of love and transformation. For now I am excited that people from all walks of life are exploring and discovering the new frontiers in consciousness. A brighter reality and a new tomorrow, filled with the miraculous and the sustainable, is not only possible it is our destiny. Welcome to the spiral to *NOW*.

I thank you dear reader for taking the leap of faith along the way throughout this reading experience. I understand if any of my experiences, as they unfolded, were hard to embrace. I suggest letting the ideas and stories settle where ever they need to. Truth is my most sacred oath. I value truth above all things and have set about to share what I have experienced or know to be true as best I can considering the limited framework of this book.

21

THE TIME IS NOW

This is the information I wrote on a flyer that I posted in 1993.
Its message and title are as true today as it was then.

This is the time of your resurrection. A quietly profound yet powerful energy is spreading throughout this seeming planet. The human mind, your mind, is ready and able to make the leap into a dynamic quantum state of being. Many are feeling the utterly restrictive condition of identifying oneself as separate lump of energy, called a body, surrounded by other lumps. Your true whole self is all inclusive and expresses as an emanation of brilliant WHOLE LIGHT ENERGY or wave! Awaken from the sleep that perpetuates the illusion of being just a particle and remember you are still as God created you. You are a co-creator who slipped "East of Eden into the land of nod." Only in dreams could you portray yourself as a fragment, cut off from the whole.

This is the dawning of the new species of Man – Spiritual Man. It's the time of your illumination and liberation from a split mind state of consciousness. The light has come and it is you! The Holy Spirit or overall mechanism of awakening is working through all your dream patterns or life scenario's and is using them to bring you to the truth of your sleeping condition. The insanity of this world is more visible at this time, as the light penetrates deep into the schism or disassociation from Source. It is shedding light on your own distorted perceptions of this reality and lifting the veil of denial.

The trail blazers of this era are already releasing to the light, whole chunks of patterns of thought that perpetuate the illusions of death, sickness and fear otherwise known as separation. Many are no longer able to live in the craziness of this world's mind set and want Truth, Light and the Love of God above all else. These bright minds are spontaneously accessing the brilliant lights of Reality and experiencing God's eternal grace. You can do this too!

It is time to relinquish all layers of fear, guilt, shame and inadequacy and step into the pure and clean NOW moment. Step off the merry-go-round by no longer referencing your sense of self from the past. Instead reach into the NOW for the true experience of SELF. The NOW is the doorway to truth. Divine revelations of whole light energy are available each moment to everyone no matter what your seeming past tells you. I am the light of your own mind calling you home from the end of time. Awaken from the dreams of death as the dream of light eternal dawns across your mind. Welcome home dreamer of the dream.

THE TIME IS NOW —A Song of Awakening

Musical Lyrics by SoLaMeé - Patricia Heneage,
Composed in 1991 ©2015
(To own a CD of her music contact her directly)

Have you heard from above the call?
It's being shared for all.
The light sings of our origins, our song.
We've been asleep, it seems so long.
Listen, listen, remember and be one.
I am light born of love, free and whole, sent from above.
Remembering in each moment, the truth from what never was.
I am you as you are me, Whole Mind we are to be.
Existing for the moment, in a dream to awaken and be free.

CHORUS: *The time is NOW (repeat)*
To begin anew (repeat)
To birth our essence (repeat)
To birth our truth. (repeat)
The time is NOW (repeat)
To look within (repeat)
And bridge the gap (repeat)
That divides all men (repeat)

SECOND VERSE:
Shine, shine all bright, the new day is here.
It calls for truth and light, to illuminate and release all fear.

The time is NOW, the time is NOW.
Let your wings fly free.
Be at home inside your heart.
Stand tall like the redwood tree.

THIRD VERSE:
The past and the future merge together within the ONE.
We are here in the moment, sharing freely God's love that has come.
What is your part?
What gifts can be shared?
We all hold within us, something needed, when we care.
The planet awaits us, as the stars hold their breath.
Will we do it; will we allow it to unfold through all actions and steps?

FOURTH VERSE:
The fires of truth quicken the pace.
They illuminate those who cannot wait.
The waiting time has ended.
The dark shelters are few.
The light brings healing to every nook and cranny of you.
Open up! Feel the flow.
Allow its warmth to make you glow.
It's time to embody the purity, spreading freedom from soul to soul.
The time is NOW, the time is NOW.

22

THE BIG BANG -
A MIRACULOUS EVENT

The following is what I wrote beginning in 1993. I expanded the article to its current length in 1998. I believe it was a way of putting into words my indescribable heart/mind awakening revelations into the Greater Reality that two years of daily light infusions had inevitably revealed. Some believe this final message is a map inward and upward towards the truth of our origins. It is what I felt day after day when I sat or stood in a ready state, launching from there into the NOW. I wrote this article for my advanced students back then who were looking for clues into how an awakening can unfold and our collective future potential as a human race.

Science tells us life began with the big bang and that this event is considered the origin of our universe. I suppose most people believe that this was a truly amazing and wondrous happening. But what if it was a response to something so odd and unprecedented that it could almost be considered an error? So much of what we base our sense of self, our sense of reality on is what we can see, hear, feel and taste.

What if the very existence of our senses and our body, is a result of a much more bizarre, yet equally miraculous moment? Now shift your mind to the spiritual paths to enlightenment throughout history. How many spiritual traditions speak of an awakening that must occur for our minds to grasp what this is all about? Did we slip or fall into something?

Books like *A Course in Miracles*, scripted (channeled) in the 1970's by Helen Schumann PhD, speak directly to this very predicament. According to *A Course in Miracles,* Jesus is directing us to wake up and remember who and what we truly are. He states that we are in a condition of dreaming because we tried to separate from our Source? Since God/source is infinite and total, and separation is not possible, a response/solution to the attempt to separate would be simultaneous. We can only dream of being separate.

No matter what a person chooses to believe about God, there is something very comforting, even compassionate about this. Despite our slip from Reality, our source created, as a result, a big bang of potential life. (Note: I will use the lower case spelling of the word *reality* when it pertains to a physical world and the upper case when referring to a Greater Reality.)

We are all witnesses to this amazing universe of shapes, texture, and the wonder of those intricate creations of beauty. Here we see the body, its senses and all the other infinitely complex bodies reflecting a seeming separateness in everything we call life. Now remember, all spiritual teachings almost everywhere state that despite appearances, there is no separation with anything. The whole oneness thing is familiar to many. Herein lays the paradox of our existence. Here is the story of the miraculous cleanup of that big bang moment. It unfolds even as we speak. And what are we when we are *not* dreaming? The answers are so many to ponder.

Let's begin again. Who are you really? Once the awakened mind becomes immersed successfully back in the true reality, it can teach to the sleeping mind that you are life eternal. "You are everything, a holy song of God, a holy son-ship, created-creator-creating, and the universal mind."

It will ask you, "How come you don't know yourself in the BEING that is you?" Instead, you find yourself *having* thoughts rather than *being* the thought. This is all in a condition of lumps of energy called bodies surrounded by many other types of lumps, all supposedly existing on a big lump called Earth. All the while, everything looks separate from everything else.

Just think about it, could this be real? Well, that is the question always asked at this point when the mind dialogues with itself. "Yes," is the response the universe can say to you, because you are real. You are *love*, made by the Creator to extend infinite manifestations of that *love*. As the sleeper, however you're in a momentary condition of lumpy consciousness. The painful state of feeling disconnected from your Source, which is God, need not continue. This is the messy error needing to be remedied. So let's review what happened to get you into this predicament.

The dreamer/you, find yourself in a pattern of energy that's within particles that are within spheres that are swirling within spirals. As part of a solution to your predicament, these patterns that began forming were intended to result in a momentary big bang lump of Beingness. *You* are this idea. However, something chose to resist the moment of the big bang of potential. This is when the fall from grace or "whoops" emerged. So in terms of messes, we're dealing with the original problem and with secondary areas of concern that rippled into a new moment of seeming separation.

One of the ideas that emerged was a hesitation within the flow of this cosmic big bang of potential. There was the idea of questioning the creator's intention. Wholeness/God/Source is a Beingness that never questions, it simply is. Suddenly we have a fragment of the son-ship lost in a need to second guess the flow of creation.

The flow was disrupted for a moment. The energy of consciousness, caught in the error of perception, actually began to believe it needed to do something different. This condition froze the energy of consciousness into a space of non-Beingness that swelled into the very dream God was attempting to correct. A dream is a seeming distance between the created and the creator.

The second error that emerged from the momentary condition was the creation of an endeavor to willfully change the creator's experiment/solution or alter the rippling big bang of *being*. An instantaneous reversal in energy results from this upside- down state of being. What emerged was an "effect" attempting to recreate its own "source." It's as if you were hoping to be your own source. Competition only exits in a dream. The third idea that emerged was that consciousness was attempting to play hide and seek with itself. It was a momentary pondering on the possibility of forgetting what reality really was, and thereby falling asleep.

You could say one experiment led to another. This idea, along with the previous ones, is in a condition of disassociation from source energy. It is a denial or turning away from wholeness. Thus, the entire event for all the ideas immediately slipped into energetic potential, otherwise known as dreaming or illusion.

The creator's dance bounced everything back into Beingness and marched on almost unaware that anything within the son-ship had slipped into a dream of its own, or so it thought. Yet even dreams include the source. Source energy is indirectly guiding us back to our moment of disassociation so that we can all awaken. All spiritual paths are an attempt to find our way back.

So it's a matter of being in denial of what you really are. You could say you're dreaming a dream. You've slipped "East of Eden into the land of Nod." The good news is you can wake up. This means you'll have to allow your true nature to draw you back into the center of the dance of creation, or life as we know it here. Then, as true peace dawns across your mind, heart and soul, you will be readied to make your reentry into *reality*. But for now, let's just become aware of the dreaming or what the illusions really are. You can also choose to become involved in changing what you're dreaming about. It's the return to the practice of conscious co-creating.

Now let's get back to what happened right after the "Whoops." Within the idea of the accidental disassociation, consciousness experienced a total sense of *change*. Caught in the momentary experience of being something other than wholeness or love, consciousness retracted and splintered into an illusion of falling energy. You were stuck in a space of resistance therefore you then witnessed a falling away from the source of light and life. The splintering or fragmenting of consciousness was and is a condition of you projecting energy away from yourself. Cause and effect seem to be blown apart or polarized. The experience of time has been invented to create illusionary distance between cause and effect.

Fragmented consciousness is a condition whereby each fragment believes itself to be a real separate thing. These thought patterns are in a condition of projection. To project away is to disown. This perceptual dividing and ordering of thought is how consciousness has perpetuated the original error or slip right up to this moment. Each moment within the dream, the error is reenacted.

Yet, the seeming slip was truly a beginning and an ending all at once. Truth answered the insane idea/experiment with wholeness, thereby undoing the momentary condition of disassociation. Sleeping consciousness is in a condition of resistance to the coming together of cause and effect. It is resisting *God's* answer, or the solution, to the original error. We're dealing with an insane idea that ran away with itself.

Throughout space/time the solution has been directing consciousness to "let go" and come to know that nothing *real* has really occurred. Wholeness, source, reality, was never really affected. "No harm done wake up and see that you never left home." Out of this experience, we've dreamed up some incredible diversity and extreme manifestations of limitation. All the while, the whole light dream has happily been reformulating each moment into brighter patterns of light.

The sleeping minds are literally surrounded by so much beauty and joy, even in the dream, but the veil of false perception inhibits their awareness of it. You see, the gentle hand of God has given us a *true dream* to awaken into first. Every second we move closer to the original moment of the slip.

As consciousness turns to face itself and the event of seeming disassociation, it begins the process of inclusion (healing). A great reversal turns projection of energy into inclusive extensions of energy or love. It's a big hug of *being* beginning to recognize itself as pure and whole. It comes to know experientially that this must include all its thoughts or projected selves. Everything you see, feel, taste or touch, is potential whole light energy waiting to be recognized. This awakening begins the holy process of merging into the solution, known in some circles as *Holy Spirit*. Consciousness begins to quicken in frequency as the light of truth starts flowing in and joyously reclaiming it. There is a dissolving into more and more inclusive experiences of the solution.

Multidimensionality dawns across the heart and mind. There is a passionate desire to *be* each moment an extending emanation of love/light, or whole communication. It becomes clear that extending true communication is the only real function here and this can take place in an infinite number of ways. Consciousness discovers that it, as an emanation of the solution, can and does make use of all the conditions of the error, but uses them to set free or undo, rather than to condemn. Everything, all thought, is being used totally each moment toward the undoing of time itself.

In order to look deeper at the progression of the slip and the return to totality, we will use a three day analogy. Another useful perceptual aid is the teaching that we're dealing with a nine dimensional cosmos. Working within the numerical value of three, or the trinity, we have three sets of three: one day to fall, one day to awaken to the complete situation, and one day to return totally.

The whole seeming evolution of consciousness, within the dream, can be plotted within the three day nine dimensional format. Through the awakening, the mind eventually can fall restfully back into the totality, before leaping back into manifestation or the dream. Each instant you're gone...then you're back. The solution is helping the lost consciousness remember the flow or dance, even within its illusionary state of separation.

Day One contains consciousness as it falls from wholeness, endlessly subdividing and fragmenting. There's a progression from simple sleep until it finds itself deep in the complex manifestations of projected unconsciousness. This is otherwise known as a third-dimensional dream reality. Here, consciousness is so certain of its inherent separateness that it is dreaming of a world of very dense bodies babbling endless forms of attack and defense. Fear rules this frequency of thought. Separation is reflected everywhere in the appearances of sickness, war, greed, hatred, loneliness, and ongoing death.

The pain of this amazing display of illusionary separation is constantly being projected around among the seeming pieces. It's like a game of hot potato. Some patterns of thought become very good at avoiding or denying the painful conditions of the dream of separation. Others only know of suffering and loss but fail to ever question the sanity of a world such as this. Survival is a main energetic endeavor for all. Procreation occurs when two pieces come together in the act of love or temporary union. The continuation of the human species is a silent understanding within the consciousness, yet cooperation amongst the races or societal boundaries, is far from being established.

The essential framework of this third dimensional frequency is built on rules, law and order or the rebellion from these. Religion and governments appear to have a desire to control the morality and patterns of behavior in groups of people. The fear of chaos underlies this activity. Changes in ways of living or being are often considered a threat to the continuity of each region's established way of life. Religious customs can hold a region together, but they can also cause endless division or wars with other people from different customs.

Day Two begins the process of awakening, as the fourth dimensional frequency starts expressing it. There is a new desire to reach out to others and unify. The fear lessens enough to allow for an opening within the heart. Consciousness, for the first time, starts looking out at its reality and asks itself, "Where am I really?" and "Who am I?" The spiritual quest for truth is kicked off and now is valued equally with survival needs. The pain of separation can be felt enough to begin seeking ways to alleviate it.

There is a new focus on healing and being healed as the new identified endeavor. Spiritualized identities pop up in a variety of formats. Teachers, guides, leaders, healers are found in every pathway of personal growth or expanded awareness. Unfortunately, among too many of these individuals, there is an underlying competitive edge to most interactions.

Despite the new interest in unification and heart energies, like compassion or being nonjudgmental, these qualities have yet to be internalized. These unhealed healers and teachers tap into fourth dimensional energies and learn to perceive the lighter body emanations. Some begin to *see* astral thoughts along with ethereal energies within the consciousness of nature.

The light of wholeness or reality begins to reveal itself to those who are willing to really see for a moment. However, the mind and heart still need the complete undoing to fully realign with the source. The difficulty lies in those basic fears that still remain intact. There is a need to fix people, events, anything that doesn't look whole.

But nothing is as it appears. You don't know what anything is really for. Wholeness emerges despite this and brings hope into the chaos. Humility is what consciousness needs to return to in order for true healing to happen. Those underlying fears come from the memory of *loss of control*. Those fears took place at the moment of the initial change or when consciousness fell into the dreaming. Wholeness has no need to control anything, because it is always within the flow of the creator. It is naturally co-creating within this flow.

For the lost ones, chaos remains, because the mind still believes it is at the mercy of people and events outside of itself. It's still hesitating to trust the universal flow of energy. Also, intuitive skills and healing treatments still focus on the effects of the original error, thereby always falling short of any true solutions. Human kind, believing still it is a body, continues to experience physical death in many varied ways. The common perception is that ill health is real. However, a spiritual body has been added to the equation.

The fourth dimensional frequency also contains the dark polarity of energies, plotting and scheming along. Battles of dark and light play out here in an endless array of dream scenarios. Certain religious faiths become immersed in the perceived importance of this activity. Here we see the original error most clearly demonstrated. One side believes it's involved in correcting or resisting the other side's resistance to the creator's plan. The whole battle is within the illusion. Other groups of faith choose to focus on the emerging heart energies and discover renewed hope. The heart energies must be tapped into and expanded to purify the former third dimensional survival instinct. The fearful ones are now lost in the battle to survive spiritually. The pendulum will continue to swing back and forth within the illusion of gains and losses until the heart is made the priority.

Eventually, consciousness grows weary of the warring within the polarized thoughts. Unification appears futile. Also, the need to heal self or others is looking like an endless process, as indeed it is. Consciousness will continually recreate more guilt and fear to be healed of, as long as the true problem is not faced. Consciousness here is truly becoming overwhelmed with the complexities of chaos. It is finally ready to give up trying to solve the problem through its complex bag of skills. The insanity of its dream world is now blatantly clear.

Here we see a critical shift occur. Consciousness truly surrenders and a real cry for *help* is sent into the universal sound, rippling across time and space. This opened, willing, singular state allows consciousness to start hearing and feeling a solution that's been there all along. Consciousness is now realizing acutely how it must become utterly dependent upon God, source, the solution in order to get it out of this unbelievable predicament. Everything it has done thus far has only complicated the situation.

Step one of course, is a directive from the solution for consciousness to begin asking for the Holy Spirit to oversee all forms of guidance. The new pattern to relearn is to follow Holy Spirit, God's angels, higher consciousness without hesitation. You, as an expression of consciousness, begin to discern the difference between opinions and an intrinsic answer your very cells respond to. You do not know what anything is for, so you release the need to make sense out of the chaos, try to heal it, or try to control it.

This is a refreshing step toward a peaceful neutrality and equilibrium. Consciousness realizes it can no longer make decisions about anything utilizing just its little mind. It becomes utterly dependent on Holy Spirit or the solution to guide it through the maze of its own mind. The letting go of the need to control allows ones attention to drop into the heart. It begins the pathway towards the center of the maze. Here lies a place of *being* that is centered, quiet, observant, neutral and receptive. This becomes the alternative to the push pull turmoil of everything outside the center of the maze.

The presence of love, (Holy Spirit), begins to loosen the tight knot of tension within the mind, as consciousness learns it must release all that the world has taught it. It begins to recognize the presence of Holy Spirit everywhere guiding and directing it toward an inward vertical association with the source. The horizontal, external search for the right teacher, healer, religious faith or group that led many times in circles is now over. More and more resistance towards the solution is dissolving, along with most everything consciousness thought it knew.

A veil of perception lifts, allowing consciousness to see and feel it is really in its own dream. In a moment of spontaneous revelation, it experiences a taste of its wholeness and purity. To fully access this, it must release the chaotic dream world of its own making. Responsibility for the chaos is no longer projected outside of self. This important step releases a lot of the need to control everything out there, since the problem is recognized within.

Only a leap of faith will trigger the necessary release energetically of all the old mind-sets. The experience of divinity is deeply felt but must be then recognized within all its projected selves. The new belief must be the following. "People are what I have chosen to see them as." Instead of the former belief "What I see is what everyone sees, and there is nothing I can do about it." It now opens up to a whole new dream script written from the clarity of innocence, purity, and wholeness or inclusiveness. It allows the solution to direct this unfolding script of miracle-mindedness.

Each moment that one releases the need to know everything or have answers, the mind quietly falls toward the center of the maze. Here, within the peace of this simplicity, you often find yourself knowing things. As you release the need to change events, correct or fix things going on around you, again the mind gently falls toward the center of its being. From this space things seem to undo and then harmonize around you effortlessly. Any action taken is so natural and swift that it often goes unnoticed. The alignment of all forces, inner and outer, exists at the center of the maze. Moving upward within the growth of consciousness, each step or level of realization always carries that standing in the center of the moment.

When you can rest comfortably within the Beingness of each frequency of consciousness, you are allowed to progress further. For you to enter this next level or frequency of awareness, each moment has to become a whole opportunity to spring into the ecstatic or deeply communal experience of its wholeness or divine self. Your passion for growth and awakening can take hold.

After what may appear to be months and years immersing yourself in this state, you might acclimate to it. You are illuminated and awake, here but not here. This occurs within the oneness of a fifth dimensional true dream of light, referred to as heaven. Here, pro-creation has been completely translated into co-creation or divine union. Co-creators live in full service to spirit within the solution. This is a resurrected world of life and light, the complete opposite of a world of shadows, ongoing death and decay and rivaling energies. Here all the miss creative dream scripts of separation have been made whole.

Co-creative endeavors explore all formats of the magnificence of a true light dream. Creative projects are plentiful within this frequency of consciousness. Happily the brotherhood/sisterhood of consciousness dances through creative energies that are devoted to exploring shapes, forms and sounds. These inspiring energies have been known to filter down to the lower frequencies of third dimensional earth.

Creative geniuses may have the capacity to receive and sometimes manifest these ideas on earth. The fifth dimensional veil is the errors umbrella that can be difficult to pass through. Only the Christ (illuminated by God) can enter here. The Christed frequency of consciousness has free access to all higher dimensional pitches. Its progress is totally conscious from here on, as it fully experiences the kingdom of heaven.

Sixth-dimensional consciousness clearly recognizes itself as the unified Sonship seamlessly dancing within the creator's dance. It is limitless in its function within the parameters of the solution. Here, consciousness experiences thought-forms in essence only. Light and tone fuse into brilliant expanses of arcing light emanations, also known as the *Great Rays*.

As **Day Three** dawns, metaphorically speaking, consciousness leaves behind all meaning and value in patterns of thought within any context of individuated form. Each dimensional frequency of expression requires the dissolving of a veil in order to be in it. The seventh inner plane however, occurs through a profound lifting by God/source itself. Like moving closer and closer to a magnet, eventually consciousness has purified and aligned enough that God sweeps you up in its arms as it recognizes you as itself. It is beyond all vision or describable qualities. To even enter this domain for an instant causes an irreversible change that secures the alignment of consciousness. One can drop back down in vibration from there and *be* in service to all that is in need of assistance.

Seventh dimensional consciousness experiences direct whole light communication. It is unable to experience any form of differentiation. There is only light extending. The original error was simply "not so." Light communicates with light. The microcosm/macrocosm of the creator's dream universe is in dynamic symphony. This collective knows itself to be the instruments, orchestras, and conductor simultaneously. Words fail to be very useful from here on. Simply put, eighth and ninth-dimensional consciousness is emanating in brighter and brighter expansions of Godhood, and does not know of the idea of the disassociation. It is receiving the source of all light, but it is not yet the totality. Its light originates directly from *reality* and flows down through the frequencies.

All nine dimensions occur in the same space/moment. Consciousness is not progressing a distance. The emanation is simply dissolving and expanding, yet accelerating. It grows inclusively brighter and brighter as the alpha and omega are brought together and then dissolved completely. Left to itself, the process of evolution in consciousness takes too long. The solution therefore includes mechanisms to shorten time.

By inserting emanations of whole light consciousness deep into its memories, the whole script can be shortened. This current picture of a dream, called earth, is an incredible display of the collapsing of the golden spiral of evolution. Frequencies from the fourth through the seventh dimensions of consciousness were inserted deep into the dreaming in order to trigger a wide path of awakening. A full scale harvest of consciousness is underway. The wheat of the world of brightness awaits its turn.

The miracle of the solution assists each emanation in re-awakening to its brightest frequency of expression. You will discover that this expression is your most natural state of being. The awakening and quickening process is not a simple linear progression, however. The analogy of piano notes or strings that play vertically is a closer picture.

Each emanation of consciousness must stretch to include everything within its awareness in order to allow the song or harmonic vibration to emerge. This is the inclusive healing dynamic at work. Consciousness flows up and down the strings or keyboard exploring each note. Certain chords or notes may feel less clear and will be returned to again until clarity comes into the sound.

Earth life, at this depth, is based on the perception that you are a physically manifested body experience. Everything you're going through each moment has the potential to realign you with your true sound. The solution is inserting higher and brighter frequencies of awareness, and they are meant to be applied or integrated into that body experience. Happy and joyous experiences are as essential to the formulation of your song as adverse situations and conditions despite the difficulty. The depth of limitation is not meant to be escaped, but rather forgiven and included completely into the awakening harvest.

For a moment there is a need for different frequency players within the master script. All frequencies share an equal value within the Solution. So embrace wherever you find yourself, in terms of awareness, at this moment. Once the right combination is actualized in the quantum instant, the whole experiment of dreams will turn inside out. This will thereby undo completely the original error for you. This will then trigger a mass awakening. It is completely astounding, given the incredible complexities of a third-dimensional dream reality.

The infusions of light seeded deep in the dream, are now being triggered to awaken. Energetically, this cuts multiple pathways in consciousness from chaos all the way back to the totality within a relatively short span of time. This could not be coming about were it not for the former brilliant embodiments, historically, that established the pathways or bridges to the higher inner planes of consciousness. Now, a massive lifting can occur within all frequencies. Like a series of spontaneous celestial events, amazing explosions of Light are being witnessed to within the consciousness of humankind.

The really bright pockets of consciousness bring in higher and higher frequencies of Beingness. Former historic accounts of spiritual awakening usually involved minimal participation with normal physical life activities. This was necessary in order to maintain a clear, pure emanation of light. At this time in the harvest, however, it is essential to not become too removed from the human dance. Each participant is asked to integrate the peaks and valleys of the universal sound until he or she can successfully thread the needle, in essence.

What is referred to as the Great Rays of light must begin to flood our consciousness at this depth and be completely integrated into our physical embodiment. We must also be at peace within the limitations of the earth experience. This very bright harmonic light has flowed down and discovered its essence hidden within this incredible illusory dance of separation.

The miracle is that the light is growing and illusions are dismantling. The energies of those simple open-hearted and willing minds are creating a ground swell of changes. We're at the bottom of the ocean of dreams. The top of the spiral is awakening to the bottom, as the bottom reaches farther upward in frequency than ever before. Eventually the spiral collapses or compresses and then turns inside out.

The particle idea called earth is very old and tired, and it is now being transformed through the ascending patterns in consciousness. Humanity has a collective sound that includes the earth and all its forms. It's an incredibly diverse human song that can be tuned up energetically and made magnificent. The wheel of karma has been revoked from the script and or accelerated, in order to allow for a more speedy harvest. God's grace is being extended to all equally.

To accept this, one must completely release the past. This is the accepting of your innocence. It is a stepping into the pure and clean NOW moment. There is a dying of all ideas about self, and its seeming past. Each moment is born fresh and new. Innocence is not withheld from anyone. To condemn anyone for anything that only seemed to occur in the dream is to condemn the self to further chaos or hell.

In terms of frequencies in consciousness, those that feel called to quicken or move into a higher domain will need a sound foundation of faith in God. To relinquish all your limited identities that are based in fear and merge with the solution requires a leap of faith. Each lifting of a costume of identity leaves the mind momentarily disoriented.

You will need wise and supportive people, and energies, around you. It does not take place over a weekend and earth time is the illusion anyway. Spirit makes use in the moment of the various dimensional expressions in frequency. It may reveal to you other relevant selves in order to embrace and then integrate them. Multidimensionality is a fluid dance that is not attached to a single self identity, but will stabilize around an identity that is most natural for you. What is all encompassing becomes the true essence of the singularity.

Through the awakening you will be forming a sense of being that draws upon every one of your brightest qualities. Consciousness is thus re-associating into brighter frequencies of self expression or *Being*. It is like being completely dismantled and then made new. Nothing is held onto. If you are learning anything in this process, it's how to let go or die each moment in order to allow in more light or be reborn.

Often, at first, consciousness will experience itself within the ecstasy and thrill of its Christed frequency, only to return to a third dimensional frame of reference (i.e. "I am a body: I am separate.") This is an example of an incomplete assimilation. As consciousness focuses completely toward the singular endeavor of its own awakening, letting no idols come before the source, the episodes of light infusion (revelation) will increase. Any truly inspired teacher would never want to undermine your own very personal direct connection with God by becoming your idol. Worship and devotion is best directed towards God. Gratitude to God and all God's servants/teachers is also good.

A key word for those who are here to fully participate in the undoing of conflict or separation from wholeness is *allowed*. Let go, trust and allow everything you feel or experience to flow completely. Be in each moment aware, awake and willing to work through whatever appears to be happening at the moment. Allow others their own personal way of processing each moment. Allow time to pass and lift the pain and struggle of grievances. Each moment is an opportunity to feel the past evaporate.

Eventually, consciousness will have been completely reversed energetically and will reference its sense of self from the Light. This fifth dimensional frequency is the goal for the bulk of humanity to reach or at least become aware of. Those embodiments that successfully integrate the Christed sense of being have a body image, yet it reflects the wholeness of life and serves as a communication device in the moment.

To reiterate, these bright emanations are here, not here, each moment. For you, they are reflecting the light of your own mind that has been thus far denied or projected. A Christed mechanism is a *Being* that is constantly translating energy into a more useful expression. All emotional and mental energetic experiences are embraced and then released easily. The mechanism is designed to undo. How you experience your undoing will be extremely personal and miraculous and every bit of it is contributing to the growing harmonic sound that will reconfigure or transform the dream for everyone.

There is a need for many different emanations of the Christ, in terms of how these communicative emanations may appear to the world. Throw out any preconceived ideas about how a Christed communication will appear or behave. Remember, you don't know what anything is really for. Be grateful for all the sisters and brothers currently in the world and what they may shed light upon.

Because everything within the dream is constantly changing, being a product of the illusion of change, the key is to associate with what is changeless: *love, light, truth, wholeness*. Become fascinated with divinity expressing itself each moment to you and through you. This way, the wild fluctuations in form won't concern you a bit.

Remember this is a dance, a life dance. Be willing to stumble through certain steps or tempos. The divine overseer (God) is silently guiding everything, if you'll allow it to. Free will simply means choices are allowed. The overseer works with and through the choices each seeming piece of consciousness is making.

The martial art of aikido is a wonderful example of this dynamic. Aikido uses no resistance, aggression or willfulness in its practice. It is a mastery of taking an energy wave, or the inertia of the opponent, and re-directing it into a more useful pattern. To do this one must first merge with the opponents' energy. From the centered space of perfect balance, the Aikido master peacefully directs the flow of energy into a less destructive direction. This martial art never intends to harm or humiliate an opponent. To merge energetically is an act of love in essence. It means they're not outside of you or split off, and opponents are respected as an integral and unique aspect of the whole.

Christed consciousness or wholeness always embraces and then redirects the energy pattern toward healing. From the center of the maze, healing, undoing and then harmonizing just happen. This is the miraculous method that is unattached to outcomes or official spiritual roles. It knows clearly that the divine overseer is the authority over each moment.

To effectively fulfill a teaching role one must be honest to self and others of the limits of one's current awareness. Then learning is a shared experience for all and healthy pathways can open for everyone. It's appropriate to assume that as long as you're embodied, no matter how bright the emanation, you're going to process personal challenges and losses.

Even global energy patterns of thought may flood your energy field. These larger patterns may emerge in your daily life experience to draw your attention to them. Whatever your attention is on indicates what you may be involved in undoing or harmonizing. A Christed or illuminated consciousness that is in the world is always aware of the necessity to stay open to that vertical inward-outward divine association. Eventually the inflow of the overseer is recognized as coming in from the circumference of existence.

This mass scale awakening to some is known as the second coming, because it is the re-membering or gathering together of all the attributes of the Christ. We're unifying streams of thought and blessing all historic ways or patterns of awakening, as it all returns to the light. The resurrection of the dream world was already a success on the inner planes. So it's a wondrous unfolding adventure completely in the hands of God. Remember to feel more and think less. Vibration leads you to the fruit.

For the third and fourth dimensional frequencies, a real urgency is being felt as it becomes aware of what is unfolding here. The time is NOW! The light of consciousness, within the dense patterns of thought known as particle mass, awaits the undoing in your mind in order to be set free or illuminated. Earth is the particle mass that you're here to uplift through your personal willingness to be awakened and realigned with the overseer's harmonic, also known as Holy Spirit. You may begin to feel the false temple of the ego shake at its foundation, if you haven't already.

Your freedom beckons. Let go of the brakes and the resistance to everything that is right NOW. Decide that you are in a dream of holding onto your separateness. The spinning dynamic of light will magnetically draw you in, if you allow it to. You will lose nothing and gain everything. *Let go* of the past a little more each moment and embrace your connection with what is here, now... LIFE. You will still be you, just much happier! God speed and remember you are loved, utterly by our Source.

This is just the beginning...

In honor of the memory of our son Harry.
"Here lies a bright heart. 1987 – 1998"

REFERENCES

1. A COURSE IN MIRACLES, ©1975, 1985, Foundation for Inner Peace, Tiburon, CA.

2. ALL I SEE IS PART OF ME, Chara M. Curtis, Illustrations by Cynthia Aldrich © 1994 Fourth Printing, revised addition, © 1989 First Printing, Illumination Arts Publishing Company Inc., Bellevue, WA.

3. ALTERNATIVE PATHWAYS TO HEALING: The Recovery Medicine Wheel, Kip Coggins, © 1990 Published by Health Communications Inc. Deerfield Beach, Florida.

4. AT THE ELEVENTH HOUR, Pandit Rajmani Tigunait ©2001 Himalayan Institute Press, Honesdale Pennsylvania.

5. CREATIVE VISUALIZATION, By Shakti Gawain, ©1978-1994, Whatever Publishing, Berkeley, California.

6. 21 DAYS WITH BRACO, Angelika Whitecliff, ©2009, Published by Awakening Within, Kealakekua, Hawaii.

7. HE WALKED THE AMERICAS, Hansen, L. Taylor, 22nd printing 2003 ©1963, Legend Press, Amherst Wisconsin.

8. INTERVIEW WITH AN ANGEL, Stevan J. Thayer and Linda Sue Nathanson, ©1997 Published by Edin Books, Gillette, New Jersey.

9. INVOLKING YOUR CELESTIAL GUARDIANS, Solara ©1986, Second Edition 1987, Eleventh Edition 2002, Star-Borne Unlimited, Los Angeles, California.

10. LIFE FORCE - The Scientific Basis: Breakthrough Physics of Energy Medicine, Healing, Chi and Quantum Consciousness, Claude Swanson, PhD ©2009, Published in 2010 by Poseidia Press, Tucson, Arizona.

11. LOVE WHISPERS, Swami Rama, page 42, ©1986, 2000, The Himalayan Institute Press, Honesdale, Pennsylvania.

12. LOVE WITHOUT END: Jesus Speaks, Glenda Green, pages 339 and 341, ©1999 Revised 2006 Third Edition, Spiritis Publishing, Sedona Arizona.

13. MATRIX ENERGETICS, Richard Bartlett DC, ND, ©2007, Published by Beyond Words, Hillsboro, Oregon.

14. THE DISCOVERY OF THE ESSENE GOSPEL OF PEACE: The Essenes and the Vatican, Edmond Bordeaux Szekely, Page 37-55 ©1975, N.p.: Academy Books-Publishers, San Diego California.

15. THE ESSENE GOSPEL OF PEACE, Edmond Bordeaux Szekely, trans. 1928, ©1981, N.p.: International Biogenic Society.

16. THE ESSENE GOSPEL OF PEACE- Book Two: The Unknown Books of the Essenes, Edmond Bordeaux Szekely, Page 31-45, trans. 1928, ©1981, N.p.: International Biogenic Society.

17. THE ESSENE GOSPEL OF PEACE- Book Three: Lost Scrolls of the Essene Brotherhood, Edmond Bordeaux Szekely, trans. 1928, ©1981, N.p.: International Biogenic Society.

18. THE ESSENE GOSPEL OF PEACE- Book Four: The Teachings of the Elect, Edmond Bordeaux Szekely, trans. 1928, ©1981, N.p.: International Biogenic Society.

19. THE ESSENE WAY: Biogenic Living, Edmond Bordeaux Szekely, Pages 41-44 ©1989, N.p.: International Biogenic Society, Canada.

20. THE HOLOGRAPHIC UNIVERSE, by Michael Talbot, ©1991, First Harper Perennial edition published 1992.

21. THE KEYS OF JESHUA, Glenda Green, Page 274, 288, ©2003, Second Edition, First Printing Sept. 2007, Spiritis Publishing, Sedona Arizona.

22. THE LOST BOOKS OF THE BIBLE, published by Gramercy Books ©1979, Reprint of the 1926 ed. Published by World Pub. Co., Cleveland. Originally William Hone's collection first published in 1920 under title "The Apocryphal New Testament." Copies date back to the 1600's.

23. THE NATURE OF PERSONAL REALITY, By Jane Roberts, ©1974, 1993, 2009.

24. THE SURRENDER EXPERIMENT- My Journey Into Life's Perfection, Michael A. Singer, ©2015, Harmony Books, New York.

25. THE SYNCHRONOUS UNIVERSE, Claude Swanson, PhD, ©2003, Published in 2003, 2005, 2009 by Poseidia Press, Tucson, Arizona.

26. THE UNKNOWN LIFE OF JESUS CHRIST, Nicolas Notovitch, trans. by Virchand R. Gandhi, Originally published in 1907. Dover Publication in 2008, Mineola, New York.

AUTHOR BIO

SoLaMeé – Patricia Heneage

Author SoLaMeé has expertise in the healing arts, intuition and meditation, encompassing thirty years of experience and training in a vast array of disciplines. SoLaMeé has earned multiple advanced certifications in cutting edge quantum consciousness techniques and healing including *Matrix Energetics* as a certified practitioner. Her sessions always address a pattern or health condition from the quantum state or energetic level in order to access possibilities for improvement. Each session with SoLaMeé calibrates the body hologram towards a higher vibration in consciousness.

SoLaMeé is a Master Instructor and has instructed and certified students in *Integrated Energy Therapy* since 2009. She has led residential silent meditation retreats and taught classes for many years. She attended *Oneness University* events in the United States and India.

SoLaMeé is also experienced in mainstream helping professions in the fields of addiction and mental health. This makes her uniquely qualified to assist others with a wide array of health issues and challenges. She graduated in 1983 from Western State University in Colorado with a Bachelors degree in Sociology, a minor in Psychology. SoLaMeé – Patricia Heneage lives with her husband of many years in Teton Valley Idaho. Visit www.thespiraltonow.com for information on SoLaMeé and her unique sessions, classes and instruction.

Made in the USA
Columbia, SC
23 December 2019